THE
GUV'NOR
TAPES

THE GUV'NOR TAPES

LENNY McLEAN'S UNPUBLISHED STORIES, AS TOLD BY THE MAN HIMSELF

LENNY McLEAN
WITH
PETER GERRARD

JOHN BLAKE

Published by John Blake Publishing Ltd,
3 Bramber Court, 2 Bramber Road,
London W14 9PB, England

www.blake.co.uk

First published in paperback in 2007

ISBN: 978-1-84454-358-8

British Library Cataloguing-in-Publication Data:

A catalogue record for this book is available from the British Library.

Design by www.envydesign.co.uk

Printed and bound in Great Britain by William Clowes Ltd, Beccles, Suffolk

1 3 5 7 9 10 8 6 4 2

Papers used by John Blake Publishing are natural, recyclable
products made from wood grown in sustainable forests.
The manufacturing processes conform to the environmental
regulations of the country of origin.

Every attempt has been made to contact the relevant copyright-holders,
but some were unobtainable. We would be grateful if the appropriate
people could contact us.

The McLean family wish to point out that they were not involved
in the writing of this book.

This book is dedicated to the man that changed
my life – and that of so many others –
Lenny 'The Guv'nor' McLean
and
Lorraine James, Elaine Wood and Canelle Hoppe
Their love and support also changed my life.

I love them all.

Foreword

Imagine what it's like to lose someone you love and respect and then, ten years later, you sit down, put on a tape and that person comes straight back into your life as though they never went away. Now you might understand what it was like for me as I worked my way through those first interview tapes. Before I began, I thought that it might be an upsetting experience, even a depressing one, but the opposite was the case. OK, there were moments when I had to pause the machine for reflection, but in the main I found listening to that 'rough, gruff' voice, to quote Lenny, very uplifting. I found myself laughing out loud at times and responding to questions Lenny threw at me.

I am reminded of Binyon's poem, written at the outbreak of the First World War, about the fallen: 'They shall not grow old, as we that are left grow old'. Ten years on, many of us have gained grey hairs, wrinkles and the aches and pains that age brings on. Yet Lenny remains in our minds as the tough, ebullient and larger-than-life character he always was, and will remain so while there are people left to remember him. My email inbox still fills up with questions about him from all over the world. The story of his life is a phenomenon that never seems to go away. The book that was launched on a thousand 'nice cups of tea' still graces bookshop shelves and sells many copies weekly.

Passing away when he did, at the comparatively young age of 49 – and very shortly after the first publication of his autobiography – he never witnessed the impact his story had on young and old alike. Ever the optimist, however, he was confident that his story would sell a million copies. He often told me to think big, aim for the top, never think any problem is insurmountable. I remember years ago, when I used to drive a battered Capri, mentioning that I dreamed of one day driving a black Mercedes, like Lenny did – and I have to say, back then that's all I imagined it could ever could be: a dream. 'Son,' he said, 'don't ever waste your time dreaming. Make your mind up what you want, aim for it and you'll get there if it's worth having.' As long ago as it was, I can recall exactly where we had that conversation and, as I occasionally drive towards that particular roundabout, in my black Mercedes, I think to myself how right he was.

Though Lenny is particularly remembered as being a hard man, an unbeatable fighter and the hardest man in Britain, to those who were closest to him, it is his humour that we remember most, and throughout these pages I think this comes across. I am confident that his legions of fans and admirers will learn a little more about this unique man as they read through what must surely be the final words from this fascinating figure.

Peter Gerrard
February 2007

The Guv'nor Tapes

Is that tape thing on, Pete?

Yes, Len.

So how do you wanna do it, son?

Well, you talk, I'll tape it and keep nudging you with a few questions, and then, once we've got it all down, we'll put it all together in book form. You know, tidy it up, put things in and take things out.

That's the stuff; good boy.

Val! Val! Peter said he's too dry to ask me any questions.

Sorry, Pete, we gotta have a drink before we start. OK, we'll just have a little chat and sort of get warmed up. Bit like going into a fight, if you don't loosen up you're all tense and it don't work. But if you do a few exercises beforehand everything works smooth, your head's clear and you feel nice and relaxed. Does that make sense?

Perfect sense, Len.

So Reggie sent you along to see me; did he tell you he thinks I'm a fucking ravin' lunatic?

No he didn't say that, he said you were old school and he's got a lot of respect for you.

Did he? Well, I've got a lot of respect for him and that ain't nothing to do with him being a so-called gangster and that he's topped a few people. What it is, that man has suffered over the years but he's kept his dignity, all his marbles and stayed strong – that's why I've got all the time in the world for him and Ronnie.

I think they should let Reggie home now, p'raps not Ron 'cos he's a different case altogether, though whenever I see him he's as good as gold, polite, immaculate and saner than half the people walking the streets. But Reg, for fuck's sake, what harm can he do? Where in the sixties he was number one, today he wouldn't be in the first 300 because he's an old man now, and they should let him home because he's not a threat to society. There's more slags out there shoving drugs up their nose, putting drugs in their fucking veins, mugging, and you read in the papers all the time about seventy-, eighty-, ninety-year-old women all been raped. In the sixties, when the Twins was working, there was violence and all sorts but here in the nineties it's much, much worse. Sometimes I think the terrible things that go on today makes what they got up to look like fuck all. Something else I think is the twins don't help themselves and what I mean is they should forget all about writing books, making films and keeping their names in front of the public day and night. OK, it coins a few quid but, if they kept their heads down, kept a low profile and played the political game while they're behind the door, no doubt about it the authorities would let them out; well, certainly let Reg out then he could make serious dough. When you get the punter in the street or in the pub talking about them constantly, all they're doing is winding up the government and making them dig their heels in about going a bit easy on the boys. I should imagine 70 per cent, maybe 80 per cent of the population in this country would say yes, let the Krays out.

What about the Twins when you were a young man, did you want to be like them?

Can't say I did, Pete, 'cos really the first time I heard of the Krays I think was when I was 18 or 19. I didn't take a lot of notice because at that age you didn't give a fuck for anybody, 'specially if they was older geezers, and you have to remember, like, I'm 44 now and the Twins must be well in their sixties so really we're generations apart. Back then, we was young and tough and the Krays and the geezers on the Firm were working towards pipe and slippers. I know now that wasn't true and really those men were in their prime, doing the business and dangerous men, but when you're a kid you're full of yourself. I never knew them personally while they was on the outside and it was only later on in life that I heard about the Krays and the things they got up to. I never actually met them until they were inside and had been banged up for years and it was only when I was into the bare-knuckle game and my reputation spread that they asked to meet me.

How was that, Pete, good start?

Good, Len, good. I love it when the person I'm working with just lets it roll off their tongue without too much thought. Trouble is when the person thinks too hard before they speak because it slows things down and isn't natural.

So I'll be all right then?

Absolutely.

Now I've done this sort of interviewing stuff loads of times, you know bits and pieces in magazines and stuff, but I ain't never thought about spilling my whole life before. I've got a feeling that you and me working together is gonna work out a treat, what with you coming from the Firm and all that. Reggie can be a fucking nuisance sometimes, but when it comes to judging a character he's pretty shrewd. I'm pretty shrewd myself and not too much gets past me, so, weighing it all up, I think you and me are gonna knock 'em dead with this book. I'm telling you now, it's gonna be a best-seller. Whad'ya say, son?

Well, I know it'll be great read and a good seller, but no guarantees on being a best-seller.

That ain't the way to think! Think big! Every time I had a fight I told myself I was gonna win. And know what? I won every time. So don't sit there thinking we'll settle for being 'alfway good; aim to be the best, OK?

Right then, Peter, away you go and ask me some questions.

What about your roots – you know, where you grew up.
Was it around here in the East End?

Not too far from here. As a little kid I spent my first years in a place called Hoxton. Have you heard of Hoxton Market?

Yes I have, very famous place.

Thought you might've. People come from all over to go there. I mean, I wasn't aware of it back then, but in previous years it was one of the roughest, toughest places you could find in the East End; turned out more villains per square inch than any other place. They say the people who lived there were ten times worse than them that lived in Bethnal Green – and that's saying something.

Gimme a second while I roll a fag.

You're the clever one, Pete. If you wanna chuck in a bit of history about the place – you know, facts and figures – you do it, because I'm relying on you to fill in the gaps.

To me, though, as a nipper, it was a lovely, lovely place; a very friendly place. Now what have we got? High-rise blocks of flats, dirty looking, riddled with crime and gangs out for trouble. No one talks to no one because everybody's frightened of getting mugged or raped. But back then – how can I say it? – just after the war it was like all the old houses had railings along the front, window boxes with geraniums in them, all painted up, because people took pride in their homes even though none of them owned them. Kids could play out until it got dark and their mothers never gave it a thought because they knew the neighbours in their street, and the next and the next, would be keeping an eye on 'em.

That's what I remember most, kids everywhere on the street playing football, playing cricket, kids running up and down and in and out of houses that weren't even their own.

Looking back, it seemed people had time for each other. There would be men standing out on the steps talking and having a smoke, old girls sitting outside their front doors shelling peas and putting them in buckets and everyone talking about everyone. It was a community. Everybody knew everybody and everyone's house was open for each other. You could go in this house, that house, and no one worried about if the street doors were left open all day or even all night. There was just a friendly atmosphere in every turning.

It was hard in them days and everyone was 'at it' in some sort of way in that area, and I suppose every other area in the East End. Everyone was hungry, everyone was trying to get a living, but it was hard; very hard. So to get a living in them days, you had to do some sort of villainy. Mainly thieving from firms and the docks and warehouses – because you didn't thieve off your own, though there was probably no point anyway, because your neighbours didn't have a pot to piss in either. So I suppose the police were the enemy then because there weren't so much money about; it was only when society started to rely on the police, in years to come, when people started getting money, when people started worrying about their own property and their own individual selves, then the police become their friends. But we know the police are no fucking good.

6

Who was the guv'nor in that area back then?

That's it, you ask me questions, son. Well, the guv'nor in Hoxton was my uncle Jimmy – Jimmy Spinks. He was my nan's brother, so he'd be my great-uncle. 'Course, I didn't know nothing about being the guv'nor then – to me, he was just a great big, lovely man. Yeah, he was the guv'nor in them days; he was a very, very hard man, a proper tearaway. He was in the race gangs and used to mind the bookmakers. I think the number-one bookmaker around that area at the time was a guy called Jack Spot and Jimmy looked after him.

His name was Comer – Jack Comer.

Who's that?

Jack Spot – Spot was his nickname. He reckoned it was because he was always on the spot for a bit of trouble, but I've heard he had a big spot on his face as a young man.

See, that's how we can graft together on this book. I put my bit in and you come up with the stuff I forget or don't know.

So you get the idea that Jimmy was a force to be reckoned with in Hoxton, and I suppose I looked up to him when I was a young man as well as young boy. I looked up to him because he was a man's man and a proper hero, but being a kid I loved seeing him, because he always gave me money. In them days, no one ever gave you money, because there was none about. But, because he was into a bit of this and that and all sorts, Jim always had money. And I mean real money. I've seen him pull out a bundle of them big old-fashioned

7

five-pound notes that could've choked a donkey. You didn't pick up that sort of folding working on a milk round.

What was he like?

Jim? He was a big man, 21 stone and about five foot nine. He had scars like tramlines all over his face, grey pushed-back hair; a very, very powerful man – a menacing man – but a diamond towards his family. In those days, men in his position had to look the business because they were figureheads, if you like. He always wore a very smart black Crombie overcoat, the big hat and a pinstriped suit – you know the kind with the wide lapels. In fact, you could say he dressed up like a typical Al Capone gangster.

Did you know that villains and gangsters didn't dress up in all that gear until that look was in films?

No, I didn't know that, but I did know Ronnie liked to get kitted out in all that mafia style, and I suppose he only got that from films.

So, going back to Jimmy, he done a stretch of five on the Moor in the days when you did the lot; none of that time off for good behaviour. Hard labour he got for being the ringleader of a battle at Lewes racecourse; hard labour then was like breaking rocks and fuck knows what else. I've heard that some people say, 'Well, he couldn't have been all that, because his face was all scarred like fucking tramlines'; didn't say it in front of me, though. What they don't know was what the other fellas looked like after he'd finished with them. Ten-man job; know what that means, Pete? I'll tell you. He was such a hard man to bring down it took ten men before they'd think of having a go at him; ten men and they still couldn't beat him. One time, he got smashed over the head from behind with a thick iron bar. Know what he did? Took the bar off this bloke, beat him senseless with it and then he walked to the hospital with his head all split open.

They say I'm a ten-man job and that makes me proud that I've taken after him. I ain't giving myself a gee, because I don't have to do that, but I took on 18 men one time; knocked the shit out of nine of 'em and the other nine run off. I'll come back to that, because I'm telling you about Uncle Jimmy. When I was a young man I looked like my father, and that's why that c**t Irwin hated me, but as the years have gone on people say I look like my uncle Jim – yeah, I'm a ringer for him and proud of it. Everyone had respect for Jimmy Spinks; he was a good man,

I remember being told that, when my father died, Uncle Jimmy went round all the pubs and had a collection for my mum. I mean, in 1953 he raised £500 and gave it to my mum. Think about it – you could buy a house back then for a grand. So yeah, he was a well-liked man and a larger-than-life character, and if television had been about then he'd have been even more well known that what he was just in the papers.

I keep jumping all over the place. Is that all right, can you sort it all out?

To be honest, Lenny, it's easier if you just say what comes into your head. Don't try and write the book as you go along, we'll do that later.

OK, but you gotta make allowances and help me out as we go along, because it ain't easy remembering all this stuff.

I just remembered something else about Jimmy Spinks: he was a Blackshirt at one time.

Got to correct you there, Len.

What's that?

Your uncle Jimmy, he wasn't a Blackshirt.

Well, I know he was taking a lot of money off that Mosley geezer, because a lot of people in the family told me.

What it is, they've got things back to front. Jimmy was taking money, but it was from the Jewish shopkeepers; he was protecting them from Mosley's mob because they were fascists – you know, they supported Germany and the Nazis in the war.

Fuck me! You reckon that's right?

I know it is. If you think about what sort of man your uncle was, he wouldn't have beaten up Jews who lived on his manor, especially for someone like Mosley. And from what I understand, he didn't always take money to protect the Jews.

I've gotta make you right, son, only it's just what I was told by family. See, you done it again. You've got education behind you and that's saved me looking a right mug putting Jimmy Spinks was a Blackshirt. Good boy.

I keep trying to go back to them early days then something else crops up.

Doesn't matter.

Yeah, you said. Well, going right back to the beginning, like

I told you, we lived in Hoxton, but life sort of changed when we moved over to Bethnal Green. I mean, when you're a kid it don't matter if you live in a shed; as long as Mum and Dad are there and there's plenty of grub, it don't matter one bit. But I remember the proper excitement of moving into a brand-new place. Dad and a couple of mates loaded all the furniture and bits and pieces on to this big old lorry; it was as dirty as fuck, wings hanging off and bald tyres. Expect it was cheap, though. Then us kids were all slung on top and away we went.

Pete, it was fucking beautiful. All painted up, new bricks, white concrete and it all smelled like a new place does when you go on holiday.

Does that sound bollocks?

No, Len, I can imagine just what you're saying.

Good boy. So anyway, we've all jumped off the lorry and we're running about all over the place – that's me, Linda, Barry and Lorraine; she was three. I think Mum might have been pregnant with Raymond – can't be too sure at that age, though, because I didn't take much notice of that sort of thing. In the end, Dad gave us some coppers to go and buy ice lollies because there was a little shop right by us. Kent Road, that was it. Still there, but like everywhere else it ain't nothing like it was the day we moved in. I like that memory, Pete, because everything was sunny and Mum and Dad was happy and us kids was happy. Don't make me sound soft, does it? Because, you know, that's the last thing I am.

Not at all, Len; in fact, it shows you've got a heart. I mean,

you say it yourself, but a lot of people think you're a raving lunatic. This book will let them understand there's a lot more to you than just being the toughest guy around.

You think so? You sure this sort of stuff ain't boring?

OK then, well, we moved into Godwin House and life for all of us was beautiful and as far as I was concerned everything was perfect. I mean, to see your mum and dad laughing and messing about is great for kids. They was like kids themselves really, because they was always kissing and cuddling. Dad was always grabbing hold of Mum and singing that old song [Lenny sings] 'Yella Rose of Texas, the only gal for me'.

Did I tell you my mum's name was Rose? Rosie he called her. His name was Lenny, same as me.

I remember one time he chucked a live mouse into the kitchen when Mum was washing up. Fucking 'ell, tell you what, she screamed so much Mrs Hayes come running down from the flat upstairs to see what was going on. He done it again a bit later. He's opened the kitchen door and he's got his hands behind his back. Now, us kids know what he's up to, but we stand in the hallway trying not to laugh. I mean, he's still got his hands behind his back and Mum's screaming blue murder and flicking him with a wet dishcloth. 'Course, then he pulls out a box of chocolates: Black Magic they was, her favourites, but she still carried on whacking him with this cloth, but she's laughing now. Us kids are nearly pissing ourselves out in the hall. Then we all burst in and had a right good laugh and then they was off again cuddling. Lovely, lovely, lovely memories, Pete.

I told you there weren't much money flying about, but we always had decent grub. Don't remember getting too many new clothes, and I seemed to live in wellies all me childhood. Did you ever hear that Scotch guy, Billy whatsisname? Very funny fucker.

Billy Connolly?

Yeah, that's him. He reckoned you could always tell who was the poor kids on the beach because they had welly-boot marks on the back of their legs. He don't know how fucking true that was.

I've gotta say, Pete, we didn't know we was poor – us kids, I mean – because we were all in the same boat, but we had a lot of love in the family.

Do you remember your dad? Because you were quite young when he died...

Yeah, I remember him like he was sitting there beside you. And I think why I remember him so much is because later on, when life was bad, what with Irwin, I thought about him and prayed he'd come back and rescue us. I'd play over and over in my head all the nice memories of him and it made my life a little bit better. Funny what kids do, ain't it?

Yeah, my dad was OK. He was what they call a good money-getter. Didn't have a proper job, if you know what I mean, but he always seemed to be able to put steam on the table and he did that – same as a lot of men in them parts – by stepping over the line.

You remember that?

No, no, I learned lots of bits and pieces from my aunt Rosie

– Rosie Wall, that is. Pete, she was the funniest woman alive and I loved being around her; in fact, all my aunts were comediennes. After my dad was gone, I spent a lot of time with her, because with her talking about him it was like bringing him alive again. Somehow I don't think my mum would've been too keen on me listening to what she was telling me, me being a kid and all that. He was a good man, but how else was he going to feed his family with no job unless he did a bit of ducking and diving? According to Rosie, he was a pretty good conman. Not one of them lowlifes who nick off old ladies, but a man who had a good line in old fanny to talk greedy bastards into parting with their cash. That's what conmen rely on: greed, greed, greed.

Did she give you any examples of any of his scams?

There were plenty. Like, he'd go in a pub – not local, though – with a pocket full of snide gold and rings with glass diamonds in them, the sort of shit you could pick up for coppers. Then he'd whisper that he was fencing the proceeds off some robbery and the mugs would be queuing up to give 'im their cash. Or he'd get big cardboard boxes that used to hold Players or Senior Service fags, fill 'em up with newspaper or straw, I dunno, chuck 'em in a borrowed van, then offer them up as being nicked. They was placed so the first box that was pulled out had a couple of layers of real cigarettes on top of the paper, but, as it was all done on the hurry-up in case Old Bill turned up, the mark didn't have the time or inclination to go through the boxes.

You're shaking your head, son, like 'Who could be that stupid?', but these idiots are so blinded by a quick profit they ain't thinking. Now, the old man ain't being greedy, so the mark thinks Dad's the mug and can't get his money out quick enough. Soon as the boxes are off, so is my dad, laughing his nuts off all the way home.

Another time, I remember we got up in the morning and the front room was filled up with boxes of Liquorice Allsorts; they was stacked to the ceiling. Dad and whoever was in on it must've been up and down in the lift all night long. Now, we think it's Christmas, but he said, 'You can eat some of them but you can't take them outside' because he was just looking after them for a mate and this mate would get the hump if he saw us eating them. Eat them? Fuck me; I ain't ever been able to face another Allsort since that day.

Let's have a break for a bit, Pete; I'm knackered with all this talking. Have a roll-up.

Nice cuppa tea, Val! You there, babe? Nice cuppa tea.

I know you live up in the sticks, but when you're down 'ere, where you staying?
With my sister in Bexley, couple of miles through the tunnel.
Yeah, I know Bexley, not far from that pub where I had my fight with the gypsy. So what does your sister do?
She's an estate agent in Eltham.
Eltham? Eltham, that's the place where that pub is.
I know where you mean – Yorkshire Grey, wasn't it?

That's the one. And what about her ol' man, your brother-in-law, what does he do to make a living?

Errrr...

Errrr? What do you mean 'Errrr'?

He's in the force. Police. Chief Inspector.

NAH! Do what? Fucking 'ell! Val! 'Ere Val, you ain't gonna believe this, Peter's relation is only Old Bill.

He's sound, though.

What – bent, you mean?

No, no way. He's as straight as they come. I mean he's a really nice guy.

I expect he is if he's married to your sister. Look, I don't mean to disrespect your family, Pete, but fuckin' hell, son – bit of a shock, that's all.

You made that tea yet, Val?

I'm knackered; this is more tiring than having a flare-up. OK, you eat them biscuits up. I need a piss...

[Lenny sings] 'Carolina moon keep shining, shining on the one I'm waiting for.'

Right, where was I? Yeah, my dad, as I said, he was a lovely man, but he wasn't a well man. He had this big scar all round his chest and when I asked him what it was he told me a load of Germans had a go at him when he was a marine, but even though he was wounded he killed them all and that was the end of the war. I thought he was a right hero, but the truth was – I found out years later – that he had a dodgy valve in his heart because he picked up some bug or a virus or something in India. Remember, this is years ago, before heart transplants and all the clever stuff they've got today, so when he had this big operation they told him he probably would only live a couple of years.

Know what? He died exactly two years to the day.

Was he a very sick man?

That's the funny thing, he didn't seem ill to me at all, but then when I used to think back on it there was signs, if you know what I mean. He used to carry me down Bethnal Green Market on his shoulders. Then that stopped, but I never questioned it; I mean, why should I? I was just a baby. He had a bad cough, but so did every other bloke we knew, because they smoked like chimneys in them days. But listen, Pete, what frightened me at the time was on a couple of occasions I'd be in bed and he'd be cough, cough, coughing. I got out of bed, crept through into the living room and Mum was kneeling beside him, holding his hand and crying. When I said, 'What's up?' Mum would wipe her face and tell me she had a little headache. But worst was finding them both crying. Mum cried at different times, little cut on the finger, or when we was home a lot later than we should've been, and even when she was happy, but *Dad* – now, that shouldn't happen. Know what I'm saying? You must've had it when you was a kid, Pete; big boys don't cry, and all that. '

'Course, later in life you learn that even the toughest guys can shed a few tears for different reasons.

But fuck me, your dad? He's a giant, a hero and Superman all rolled into one, so something had to be up. But they never told us nothing. Perhaps they both thought some miracle would happen, but it never.

Was your dad in hospital when it happened?

You nicked my lighter? Where the fuck's that gone? Gis a light, son.

Hospital? Not too sure about that. He might have been in and out, but the details have gone right out of my head. What I do know is that one minute that lovely man was in our lives then he was gone and we never saw him again. Very sad. I can't really describe it, but sad don't seem enough to cover how we all felt.

I can tell you how it happened. Not his dying, but how we found out.

The only people in the block who had a television at that time were the Hayes family, who lived in the flat above. I suppose with their fruit business and a few of them working, they had a lot more folding than anybody else. They weren't flash or nothing, and I distinctly remember Mrs Hayes – lovely woman – bringing down decent bits of clothes that her kids had outgrown, even though Alfie was the same size as me and a couple of the girls was the same size. Leaving Mum a bit of pride, you see. Same with food: she'd bring all kinds down for us that her family couldn't eat, yet a family that size could've eaten a warehouse full and none to spare. Pride and respect, that's what the old East End was made up of.

What was I saying?

About the Hayes having a television.

Good boy, you're listening. Yeah, so every chance we got we was flying up them stairs to watch this telly. There was a kids' programme in the afternoon after school was finished and my favourite was something called *The Flowerpot Men*. Daft, really: Bill and Ben was like flowerpots and the girl one was a flower called Weed because all she ever said was 'Weed, weed' in a high-pitched voice. So, anyway, me, Barry, Lorraine and the Hayes kids were all sitting on the dining table watching this, with the curtains drawn because people thought you had to watch telly in the dark, and Barry is driving us all fucking mad going 'Weed, weed' in our ear'oles. Mrs Hayes come in and said that Mum wanted us, so we kicked up a right fuss, you know, moaning and shouting, 'Just give us five more minutes.' Then I've looked round and she's crying. Mrs Hayes crying? Nah, couldn't be, but she was, so I've jumped down and the others followed me. We was led to the front door and there was Mum holding Raymond, because he was only little, and she was crying as well. That was it then, we all kicked off crying and we don't know why except we're all frightened, I think.

We get indoors and there's Linda crying as well. Mum kneels down and pulls us all together in this big hug and says, 'Your dad's gone to heaven to be an angel.' To be honest, Pete, at that time I thought it could've been a lot worse, because I didn't understand, so I give her face a wipe with me sleeve, give her kiss on the cheek and told her he'd back when he'd finished being an angel. Then I got the shock of my life because she said, 'Oh, Lenny, he ain't ever coming back, but he'll always be looking down on us even though we can't see him.' I don't remember nothing at all after that except Mum crying and then the funeral.

Was it a big send-off?

That's the funny thing, when you consider what he meant to me – to all of us: I can't remember. Doubt it, though, what with money being short. All I do remember is a great big church full of people crying and a coffin going into a big hole in the ground. Tell you what, Pete, we'll go down the cemetery and I'll show you. Is that good? None of that seemed to have anything to do with my dad.

Don't get me wrong, all us kids loved that man to death. But we was kids, and kids can't grieve for too long, no matter how much we missed him. Mum took it very hard, though, she got thin and sort of old even though she was only 24. Fucking shame, really, because looking back she was really only a young girl and she was a widow with five kids to look after.

What sticks in my mind is me laying in bed – now, this is months after – and I'd hear her going, 'Oh, God, oh, God, why, why? Oh, Lenny, where are you.' First off I thought she was shouting for me, so I'd go to her bedroom and we'd have a cuddle until she went to sleep. Don't think, Pete, that it was just me that did all the cuddling and stuff, but because I'm telling my side of things I can't keep going off to talk about my brothers and sisters. You understand what I'm saying?

This ain't easy, you know, because you're making me think back to times I ain't thought about for years and years. Something else: thinking about my dad and my mum, who's gone as well now, is giving me a bit of a lump in the throat. **Shall we talk about something else?**

Yeah, just for a bit. No, we'll have a fag and a nice cuppa tea.

Val! Val! Peter said should he go round the café for a cuppa?

So your brother-in-law's Old Bill? Still can't fucking believe it...

I'll tell you a bit about the Hayes, because they were a diamond family, every one of them. I honestly think they helped keep our family together, what with the help and support they gave us.

I remember Billy Hayes. I ain't seen him for about 35 years – actually, no, 37 years. I'll never forget him, because he was one of the few outside the family that was good to me when I was a little kid. He used to take me out every Sunday and meet his girl. He used to take me in a cab, just take me wherever in general. I can remember I was about seven years old, so to me Bill was like a grown-up man, but don't suppose he was very old at all – probably in his early twenties. I used to think, yeah, he fancied my mum, because she was very pretty and over the years I often wondered how life would've turned out if they'd got together. Shame how you lose touch with people, because I've got no idea where Bill is now. I mean, I ain't seen him in 37 years. I'd love to meet him and shake his hands. Bill's got to be about 60 now. It was a very big family of Hayes and they were very good friends of ours: Pauline Hayes, Freddy Hayes, Timmy Hayes, Julie Hayes and Patsy Hayes.

You know, years ago, when we was all little kids. I used to go hop-picking with Mrs Hayes. She used to take me away with Alfie, because she knew how spiteful Jim Irwin was. I ain't got to all that yet, but you'll see what an evil bastard he was when I do. To me, hopping was like going on holiday, and in a way I suppose that's what it was for all East Enders. We used to go to some place in Kent – Tunbridge Wells, I think. We'd go off in a lorry and it would take all day to get there because the lorry done like ten miles an hour. Apart from living in a big wooden shed and pissing in a bucket, what I remember most is the smell of them hops. Can't describe it, but it was lovely and it clung to us all the time, even after we come home. You ever smelled it, Pete?

Yeah, I have, so I know exactly what you mean. I haven't picked hops, but I've worked in the drying houses – you know, oast houses.

You don't half get around, don'cha?

When I think back it was hard, because those hop leaves tore your hands to bits and it killed your back. But it was fun. It was just like a community where everybody mucked in together. Know what? I don't remember having a wash the whole time I was there; must've gone home as black as Newgate's knocker. I used to bring home a few bob, but I give that to Mum.

I liked the Hayes, because, like I say, they all worked down the fruit market and they used to have loads of taters and apples and cooking apples and things on their back balcony. Our balcony used to lead up to their balcony, so me and Barry used to creep up there in the middle of the night and nick all their cooking apples and take 'em back to ours and eat 'em. We suffered, because next day we used to have belly ache – but that's neither here nor there.

I think John might call in later. Have you met John?

Which John is that?

Johnny Nash.

No I haven't. I've heard a lot about him, though.

Nice man, John. Comes from a good family of well-respected people. I think you'll like him, Pete. When I was away he looked after my Val; he was always calling in – not on his own, though, because you don't do that when a bloke's behind the door. Respect, see: he always brought his wife Linda with him to make sure Val was OK.

Apart from hop-picking, did you ever go away, you know, have trips away with your family?

Yeah – very occasionally, we'd go to Southend for a day. That was like the main place for people in the East End, because it weren't that far. I mean, I never did it, but some kids would cycle there for the day. Fucking hell, you can't let your kids out the front gate these days, but then it was different.

Anyway, we'd go to Southend, take a basket of food and sit there playing in the sand. She would be sitting in a deckchair, Mum that is, and if I remember right she looked happy, because she was away from it all. Weren't no money to spare, so there weren't much ice-cream flying about, but we all just loved running in out of the sea and making sandcastles an' all that. Sometimes there'd be a Punch and Judy show on the beach and we'd holler and shout and scream at them puppets. That was free, I think – 'bout the only thing that was.

I know I went off the rails later in life, but then I was just a proper little kid. Shouldn't really say it in a book, but I think I was what they called a 'mummy's boy' at that age. You know, didn't want to lose sight of her. What it was, I was frightened she might disappear like my dad done. I mean, I loved that woman to death.

You could always tell when us kids was enjoying ourselves, because someone was always crying [laughs]. And you could always rely on my brother Barry to have a runny nose and be bawling most of the time. I used to say to him, 'Pack up grizzling' and he'd say, 'I hate it down Southend, I wanna go home.' Every kid you looked at seemed to be crying with a snotty nose and that was what was funny about it.

Overall, as kids we had a violent childhood – very violent. That's why when my brother come of age he got out of it, he emigrated to Australia. I was banged up at the time.

What prison?

No, no, no. Borstal, come to that in a bit. What happened was, we got a special dis-something or other.

Dispensation?

24

Good boy, that's the word. Yeah, we got one of those from the governor so that Barry could visit and say goodbye. Funny really, we were never what you'd call a touchy family. Don't know why, because we all loved each other, but I think that's the way it was back then. So me and Barry had a nice visit, a long talk where the both of us fucked Irwin into the ground for ruining our childhoods, said our goodbyes and, being tough guys, shook hands and off he went. Well, almost. As I watched his back I got this lump in my throat enough to choke me – remember, I might never see him again. I shouted after him and he come back and I said, 'Come 'ere, you ugly bastard' and I gave him a big hug. Ain't ashamed to tell you, Pete, we both had tears in our eyes. Later, when I was in my bunk, I laid there thinking I'd like to kill Irwin for making me lose my brother.

Barry was just a baby, really and there he was taking off to the other side of the world. I must have been about 14 then and thought he was as brave as fuck, you know leaving everything behind and starting a new life. Really he wouldn't have done it if it wasn't for Irwin. He bought a big house out there with a fishing lake at the bottom of his garden and everything was lovely. He done well for himself working for the government in the water industry, had kids, and them and his wife Judy was the love of his life. Then, one morning, she was taking the kids to school and she's gone to pull out and there was a lorry coming along... anyway, it went straight into the car and killed her stone dead. Terrible, terrible thing to happen. But the two children, they were saved, and Barry is coping well the last time I spoke to him. He's a proper McLean, a strong character, and he knows life must go on and he's got to look after them kids and bring them up. I said to him, one day I will come out to him and meet his family, because I've never met them, but his kids have heard all about me and want to meet me and see me, so I shall go out there one day.

Yeah, Barry just got out of it. He didn't suffer as much as I did, but life weren't good for none of us. He only come back once for the funeral when my mother died, then he went back and I've never seen him since. He never used to get as many beltings off Jim as bad as I did. Looking at photos, Barry has grown up looking like me, but he didn't look like me as a kid. That was the problem: I reminded Jim of my dad and he knew my mum still loved him, so he knocked the bollocks out of me. Barry was quiet; he didn't say too much.

We used to have a laugh when we was kids, me and Barry. He was a really smart kid, always immaculate and well dressed, you know, where I was always rough and ready when I was a kid. I remember when he saved up for months and months and then spent £30 on a suit – you won't remember, Pete, but that was one helluva lot of money back then. He was proud of this suit. Then, one Friday night, he's hung it outside the bathroom while he had a bath; bathroom was so fucking small you could hardly hang a towel up. All of a sudden I come in, see it all hanging outside the door, the lot: shirt, tie and that suit. I've slipped out of my gear, had a quick wash in the sink, put his gear on and went out [laughs]. That caused murders when I came home, because Barry was sitting in his vest and pants and socks and I come in looking the bollocks in his suit.

Were you closer to him than the others?

No, I was more close to Lorraine, I suppose. I mean, I loved 'em all, but she was my favourite – and Kruger, because he was the baby. Me and Barry got on more as we got older, but as I say, I ain't seen him for 20-odd years now he's in Australia. But I will go out and see him one day.

Shall we have a nice cuppa tea? Val! Val!

Give us a roll-up, Pete, I'm right out. So, how am I doing? If somebody told me this was going to be hard, I wouldn't have believed them. These stories ain't boring, are they? Pete, my son, you got to understand, it ain't too easy for me trying to remember everything. It's not boring you, is it? Because you'll jumble it out and jumble it out, won't you? There's little bits like the milkman throwing carrots at the horse, and when I was about two I wanted a pet and my dad bought me a cat, it was about six weeks old. Me and Dad were downstairs and next we see a fucking dead cat come flying out: Mum gassed the cat and slung it out the window. It's fucking hard to think, innit?

You're doing great, Len. You seem to have a good memory for detail.

Yeah, I'm surprising myself. I ain't jumpin' about too much, am I?

Don't worry about it. Like I said, we tape everything then straighten it all up later.

That's good. I'll get to some better stuff later.

Going back to Kruger, did I tell you why he was called that? Well, when he was a tiny baby, he was the spitting image of an old German man who lived downstairs – must've been an ugly little fucker. His real name – like, his christened name – was Raymond.

[To Val, who brings in the tea] Thanks, babe... 'Ere, drink your tea, son. My Val, ain't she lovely? Know what? I love that girl a bit more every day.

Talking of stories, I bumped into Allan Dixon the other day and he reminded me of a funny thing that happened years ago. The first time I met Al was when I was introduced to him outside the White Swan in Commercial Road. I was minding the gaff and he hadn't long been out after doing a nine stretch. I knew about him and his brother George because they was really well known faces years back; now they're both businessmen.

I said, 'How's it going Al?'

He said, 'Lovely mate, lovely, you the minder in this place?' I've gone, 'Yeah, brings me in a pension, what are you up to?'

He said, 'I've got this jellied eel stall here and four or five others all round the East End, they make me a few quid and help keep my head down if you know what I'm getting at?'

I said, 'Well if you get any problems, gimme a shout.'

He said, 'Thanks for the offer but I'll be ok Len, it's only a fucking eels stall, shouldn't have no problems with that.'

Anyway, one night we had a right fucking tear up in the Swan with the Watling Street mob; load of young kids in their twenties, all smashing the gaff up and wrecking the place. I've gone through the lot of them, belting them and throwing them out the door; one or two at a time I'm giving it to them and chucking them outside.

Now I've got my hands full so I ain't even thinking of nothing else, but over all this ruck all I can hear is Al hollering about his eels and crabs. 'Lenny, fucksake mind my jellied eels stall – hold up, hold up, you're wrecking my business.' After about twenty minutes it's all over and I've stepped outside to see what Al was shouting about. There's geezers laying all over the place and it's knee-deep in shellfish. What happened was, as I've slung these boys out they've gone crash into the eel stall and knocked it clean over. I've rounded them up, made them tidy up and then dug deep for a bit of compensation for Al. He weren't laughing at first but he saw the funny side later.

OK, what shall we talk about now, Pete? Ask me about my sister Lorraine, who we always called Boo – no idea why.

[Val speaks] **Tell Pete how you used to get Boo in trouble.**
He don't want to hear that, babe.
[Val] **All right then, tell him about Boo when she was in America and she nearly got murdered.**
Oh, good gal, you come and sit here and help me if I get

stuck. See, Pete, my Val don't forget nothing. Yeah, about my sister Boo. See, we all tried to get away from Jim Irwin in our own individual ways. I got married early to get away from him...

[Val] **Oh, that's nice – I thought it was because you loved me! [Laughs]**

Babe, you know I've loved you every minute of every day since I first met you.

[Val] **I know, love, I'm only winding you up.**

Now I've lost me thread; what was I saying, Pete?

About how you all wanted to get away from Jim Irwin.

Oh yeah. So I left home because I loved my Val. Barry went to Australia. Kruger got married and moved out. My sister lived with me nan. And Boo emigrated to America and married a Yank. Well, really she married a Yank to get out there but things didn't work out and they split up. Bit like myself, Boo could take a knock back and move on, so she got a job as a waitress in a bar to make ends meet, didn't she, Val? Then, one night, she's come out the bar where she worked, is just getting in her car and a big black bloke got hold of her by the neck and dragged her into another car that had two other blokes in it. They've given her good belting, slung her on the floor of the car and driven off. Now, Boo ain't a McLean for nothing. She kicked like fuck and, as they was going out the car park, managed to open the door, throw herself out and call the police. They said she was lucky to get out because those guys would've took her and murdered her, no doubt about it. Seems the law was looking for these lowlifes because they'd tried this attempted kidnapping stunt before and not long after Boo's run-in they was cornered by the police and the three of them was shot dead. My sister decided to pull the plug on America after that and come home. Now she don't live far from me and feels safe.

Let's 'ave a sandwich, Pete, then I'll catch up on some early stuff. That all right with you, son?

That's fine with me, but, like I said, tell it however you want. Good stuff. Get that sandwich down you, you need feeding up.

I just remembered something else about me dad that happened a few years later. I'd be about 12 by then, and me and my cousin Tony McLean – proper livewire, him – were kicking about the streets because we'd hopped off school. I dunno why it come up, but we was talking about my dad and Tony said, 'Let's go and see where he's buried.' Hard to believe, Pete, but I'd never been there since the funeral and didn't even know where it was. So we shot round me aunt Rosie's and that lovely woman never even questioned what we was up to or why we weren't at school when we asked her where the cemetery was. She's written it down and we set off for Stamford Hill.

What, walking?

You're joking, ain't ya? No, we had to get a bus, but because we'd been up to a bit of thieving or something we had a few shillings in our pocket so it weren't a problem.

Yeah, just come to me: Albany Park cemetery, that's the

place. Tell you what, we thought it was the bollocks: big archway over the entrance and all that, sort of place where you'd expect kings and queens to be buried. We've walked in and it's like a big beautiful park, trees, flowers, the lot. And – silly, really – we're both sort of excited about seeing what sort of headstone Dad's got. We run up and down looking at all the marble things and them with big angels but we couldn't find it, so we've gone up to this wooden shed where a bloke was sitting. First thing he said was, 'This ain't a fucking playground.' I thought that was nice talk in a cemetery but, instead of, like, telling him to fuck off himself, like we might 'ave done, we was polite and asked where Leonard McLean was. He's looked through some old books and told us it was number four, straight up and follow the path.

We've done that, and ended up kicking our way through a load of nettles; so back we go to the shed. I told the old bloke somebody had nicked me dad's headstone, because it weren't there and that c**t laughed, Pete, he fucking laughed at a kid that was trying to find his dad's grave. So he thinks it funny when he tells us me dad never had no marker 'cept a number because he was a pauper. I might not have been too educated, but I knew what that meant and I felt right choked up. As we're walking away he's shouted, 'He's probably got twenty people keeping him company down there.' We got a bit away, then picked up a few bits of broken marble and smashed them against the shed, then run like fuck. I was gutted.

So I never found it and never went back. But what we could do is, you and me go and find it; how does that sound? P'raps you could take some pictures for the book when we do.

Sad story that, innit?

I was going to talk about the time that changed my life. I know I've told you bits and pieces, but I'll go back to the beginning.

This is that Irwin, your stepfather?

Dead right, son. Who knows how I would've turned out if it wasn't for that child-beating slag? I'll come to it in a bit.

My turn now.

Yeah, go on, I'll make a roll-up while you're gone. Don't forget to wash your hands.

[Lenny sings] 'Love me tender, love me do...' Val! You there? Val!

She's gone out.

You was quick. Didn't pee on the floor, did you, because she'll go fucking mad.

It's OK, Lenny, I'm house trained.

I'm just joking with ya.

So, like I started to say, my mum took my dad's death very hard. She seemed old and didn't do nothing, and what I mean by that is that she never went out, never had her hair done proper and seemed to live in one of them pinny-dress things women used to wear for doing housework. Don't get me wrong, Pete, she still had time for us kids, but there weren't no spark there. This went on for a long while, probably a couple of years, then, all of a sudden, like almost overnight, she changed. She had her hair permed, got a new dress and went back to our old mum again. Laughed a lot and all. She even went out with Mrs Hayes while one of her daughters kept an eye on us. Now, we thought this was brilliant. We wouldn't have been so happy if we'd known what was coming.

Now, I come in one day and there was this big bloke standing in our sitting room. I'm thinking, 'Who the fuck's this?' and he goes, 'All right, boy?' I s'pose I was a bit possessive of me mum, so I blanked him – instant dislike, see. Probably would've been the same with any man, but, really, I didn't like the sneering look on his face. Mum was making a cuppa tea, so I've shot into the kitchen and, a bit stroppy, I've asked her what this bloke's doing here. A lot of women might've said, 'You're a kid, it ain't none of your business, so have a clip round the ear'ole,' but she knelt down, put her arms around me and told me, 'His name's Jim and he's gonna look after us.' I'm only a baby but I'm thinking, 'Fuck this for a game of soldiers,' so I put up a few arguments like, 'We've got an uncle, there ain't no room and Dad's looking after us.' Waste of time and next thing that fat bastard's moved in.

Little Raymond and Lorraine got sucked in by him and so did the other two to a degree, because he always come with a bag of sweets or bits of toys. Me? I saw something, so even then I had a knack of seeing through people's old bollocks, like I have now. There's a lot of blokes out there who want the woman but don't want the baggage they bring with them, and he was definitely one of them sort.

Did he move in straight away?

No he didn't, because I should think Mum was a bit old-fashioned, but to a kid's mind it was almost like straight away. First off, he'd come round a few times a week and it was always the same old thing: flowers and chocolate for Mum and sweets for us. I never ate nothing; it would've choked me. Let's face it, I hated him for replacing my dad and he hated me because I got between him and Mum at every opportunity.

How was he with you at first?

Well, he'd put on a bit of show, you know, turn it round so it looked like I was the problem. 'C'mon, boy, don't be moody' or 'Cor, you ain't 'alf a sulky soldier, Lenny.' I think even Mum swallowed that. Now, he'd mess around with the others, 'specially Raymond, what with him being a nipper. Like he'd tickle them or have little play fights and do tricks and stuff, but when it came to me that tickle in the ribs was a vicious dig, or he'd ruffle my hair and I could still feel his knuckles an hour later. I never said nuthin'; not a word.

First time I found he was sleeping in my dad's bed, it was like a punch in the stomach or a knife in the chest; terrible, I felt. It was like, 'Now Dad's definitely not coming back.'

Then they got married and the gloves was off. I was only a little kid, but I'd been making tea for years, so one day when Mum was out he's told me to make him one. I done that, took it through and spilled half in the saucer; didn't use mugs in them days. He's took the tea, put it on the little table and smacked me, full hand, straight round the face. Pete, remembering it today, I wanna tear that c**t's face off.

I couldn't breathe because I was too shocked. I didn't cry, just looked at him, and he looked at me and said, 'That's for being a clumsy little fucker.'

Know what? When Mum come in, she never said a word about my face being bright red on one side. What was all that about? Was she frightened she'd lose him if she kicked up a fuss?

I've gotta have a smoke, because I've wound myself up over that gutless coward.

You took on a couple of kids, didn't you, Pete?

Yeah, two girls. They were only little then.

Don't matter. Did you hate them, did you belt them, did you knock 'em about?

Of course not, I loved them like my own.

Of course not, just what I expected. And you know why? Because you're a man, a proper man. There ain't a lot of you but you was a bigger man than that piece of shit could ever be.

Let's have a cuppa, eh?

OK, then. I don't think I was a bad kid, but I was probably a stroppy little fuck when he was around – but only because I'd lost me dad at a very impressionable age. Make me right, Pete, – only natural, innit?

In between that slap and what come next, I suffered loads of digs, but only when Mum weren't around. I mean, you read about kids suffering abuse and all that and you think,

'Why didn't they tell somebody?' but what happens is, the kid thinks it's their fault for some funny reason, so they keep schtoom. Now, I'm always a bit wary around Jim, but I must've let me guard down this day. Mum and the others was off up the market and I was playing on the sitting-room floor. I still remember it: I had a few Dinky toy cars and I was pushing them up a tray or bread board or something and crashing them up the skirting. I'm giving it large with the engine noises. Jim was sitting in my dad's armchair, drinking bottles of beer and listening to the wireless. I heard him mumble something but I thought he was talking to the wireless. Next thing, he's kicked me right up the arris and shouted, 'Don't fuckin' ignore me, shut that noise up.'

I'm six, Peter, so two minutes later I'm at it again. Crash, crash, crash. Next thing, he's flung hisself out of the chair, grabbed me by my jersey and shook me like a rag doll. Tell you what, me teeth were rattling in my head. He's red in the face and spraying spit all over. 'Shut your fuckin' noise! I'm the guv'nor here and, if I say shut it, you shut it.' He's lifted me right up and screamed, 'Who's the guv'nor, who's the guv'nor?'

I'm strangling, I'm nearly shitting myself and I don't know what to say.

'Fuckin' well answer me!'

So what am I gonna say? Who else? 'Me mum,' I said.

He went crazy, spun me round and flung me against the wall. Fuck me, I've hit everything before I hit the deck: my head, my arse, my knee – and that was the worst, because it was broke. And he stood over me shouting, 'Get it right next time, you little c**t, I'm the guv'nor.'

Wasn't he concerned when he saw that you were hurt?

Don't make me laugh, he's dragged me by the scruff and slung me in bed and I just lay there with my leg on fire. I heard Mum come in and then heard him giving her a load of shit about me chucking myself down on the floor in temper. Then they both come in the bedroom, and while Mum's checking me over he's standing behind her giving me the look that said, 'Keep it shut if you know what's good for you.'

Cut a long story short, one of the Hayes took me to the hospital and got me sorted out, plastered up and all that. I think I was in a couple of days.

Didn't the hospital report what was obviously not a simple fall?

Peter, my son, this weren't where you come from. Where was you from as a kid?

Welling – Welling, in Kent.

No disrespect, but that's a million miles from the East End. Where I grew up, nobody give a flying fuck for some scruffy little kid outta the backstreets – at least, they didn't back then. Funny thing, though, I'm thinking Mum ain't gotta clue about Jim Irwin, but on a visit one day she stroked my head and told me that she was so sorry. Now, she wasn't saying sorry because she thought I chucked myself down, but, in her own way, without using the words, she was saying sorry for bringing that beast into our lives. Years later, she did actually say it, but not right then.

Do you think your mother knew the full extent of what he was doing?

To be honest, I don't think she did. I think what she did know about she put down to him being a bit strict, but then we'd all been a bit wild for a long while so Mum probably didn't think it was a bad thing. A lot of it she never saw and some of what she did she blanked right off. I can't find it in my heart to blame her, because life must've been very hard for her.

Something else he did was give us points for being out of order and he reckoned being out of order was if we just breathed. 'Spare the rod, spoil the child' – if I heard that once, I heard it a thousand times, and then you knew you was in for a belting. That points thing. At the end of each day, he'd see how many points we had, then give us a belt for every one, and in my case a few extra just to be spiteful. This weren't a little smack, it'd be a good punch, even for the girls, and if you got on the floor and curled up he'd use his feet in the ribs.

Wasn't there anyone at all who could've protected you?

I suppose there was, like Jimmy or the older Hayes boys, but there was this thing about keeping what went on behind closed doors. A way of life in the East End, and I s'pose it rubbed off on us kids. Know what? We spent so much time in bed for something or other, it's a wonder we didn't get bed sores. I ain't kidding, loads of times we'd be sent to bed at five o'clock because he was in a mood. Imagine, Pete, summer nights, broad daylight and kids outside screamin' and laughing and playing and we're stuck in that little poxy room.

You know, I think Irwin had a screw loose, because the way he went off weren't normal. We was larking about in the sitting room, all us kids, Mum was doing our tea and because we were making a load of noise he's started shouting and bawling. Next thing, we're on our way to bed – quarter to five. I think Mum tried to talk him out of it, but he weren't having it. I remember him screaming at Mum, 'If you won't discipline your fucking kids, somebody's got to.' Then he's crashed out the front door.

Did your Mum let you up when he wasn't around?

Fuck that, no.

Now, this is an example of why she didn't risk it. How that crafty bastard done it I don't know to this day, because he'd gone out. We're laying in bed whispering to each other and Mum come in, quietly shut the bedroom door and she's got a plate of bread and jam in her hand. She's gone 'Shhhhhh' and put her fingers to her lips. God love her, she tried her best. I've just leaned up to grab a sandwich and, CRASH!, the door's flew open and Irwin's standing there like a maniac. He was shakin' and his face was bright red. 'Wha'd I say? Wha'd I say? No fuckin' tea for that lot!' Mum just said, 'Jim?' and he grabbed the plate and slung it straight through the window – CRASH! again.

We're all babies really, we're covered in bits of glass and we're screaming in fear. He's grabbed Mum by the hair and I've shouted, 'Leave her alone.' That was it, he's gone mad,

40

trying to get at me or one of the others. Mum threw herself over us all so he started punching her in the back. An 18-stone man belting an eight-stone woman. Pete, I could feel every punch and Mum never said a word, just groaned every time he hit her. All the time he's screaming, 'Greedy c**ts, eating my grub when I said don't.'

Then he just went, slamming the door behind him. Mum rolled off the bed and just sat leaning against the wall, with blood coming out of her mouth and I wanted to kill him stone dead for hurting my mum. Mrs Hayes come down from her flat because she'd heard the ruck and wanted to call the police, but Mum wouldn't have it. Turned out that excuse for a man broke her ribs.

You ain't finding all this kids' stuff boring, are you?

Not at all, Len, I find it very sad that you all suffered like you did.

Good boy. Why I'm saying all this is because I think it turned me into the man I grew up to be. You know, a lot of violence and hate inside me.

I remember one night Jim Irwin had a party in our flat; my nan was there and because she always wore them big black shoes old women used to wear I knew it was her walking up the passage. She was on the way to the toilet, so I opened our bedroom door a crack and as she come back I whispered for her to come into the bedroom. She come in and I said, 'Nan, Jim don't stop belting us.' She said, 'Do what! When did he do that?' I've said, 'All the time, Nan', and showed her the strap marks and knuckle bruises I'd got over the last week.

41

Behind me my brothers and sisters are whispering that they've had some as well. Nan's give me a hug that nearly smothered me and said, 'I'll give 'im belt my babies', and she's flew out the bedroom. We're all grinning like monkeys waiting for it to kick off and you ain't heard nothing like it when it did – it was fucking murders – then she got slung out the flat. Well, I must take after her because sometimes enough ain't enough and she's come back the next day and given him a right-hander on the chin, so she's slung out again. Give you some idea Pete; my nan was like Rocky Marciano. Remember 'im? Blinding fighter. Anyway, she was a big woman, you know, like what a typical Nan was like in the old days. Big arms on 'er, always wearing one of them pinny things and either slippers or black leather shoes. Lovely woman, tough outside but a big heart of gold and soft inside. Now, Jim's already suffered a good couple of digs and, 'course, he can't retaliate because he knows that lay one finger on Nan and Uncle Jimmy would've cut 'is lights out. Right, so he can't do nothing about Nan giving him a seeing-to, so he does the next best thing. You're nodding your head, Pete; because you know what I'm gonna say. Yeah, he give me a belting. 'Course, he don't say why he's kicking and punching me, but I knew and I made sure Nan knew as well. Remember, Pete, I'm just a baby, so being a grass don't come into it. I found out what happened from one of the older Hayes brothers after Nan went barging into the drinker Jim Irwin was using. She's gone in, picked up a big old glass ashtray and done him right across the back of the head and split it wide open. I was told he never said nothing, just sat there like a lamb with blood pouring down his neck. I ain't fucking surprised; he must have been practically unconscious.

When Billy Hayes told me what went down, it put a grin on my face from one ear to the other like I'd been cut right across me mouth. Tell you what, that cheered me up for ages, because every time I looked at Jim I used to see like ten stitches in the back of his head and thought to myself, 'Good girl, Nan.'

I won't say that Irwin learned his lesson, but for a long while after he kept his hands in his pockets and made do with sneering and snarling at me. I could suffer that.

I used to love to go round my nan's, because she made a terrible fuss of me. I was her favourite and I was always round there telling tales about Jim so as to get him a belting because he was a horrible man, and I don't think I will ever forgive him till the day I die – I mean that.

Things went back to normal after a while, though I've gotta say normal in our place wasn't like anybody else's normal. Then something happened that made my mind up to get Irwin a proper taste of his own medicine. You know, I hate grasses. Make me right, they're scum, but when you're a baby, what you gonna do? I've come home from school one day and little Raymond is sitting on the doorstep, he's crying because there ain't no one in, he's cold because it's like winter, and on top of that he's pissed hisself.

He's forgot the door key is on a bit of string through the

letterbox, so I'm just getting me hand through, and the lift door, that's right opposite our front door, opens and out steps Jim Irwin. Raymond's still grizzling, so he's gone for him straight away. 'What you crying for, you baby?' Raymond could've said he'd fell over, but no, 'I've wet myself,' he's gone. 'Fucking hell, that's done it,' I thought to myself. Jim's managed to slap him and open the door at the same time. He's slammed it in my face and I could hear him belting that baby. Raymond's screaming at first, then he went all quiet. I still feel I let him down that day, because I sat on the step 'til Mum and the others come home.

Soon as we got in, Jim started covering his arse. He told Mum that Raymond's had a little slap and to leave him alone; and Mum did. It weren't until we went to bed that I see what a state that boy was in. His legs and his little bum was covered in welts and bruises and I've guessed Irwin's used the belt buckle on him. We've all give 'im a cuddle and he's going, 'I'm sorry, I'm sorry.' Yeah, I thought, sorry for being beaten like a fuckin' dog.

Let's have some tea and a fag. You up for that, because all this talking's wearing me out.

Yeah, good idea, mate.

[Val brings in some more tea] Blimey, Val! That was quick, I ain't even asked yet. Peter said have you got any of them custard creams? He's costing us a fortune and we ain't even sold a book yet. Good girl, Val, ta. She's lovely, my Val, she's stood by me all the way, no matter what come along, and I love her to death.

About my little brother, then. What happened was, I lay on the bed cuddling Raymond and I'm steamin' inside because of what's been done to him. Me nut's going round and round for hours. I heard Mum and that slag go to bed, waited for about an hour, then got up and got dressed. I had this plan to fuck Irwin up.

I've woke me brother up, and he doesn't even know where he is, slung some clothes on 'im, and – whispering to him to be dead quiet – we've crept to the front door and slipped out; took me ages to shut the door so it didn't bang. This was winter and cold enough to freeze your nuts off, but I've wrapped a coat round Raymond and led him downstairs. Now, tucked behind the waste bins was a go-kart me an' Alfie had made. Did you ever have one of them, Pete?

Blimey, yeah, every kid had one made out of pram wheels and bits of wood.

You got it, bit of string to turn the front wheels. Anyway, I've dug this out, laid Raymond on it and pulled him along. Know what? He never even asked where we was going. I'm getting on seven and that little blighter's about three, I think, and we're wandering the streets in the small hours.

What, were you running away?

Not running away. I was heading to our nan's, because she sorted Irwin out before but, at the back of my mind, even though I was only a kid, I knew she would involve her brother Jimmy Spinks.

Fuck me I was cold, because I'd put my coat on top of Kruger's to keep 'im warm. I ain't making myself out a hero;

because to be honest I was shittin' myself, but I weren't gonna give up. Seemed like I walked miles and the string was cutting my hands to bits, but I kept going because every time I looked round all I could see was Kruger's eyes looking at me out of the coats and I knew why I was doing it. I seen a police car coming up the road, so I dragged the cart into a gateway and crouched down 'til they went by. Might have been a good thing if they'd seen me, but right or wrong I had this fear or distrust of Old Bill. No reason – well, not at that age, anyway. By the time I've reached Nan's, I was completely bolloxed, and when Nan opened the door all I could get out was 'Jim hurt Kruger.' That night's all a blur after that, though I do remember praying to God that night for Irwin to die or get run over or something.

Were you a religious family, then?

No, no, but what it is, you might not believe in God and that but when things are rough it don't hurt to try and get a bit of extra help. I mean, in the nick I've heard the roughest, toughest evilest men saying a prayer before they're up in court or when they've been lifed off.

I did go to Sunday school, but before I did I used to go to a shop called Morgan's and buy a penny ice block with me collection money then suck the life out of it, so, by the time I got to church, all that yellowy ice used to be white and I'd go and sit in there and be bored for an hour and half. I supposed the reason Irwin wanted me out of the way so he could have a few private hours with my mum, I don't know, but I suppose that was the move in his head. As you get older, you realise why they wanted you out of the way, and fuck all to do with God.

So, did your nan go round to your flat with the big ashtray again?

Better than that, Pete; like I hoped, she got in touch with Uncle Jimmy. I found out what happened later, and I think it must've been Rosie who told me – can't be too sure about that. Whatever, seems Jimmy's gone round our flat like a fuckin' ravin' lunatic – or so I was told, but knowing Jimmy, who was a bit used to violence, I bet he was angry outside but calm inside. I would've loved to 'ave been there.

Seems he punched his way through our front door, then knocked seven bells of shit out of Irwin. What with Jimmy being old school, out come his cut-throat razor and the only thing that saved him being striped was my mum, who begged Uncle Jimmy to stop. Fuck knows why, because Irwin hadn't done her no favours – well, he certainly hadn't done her kids no favours. So Jimmy stopped short of cutting him as long as he fucked off there and then and didn't come back. Know what? That gutless coward, that fucking animal, took off like his arse was on fire. So we were on our own again.

[Sings] 'Da-da da-da da da da' – *EastEnders* is on now, so that's fucked havin' a cuppa tea for half-hour, because my Val watches it. Gotta tell you, Pete, I minded some of that lot one night. The *EastEnders* mob was having a big party at a place in Beak Street and at the time they were right on form, right on top of the hit parade, so there was a big-time lot of reporters there. The new producer, Jill something or other, give me a bell and asked if I'd come and mind them while they had our private party. I said, 'Yeah, as long as the money's right.' We agreed a figure and I kept all the photographers away and made sure there was no agg from anybody getting drunk or gatecrashers trying it on. In the meantime, a pal of mine who was also a pal of that Dean whatsisname – Peter Dean, what acted that soppy pratt who had a veg stall in the market – anyway, my pal Oggy used to got to school with Dean, so, when he asked me if he could get in the door, which p'raps he shouldn't have done, I said, 'Come on up and I'll slip you into the party.'

So the stars are all turning up and they was all polite, saying, 'Cor! You're a big fella, you're Lenny McLean, we've heard about you so we know we're well minded tonight.'

Then, Peter Dean come in and went, 'Hello, Lenny, all right?' and tried to give me his coat.

I've gone, 'Don't give me your fucking coat, the cloakroom's over there. I'm fucking minding your mob; I don't take coats of off no one.'

'Oh,' he said, and sat hisself down.

After a bit he come up to me again with a bit of a face on, saying, 'I see Peter Oggs is here, why is that?'

I've gone, 'Well, he's your mate, ain't he?'

He's said, 'In a manner of speaking, but he's not a member of cast so he shouldn't be here.'

I've said, 'Well, you're a fucking nice mate, ain'cha? But

listen, straighten your mug up and listen: Peter Oggs is with me, OK? Don't you worry what he's up to, just go and enjoy the party.'

He's gone all red and said he'd report me – fuck knows who to, though.

To be honest, most of the actors were OK, but the one I took to outta the bunch was Dot Cotton – can't remember her real name. She was one of your own, was Dot.

D'you watch it, Pete?

On and off, don't make a habit of it.

And who's your favourite?

I suppose I'd have to say Peggy – Barbara Windsor – because I think with her what you see is what you get.

Yeah, she's lovely. I think we've all got a soft spot for her. Did I tell you she come round ours when I was a kid?

It's a funny old world, Pete, and a very small one. See, back when I was a little kid Barbara actually visited my house – well, wasn't a house, it was a flat, but that's what you say when you're talking. Anyway, what it was – and obviously, unknown to me at the time – was my stepfather Jim Irwin – fucking slag, I don't really like mentioning his name – used to do a bit of work with Ronnie Knight. Fuck knows what it could've been, because Irwin weren't nowhere in Ronnie's league. So, for whatever reason, Ronnie's come up to my place and he's brought Barbara with him. Now, I was only little, but like everybody in them days I knew who she was because she was a big star. Tiny woman, all the bits in the right place, and very, very beautiful. I'll never know why, but

49

for some reason I ended up sort of standing behind the settee. Probably I was either very shy or half expected Irwin would give me a punch in the head in front of this lovely woman; never even opened my mouth. Different story when I got to school, though, because according to the way I told it Barbara gave me a big kiss and a cuddle and we chatted like old friends. Them that called me a lying bastard – which I was – got a smack in the ear'ole. Blinding story that, weren't it, Pete?

Ronnie was there as well, and strangely I come friends with him years later. I mean, a long time after I met him I asked him what he was doing working with Irwin all them years ago. Turned out Jim was nothing but a runner and Ronnie had knocked him on his arse for messing with a girl in his office. If Ron had known what he was doing to us kids and our mum he would've had him disappear.

Ron's old now, though I hope I look as good when I'm his age. He's got a club in Fuengirola; he's there five or six nights a week. He just minds his own business now, keeps a low profile, so people tell me, and I say good luck to you, Ron, and keep strong. I think they should leave him alone now, as he's really done his sentence out there. When I say that to people, they say, 'But he's gotta lovely life in the sun, nice villa and a beautiful wife.' I say, 'Yes, but he's a prisoner; he's stuck there and can't go nowhere.' Don't matter how much money he's got, he is out there miles from home away from all his friends and family and he is a prisoner. You know, you go away on a fortnight's holiday and you've had enough, you don't want another fortnight, you just wanna get home to your own bed. I think it's time they let the man come back. I dunno, I just think different from a lot of people, I suppose.

On the quiet, did you know he's talking of coming back?

Nah! Who told you that?

He did.

Fuck me. They'll nick him straight off the plane, tell him.

He knows that, but he's hoping that after all this time they'll go a bit easy.

Well I fuckin' well hope so. You gotta take your hat off to the man, he never hurt no one, never hurt no one at all. All right, perhaps he nicked a few quid over the years, but ain't we all? Fuck's sake, just leave the man alone. I met Barbara about a month ago up West. I see her walking along with some actor fella that was doing a show with her in a West End theatre – dunno what it was called. I was outside with some people and I shouted over to her and said, 'What you doing up the posh end of the street?' 'Course, I was only having a laugh. She come over and said she was just going to a restaurant for a bit of lunch. I said, 'Have you seen Reggie?' and she said, 'Yes, I had a nice visit with him a few months ago.' I told her that Mike Reid and Helen Keating went up last week and I went up the week before. How's Ronnie? 'Oh, he's OK as far as I know, but I don't see him much these days, just a phone call every few weeks.' I said, 'Well, I'm going to Fuengirola in a few weeks and I will probably pop in and see him.' She is a generation before me, so I don't really know her, but believe me she is as good as gold and just like she appears in films or on telly: 'Ullo darling,' and all that.

Talking of Fuengirola, I met another geezer out there. D'you remember Lonnie Donegan?

Not much. That man got me and my mates started with a skiffle group like every other teenager. I thought he was dead.

Well, he weren't when I saw him. Me and my mates did the same thing. We were fuckin' terrible. We went into this singing talent thing and come fourth outta four.

No, what I was saying, I see this bloke in a bar and I said to my Val, 'That's Lonnie Donegan, I'm gonna shake his hand,' and I did. What a lovely man. He told me he lives over there and mainly just writes songs for other people now; funny who you bump into when you're miles from home.

Doesn't matter if I jump ahead, do it?

No, we'll sort it later.

Talking about Ronnie made me think of something else about him when I was in prison. One time I was having dinner and one of the cons by the name of Carl, bit of a mouthy git, came down and he had a paper under his arm and he said, 'Read that, Len.' I've had a look and it was saying that Ronnie Knight had been bashed up in a club in Fuengirola.

Now, this geezer's laughing while he's watching me read the paper and I said to him, 'What are you laughing for, you c**t?'

He's said, 'Gangster? Hard man? He ain't so tough now, letting himself get a seeing-to.'

I've gone, 'So that's why you're laughing, you fucking mug. Well, whoever done that to Ronnie took a diabolical liberty: the man's 60 years old.' I said, 'Get outta my sight, you arse'ole, before I slap that laugh off your stupid mug.'

As he's walked off, he's said, 'Fuck you.'

So I said to a fella sitting near me, 'See him? I'm gonna belt him fucking senseless.'

This guy said, 'Not now, Len, we're being watched.'

'No,' I've said, 'later I will slip out and knock him spark out.'

He went, 'All right, I'll watch your back.'

What we done, we found out which cell he was in; I was one of the number ones, so I could walk about without any trouble. Later, I stepped into his cell while he was slopping out and stood behind the door waiting for him to come back. As he stepped inside the cell door, I've hit him on the side of the head and knocked him unconscious, picked him up, laid him on the bed and chucked his blanket over him. His cell mate come in and I told him to say nothing or fucking else. The next morning I see him coming down and he couldn't look at me – he kept looking at the fucking floor when he walked past me. I'll give him his due, he never screamed.

His pal kept laughing and I said, 'What you laughing at?'

He said, 'He didn't wake up until four o'clock this morning.'

You want some more of that earlier stuff, son?

Yeah, you were saying Jim Irwin moved out.

No, I was saying he was chucked out on the end of a razor, but, good boy, you ain't forgetting what I'm saying. You sure that stuff ain't boring?

Not at all.

Good stuff. OK, we'll have a nice cuppa tea first. Val! Val!

Look atcha, you've got ash all over her floor. She'll go fuckin' mad.

So have you!

Nah, it's blowing over from your side.

Anyway, we had a bit of a break from Irwin and it was lovely: no tension and no agg. We was all smiling again, though I've gotta say Mum didn't seem as happy as we were. I mean, what do little kids know about adult relationships? Perhaps if we weren't around the two of them could've been happy and he might have been a different person. But we was, so it's hard to understand what she saw in 'im.

This geezer kept popping in and out and he was a skinny little c**t with a face like a rat, so I'm thinking, 'Hope he ain't after Mum, because we just got rid of one bad bastard, we don't wanna go there again.' Know what it was? Irwin was using this bloke to pass messages to Mum, asking if he could come back. According to Rosie – bless that woman, she told me everything; too much, sometimes – Mum's gone to Uncle Jimmy and begged him not to hurt Jim if he come back, said he'd learned his lesson. So, getting to the point, that smirking, horrible beast of a man come waltzing in one day with a suitcase like nothing had happened. Two minutes later, he's giving me the boot again. Remember, the last time I see him was when he give Kruger that belting and I was waiting for something to kick off.

I've got in the lift one day just after he come back and, fuck me, he got in right behind me. The door shut and he got me by the throat and pinned me in the corner, shouting, 'You're a little fuckin' grass and grasses always get what's coming to 'em.' I never said nothing. As I got outta the lift, he said, 'Be careful you don't trip one day and fall over the balcony.'

Make me right, Pete, does that sound like somebody who's got all his marbles?

Seems like he definitely had some sort of mental problem.

You've got it. No grown-up should talk to a young kid like that.

Pete, my son, I could talk forever about the bashings I got, but one sounds like another after a bit so I'm gonna move on. Is that all right?

That's OK, Len, but, before you leave it, did the ill treatment stop as you got older?

I suppose it got a bit less, but he never missed a chance to have a dig. Mum got pregnant and then she had a little girl and I thought things might change, but they never did. You'd think us lot would be jealous of this new kid – Sherry, her name was – but we weren't. She was a proper little darlin' and she followed me everywhere when she could walk. Lost touch with her when she grew up, over a thing that happened, but that's something else.

So, as the years have gone on I've filled out and started running around with a little firm. There was Tommy Green, Andy Bradshaw and Joe Kyle, good lads who lived local and after a bit my cousin Tony joined us. Fuck me, we got up to stuff. You told me your dad was a copper and you lived in Kent, Pete, so life would've been worlds away from my background. So you might not understand what it was like for us kids in the East End. Thieving to us weren't dishonest; it was a way to get by, if you know what I mean. It was everywhere – not indoors, because Mum was funny like that. But, like I said earlier, everybody was at it, so it seemed like normal.

To be honest, we was a right bunch of toerags. We'd all been nicking since we could walk; fuck me, there weren't no money coming from indoors, so we had to do the best we could. Little stuff at first, like a few sweets from Morgan's. Usual lark: ask for something off the top shelf, then up the jumper with whatever when his back was turned. Caught me one time and nearly knocked me head off me shoulders; you couldn't get away with hitting a kid nowadays, but it never did us no harm.

Jump-ups, now that could be an earner. We'd hang about until we saw a lorry doing a delivery, then, once the driver's taken his first box into the shop, we're up, grab whatever and away.

I did the same.

Nah! And your ol' man a copper?

One time when I was about six, I got in the back of a fruit

lorry, filled my jumper but I didn't hear the driver come back until the engine started. I had to jump out while he was doing 20 miles an hour. It's a wonder I wasn't killed.

P'raps things weren't that different over your way, then. Fruit was a waste of time, because you pick it up for fuck all down the market, but we still done it anyway. Sometimes we got a right result, like if it was shoes or dresses or spirits, but that didn't happen too regular, because they kept their eyes open. We had it all worked out, though. I was always the one that done the business, a couple of us catching the gear and one, usually Tony, waiting by the shop to ask the driver something stupid if he came back too quick.

But what we never done was nick off our own. I mean, some old girl could have a thousand pounds in her purse and we wouldn't have dreamed of touching it; not like the scum today. Sometimes back then you got the odd bit of trouble with lowlifes and I remember one time we was all down the Roman and we see this geezer snatch a bag off this woman who had a pram and a couple of nippers. We've chased this piece of shit and got hold of 'im after Tone tripped him up and we beat the fuckin' livin' shit out of him. We weren't heroes and we didn't want no fuss. But you know, there's things you don't do.

As we all got older, we got into heavier stuff, like proper thieving. We worked our nuts off one night stripping lead off this roof; how the fuck we got up there I dunno, but we're black as arse'oles, hands are cut to bits and sweating like bastards. That's OK, because we're gonna have a good earner. So we're ready to start chucking the lead down. Joe or Tony, I dunno which, leaned on the edge of this roof and one of them big stone things fell off and dropped right on top of a motor down below and flattened the fucker. Tell you what, we got down and away quicker'n we got up.

You were youngsters, so how did you turn whatever you stole into cash?

Ah, that's the thing, it ain't easy to find the right outlet for hooky gear and we got turned over a few times before we found a decent fence down the Nile. I mean, the guy we used give us shit money, but at least he did give us a few quid. One time we took a bag of jewellery to this guy we'd been told was sound. He said come back in an hour, and when we did he can't remember who we are – he's rumped us. Remember, we're still youngsters, so what we gonna do? He's got a minder giving us the look and we ain't big enough to take him on, but we can run. I've called this fence a big, ugly, no-good fucking wanker. Then, as his bloke's come at me, I've given him me boot right up the knackers. He's gone down like a sack o' shit, screamin' like a baby, but that's about as far as we can go, so we legged it; Learned a good lesson that day.

Did you ever get caught by the law?

We was lucky really, or clever – probably just lucky, thinking about it; though we did have a run-in that could've seen us behind the door. Now, because we're getting a bit daring about what we got up to, we had to get further away from our patch. Ain't got a clue what we'd find in Romford that we couldn't find a bit closer, but Andy, Tommy and me jumped on the train one day and headed for Essex. Don't have to say we was having a right laugh; empty carriage and getting bored. Tom's unscrewing the light fittings and picture frames with a penknife and me and Andy are having a friendly punch-up. He run at me and I've walloped him up the side of the head. As he's falling backwards, he's grabbed the cord that stops the train in an emergency and we've run into a brick wall. Well, that's what it felt like.

Serious offence.

Yeah, I know, but that ain't the half of it. We've flung the door open and slung ourselves down the banking. I've tore me arse on the fence, Tom's lost his shoe and Andy's fell in a ditch and got soaked to the waist; what a fucking mess. Geezers are shouting at us to come back – as if that would make us give ourselves up. We just kept running, until we couldn't run no more. We ain't got a clue where we are but we can't ask nobody in case Old Bill's put the word out.

This must've been winter, because I remember it getting dark. We're cold, knackered, starving hungry, lost and proper pissed off. We come over a hill and there's a little garage, one of them one-man jobs they used to have back then. I've said to the boys, 'If we could get a few quid outta that gaff, we could get a taxi home. D'ya reckon you can cream the place, Andy?' He's up for that and creeps over and hides behind some old lorries. We're watching. Ten minutes has gone by and I'm getting the arse'ole, then a van pulled in and this old boy comes limping out. He's got one of them big boots on.

Club foot?

Yeah that's it, so he's dead slow.

We see Andy slip into the door the old fella's left open. Piece of piss. One minute, then we hear a crash – told us later he's grabbed the cash and walked straight into a pile of oil cans. He's come out the door like a fucking greyhound, straight past these geezers and off down the road. We've caught up with him a bit later; we're outta breath, but we're laughing like c**ts while we divvy the money up. Sixty-nine quid – a bloody fortune. Now all we've gotta do is find a phone box and order a taxi and we're home and fucking dry.

Talking of dry, 'ere,

Val! You up for a break, Pete?

Yeah, I'm spitting feathers

Val! Peter says you're fucking slow with that tea.

You'll get me bloody well shot.

So, we walked a couple of miles and we're laughing because Tom's only got one shoe an' his sock's cut to bits; he weren't laughing, though. Anyway, one minute we're Jack the lads and full of ourselves until we're all blinded by headlights in front of us and the same behind. Next minute we're sitting in a squad car being driven off to the nick. As it turned out, we weren't put in cells or nothing, just shut in an office with a policewoman until our parents came. Mine didn't, because my uncle Bobby Warren come instead. He was a bit stern in front of the coppers, though they didn't know nothing of his rep, but once we was released he was OK.

End of the day, we got a bit of probation each. Andy and Tom got a right bollocking from their parents and kept indoors for ages. I got a punch in the side of the head that made me go cross-eyed and a kick in the kidneys while I was on the floor that made me piss blood the next day. See this?

What's that?

This scar on me eye. Caught me with his ring when he belted me, so I ain't likely to forget that day, am I?

Good story or what?

I think you said you had a great respect for your uncle Bob.

Not 'alf. He was another man's man, like Uncle Jimmy: proper old school, a nice man, a tough man but a very fair man with proper old values. He wasn't whiter than white hisself, and, though I can't say he encouraged me to play up and get into trouble, he understood what it was all about.

Back in the fifties, he'd got a seven, along with Frankie Fraser, for doing Jack Spot, the man we was talking about before. What it was, there was trouble between this Spotty bloke and another bloke called Dimes because they both wanted to be top gangster, or godfather, or whatever. Uncle Bob was a good pal of Albert Dimes as well as working for him. These two were always at each other for one reason or another, and they ended up having a bit of a straightener up in Soho – Frith Street, I think. Both of them had knives and they've gone at each other and they've both ended up in hospital. Cut a long story short, Pete, Dimes got Bob and Frankie Fraser to give Spotty a seeing-to: slash 'im up to frighten 'im to get outta the business.

They've done the job but got nicked afterwards and got a seven each. I remember Bobby Warren telling me a story about their first morning at the start of their sentence. Bobby said, 'We come out the cell and straight off Frank pulls a knife out, I don't know where he got it from but he grabbed a screw, put the blade to this geezer's throat and said to him, "How we gonna do it, the hard way or the easy way?"'

The screw is shitting hisself and saying, 'I don't want no trouble, Frank.'

Then Frank turned round to Bobby and said, 'Bob, the next seven is going to be a fucking hard fight all the way so I'm gonna get you moved.'

Bobby said, 'No way, I'm staying with you, we're in this together.'

I dunno what stroke he pulled but Bobby got shipped out, done a few years and come out. Frankie served every single day of his tariff.

Know why that was, Pete? I'll tell you: principles, principles, very, very stubborn principles. You know, if you get a ten or twelve or whatever, you only serve two-thirds?

Yeah, or less.

Or less even, but to get that you have to sign a bit of paper to say you'll behave and all that bollocks or they can pull you back in. You're then known as a 'ticket of leave' man: nick a sweet from Woolies and you're straight back in to finish them years they let you off. Most cons would sign the paper and swear on the Bible they was gonna go straight for ever – even though they knew it was bollocks. But Frank didn't wanna give them nothing, wouldn't sign the papers and served every day of the seven. He didn't want parole or nothing. It was his pride; his principles are so high. Some people might say he was a mug but, whatever, you've got to admire somebody who sticks with what they believe.

So, going back to myself. We had a right result when Jim Irwin got hisself lifted for conspiracy – that's law talk for trying to get gear or money by fraud but that ain't got all the facts right. Always good for at least 18 months, and that's what he got. Should've done time in Brixton, 'cos that would've knocked the smug smile off his face. But, no, that jammy bastard gets sent to Ford Open and, like everybody knows, that's a piece of piss.

The police actually raided our gaff early one morning and it'll give you some idea that I was well at it myself because I almost surrendered myself without a fight to save Mum the agg. I'm pulling me trousers on ready for walking out to the van when a copper stuck his head round the door saying, 'All right, kids, no need to worry, just gonna have a word with your dad.'

Fuckin' hell, I've got a bundle of them little Dansette record players under me bed – remember them? Don't have to tell you, me arse was really going. Didn't seem five minutes before Irwin was back in the flat, though.

Funny really, when I think of all the stuff we were nicking regular, I got myself lifted for nothing, fuck all to do with thieving. I weren't with the boys this night; I was knocking about with a pal called Charlie. We ain't doing much in particular, just wandering about, really. Now Charlie's got this penknife and it was the bollocks. What do they call them famous knives that do everything?

Swiss pocket knife?

You got it in one, my son. Swiss, little badge on it, and done everything but make tea.

To keep up with him, I've got hold of a bayonet, because there was loads knocking about for years after the war. This thing's over a foot long and razor sharp, could've cut your fucking head off. But that ain't what I wanted it for. I just wanted to be the dog's knackers, because I never felt the need to carry a tool to do damage or hurt anybody as a kid, or an adult.

So we're walking down the road and next thing we're shoved in a shop doorway by two coppers and turned over. No reason given; none needed, I suppose. They can't do that sort of thing today, but back then they could do what they liked with you. So we're lifted for carrying offensive weapons in a public place. They've called up a van and we got taken to Old Street nick and slung in a cell after getting the works: belt and laces off, in case you try and hang yourself; prints; picture took. What a fucking lark.

You ever been lifted, Pete?

Two or three times.

You know what I'm saying then. I'm giving it a bit of front, but really I ain't feeling too good. We're put in different cells, but we shouted to each other until we was told to fuckin' well shut our gobs. I'm thinking, 'If this is what it's like being in prison, I don't want none of it,' because the place stunk of piss from a little bog stuck in the corner and it was bloody filthy.

I s'pose I laid on this little wooden bunk for about an hour and I'm feeling a bit more confident. Then the door come open and I was told to shift my fucking arse on the quick. I ain't quick enough, so this copper grabs me by the arm and I've said, 'Get your hands off, you bald c**t.' Know what? He's given me a clout round the ear'ole that made my head spin. I told 'im, 'You can't do that, it's police brutality.'

So he said, 'D'you want another one?'

I'm new at this game, so I've just said, 'No ta, one'll do.'

When me Mum turned up with Mrs Hayes, she was crying and this copper's saying, 'See what you've done, see what you've done.'

He didn't 'ave to point it out, I weren't blind, and I tell you, Pete, I was gutted because I hated to think I've give that woman more grief.

We're soon out of it – bailed to appear at Bow in a month.

On the way home, Mum said, 'Jim ain't best pleased.'

I just said, 'Sorry, Mum,' but inside I'm thinking, '"Ain't best pleased?" That horrible fucker's just done 'is own bit of bird and he wants to dig me out?'

I took his good hiding and I didn't say a word. I was good at that by then.

Why did you put up with his constant violence? Didn't you feel like hitting back?

Funny you ask me that, because I've asked myself the same question over and over and I still ain't come up with an answer. It weren't nothing to do with 'im being twice my size, because what with what I'd been through since I was a kid I wasn't afraid of nobody, didn't matter how big they were. I dunno, p'raps I was so used to wiping my mouth over it all, I just accepted that's how it was.

There was a time when I was older, though, that I struck back. How it was, I'd been out all night one Saturday and I was fucked. I'd been drunk as a sack and fell into bed about half five; I'm dead to the world. Seemed like next thing I'm woke up with a punch in the head. I think I'm dreaming until Irwin's got his face right in mine screaming, 'You bone-idle little c**t, this ain't a fucking hotel.'

Now, I've already got a bit of a local rep for being a bit tasty with me fists and I've bashed up tough guys and even bouncers, even though I'm not all that old. He's gonna gimme some more, so I've jumped outta bed and given him a right-hander; he's gone red, white, then green, and fell back against the door. Now the lunatic's come out in me and I wanna kill him, but Mum had heard him shouting and pushed her way into the room and come between us. Showed I was getting past being knocked around, though.

Still, never mind that, I was telling you about me getting in trouble.

That month was the quickest and longest in my life. I ain't got time to think, then bomp! I'm standing in front of this bunch of old people in a sort of library-looking place. Charlie's already been done; gone in with his mum and dad and come out grinning like a fucking cat. He's held up three fingers and given me the nod. Sweet: three-quid fine and all dusted.

I'm thinking this is all bollocks, and I'm working out how to get hold of a few bottles so me and Tone can get pissed to celebrate. I can hear them going on about me being a menace to society, a teddy boy and a thug, and I don't give a shit. Two pigeons are at it on the windowsill, dirty bastards, so I'm watching them and me mind's well away so I only just caught a bit of it when this geezer gimme the three quid. 'Have it,' I thought, so I've put the big smile on to cheer Mum up, because she looked like I'd been fined a thousand pounds; and there was tears again. Fuck's sake.

Then this fat bird in a flowery dress shouts, 'Leonard McLean! If you imagine three years in an approved school is something to smirk about, I suggest you think again.'

Fucking stroll on! What! I couldn't speak, I was so shocked. These mugs, these muggy straight-goers, have practically lifed me off. How come Charlie got away with it? Because he was a straight kid with an apprenticeship, I expect.

What got me, Pete, was that these people never stopped to think how I'd suffered all me life; didn't give a fuck that I'd been bashed a thousand times. All they saw was an East End kid who they thought was no good. Never mind how it hurt my mum or that I weren't a bad person inside. Fuck it, let's bang 'im up and get home to feed the cat.

I wanted to stick two fingers up and tell 'em they was all c**ts, but that wouldn't do me no good and Mum had had enough upset.

I dunno where all this is coming from, son. I don't s'pose I've given any of this a thought in years and years, and it's just turning up in me head.

To be honest, I'm amazed at the small details you remember. Yeah, me too; let's have a nice cuppa, eh?

Anyway, I'm taken off and shut in a room with some other guys in the same boat. After about half-hour, Mum was brought in and a few other families. Well, she sets to crying again once she saw me and I said something I'll regret for the rest of my life, even though I've said sorry a hundred times. Know what I said? I said, 'Mum, pack up them tears because you're showing me up.' It was like I hit her with a brick and I can still see that look on her face now – like all crushed, and I wanna give her a cuddle and tell her I didn't mean it. But I can't, God bless her.

Suddenly we're all on the move, quick march, hurry up, hurry up, and I realised that this was what it was gonna be for the next few years. Gotta say, I was starting to feel a bit sick about the whole business. Next thing, I'm on this bus looking out at this little woman with a hanky stuck in her mouth and it broke my heart. She pushed up to the bus amongst all the other kids' families and said, 'Be strong, son.' I just got a minute to say, 'I love you, Mum,' and we're off. I thought I was a pretty tough kid, but I've gotta say, as I saw my mum disappearing in the distance, I felt the tears starting up so I kept me face to the window so nobody could see. Though from all the sniffing noises coming from all over the bus, I think we all felt pretty much the same.

We were all given a card to take with us. It had names, offence, tariff and across the top 'Stamford House Remand Centre, Stamford Hill' – so that's where we was heading.

That rings a bell. Didn't Ronnie Biggs start there?

Ronnie, yeah, Charlie Richardson, too many of the faces to put names to. That was – and not sure if it still is – where if you was gonna be a villain, it was a sort of infant school before you got older and moved up.

Talk about the old hurry-up, our feet never touched the ground. We weren't allowed to talk, we had to march on the double, we had to get processed, then shower, new clothes, then off to the dining hall. Bread and fucking jam; I ain't eaten all day and that's what they give us. Now, I wasn't the fighter I was gonna be, but, when this fat Geordie kid shoves me out the way so's he could grab a handful of bread, I've given him some knuckle in the kidneys. He's yelped his head off and fell on 'is knees and I got put on report. Fucking great start.

After that, we're shunted off to our allocated houses. Mine was Amby House. Because how it worked, the place was broken up into different buildings, like it wasn't one great big prison. Bed was relief, I tell you.

Lights went out and that was like cue for most of the kids to start letting themselves go. That all died down after a bit, 'cept for sobs here and there. I laid there and to be honest I was more angry than upset. I wanted to hit out at anything and in me head I blamed Irwin and for the hundredth time I wanted to kill 'im. Thinking about it now, it wasn't his

69

fault that I got caught with that bayonet, but at the time he was – what shall I say? – a sort of focus. Does that make sense, Pete?

Perfect sense, Len.

Once I cooled down, I started to think about my family. I'd never been away from home before and the thought of not seeing them for a long time cut me to pieces. Stupid, but I had this idea they would all forget me. I felt myself getting a bit tearful, so I bit me lip, then said 'Fuck 'em' so loud the kid in the next bed jumped up looking dead frightened.

Considering I was a proper tearaway at school and what with the shit atmosphere we lived under at home most of the time, I settled into the routine not bad. I mean, I managed to avoid too much agg. I had a few little tear-ups, but it weren't too bad. Now, because of Irwin, I hated bullies, I detest 'em and always will. So I'm laying on my back out in the playing fields, taking it easy, and I see this big ginger c**t giving one of the little kids a seeing-to, shoving 'im around. So I said to this little kid standing beside me – Rubber we called 'im, because 'is name was Johnny – I said, 'Who's that pratt over there, Rubber?'

He'd been here for a bit longer than me and he said, 'That's the Daddy.'

I've gone, 'Fucking Daddy, what the fuck is that?'

He says, 'He's the boss of us all and he's a Scotchman.'

Oh, yeah, is that right? I've shouted over to this lump, 'Oi! You haggis-eating piece of shit, leave him alone.'

Well, he's run over to give it some and I've done no more

than put a good bit of leather right up 'is knackers and he's gone down like a sack of shit. I've jumped up and give him a dig in the head and I'm just gonna give him a bit more when I'm grabbed from behind by a teacher. (I'm calling these people teachers because they weren't like screws and the whole place was like a very strict school.)

One of the rules in that place was, if you were caught fighting, you had to have a boxing match in the gym with whoever it was you'd had a ruck with. Right, so next day we're both in the gym and ready to go. It was all done proper with a teacher as a ref and rounds and all that. I give 'im rounds: first two minutes, I've knocked the bollocks out of 'im. I'm giving it the big un, you know, 'I'm the Daddy, I'm the Daddy,' 'til I was told to shut up.

Didn't do me no harm to get a bit of a rep, because by the time I was moved to Redhill Borstal my name had already been mentioned and they was already a bit wary of me before they see me.

You said something about running away from Borstal.

Yeah, I did, but it wasn't Borstal proper, it was Stamford, which is a remand place. Yeah, and funnily enough it was with the Scotch geezer who I had the fight with. Typical kids, we come mates after I battered 'im.

Now, we was caught nicking chocolate from the little store they had and was going to get a right seeing-to from the governor. So, what we gonna do? Over the wall – well, it weren't a wall, because as it weren't a prison we just walked out one night. We walked for fuckin' miles and haven't even got a clue where or why we're going. Sod's law, we're on our bastard knees when the same copper that nicked me for the bayonet recognised me and I was lifted again; all a waste of time. For a copper, he weren't a bad geezer. I remember him laughing and saying, 'Nice try, boys,' then he got us teas, cakes and smokes while we waited for the van from Stamford House.

We both got six strokes of the cane for nicking the chocolate, which we would've done anyway, and 12 for running away. They fuckin' well hurt and all, but it earned us a rep as tough gangsters from the other kids.

Was Redhill a tougher place, with it being Borstal proper?

Nah, same as the remand place, really. I've gotta say, don't forget I've got this rep, so the way I got treated might have been different for kids who weren't as strong. Mind you, I never let none of that bullying shit go on anywhere near me.

So I kept me nose reasonably clean and managed to walk out after less than 18 months. I was about 14 by then, and I'd put on two stone, what with all the stodgy grub they filled us up with. Tell you what, I was up for anything, but first I couldn't wait to see me mum and the rest of the family.

I've walked in the flat and, before I could even give Mum a hug, fucking Horrible Bollocks has said, 'Oh, you're back then, well, you can get yourself a job first thing because this ain't a doss 'ouse.'

Some welcome home.

Y'know, Pete, this ain't easy at all. How am I doin'? Good? Or fuckin' brilliant? Or boring?

Fucking brilliant... Sorry, Val, didn't see you there.

[Val] **Heard a lot worse, Peter.**

Ta, Val, bring the sugar bag in, he keeps complaining you ain't putting enough sugar in. Ain't she lovely, Pete? She's my world and has been since I met her in the Standard. Come to that later.

I keep saying it, Lenny: you're doing very well. Better than I could do if it was the other way round.

I lay in bed some nights and my nut's doing hundred miles an hour over things that's happened to me in my life. You should let me have one of them recorder things, because I think, 'That's a blinding story to tell, Pete, when I see 'im,' then I forget.

It'll come to you, don't worry.

Can we add bits in when we sit down to put it all together – you know, if I remember stuff we ain't taped?

We can do anything we want, mate.

Lovely, good boy.

I just remembered something I want to put down and I don't want you pulling faces. Is that tape on?

It's on.

OK, you ready? I met Peter Gerrard through Reggie Kray; he's a very pleasant man, very professional. He don't put things into my mouth, he lets me say my own thing and what I like about this man is he sits next to me like a friend, treats me like a friend and I class him as a very, very good pal. I've told him stuff that could get me or other people a few years and he sits there and don't say a word. He don't judge, he don't talk to anyone. I trust him and I love him like a brother. Now I'm gonna shake his hand.

How's that?

I'm touched and right now I can't say anything but thanks, Lenny. I'll treasure those words.

Now don't get all soft, I'm just telling it how it is. Make sure you put that in the book.

Where was we? Let's talk about some of me family. What about my cousin Tony McLean? Good kid, Tony, smashing kid. I've always been like a brother to him, always protected him ever since he was a kid, because I class him as a brother not a cousin, and if anyone fell out with him I'd belt 'em. Even when we was in Borstal together another time I protected him. I wouldn't let none of the other kids dig him out, because if they did they knew they'd get a good hiding.

'Course, he thrived on that, especially when I used to dish all the food out when I was number one in the kitchen. Everyone had to be on parade in the dining room at seven in the morning, all dressed full kit and then all queue up till half-past seven. Tony used to walk in at half-past seven with his slippers and dressing gown and walk straight to the front of the queue and get his breakfast in front of all the others and then walk back past 'em, smiling like a Cheshire cat. In this place, we had a lot of very hard boys, half of them was nutcases and they come from all over: Liverpool, Manchester, Birmingham, boys that come from the toughest places. They used to say, 'If it wasn't for that horrible fucking c**t Lenny, we'd kill him,' and, even though he knew that, he'd still take the piss and walk about laughing his cock off. I used to say to him, 'If I get discharged before you do, they're gonna kill you stone dead.' He went, 'I know, boy, that's why I'm gonna be right on your heels when you step out them gates.'

So how come Tony ended up in Borstal with you? I thought it was just you and Charlie.

Ah, that's because I'm jumping ahead. You said that was OK, didn't you?

That's fine. It's just that you didn't mention Tony earlier.

Well, I wouldn't, because this is a different time. I thought I told you I done a couple of spells in Borstal?

What happened was, me and Tone are getting up to all sorts. I told you about jump-ups earlier? Well, about the same time we're nicking gear from offices; now we're talking a bit more serious stuff, though you gotta remember we're still only kids. We'd blag a train ride up into the Smoke, look for a fancy office building and just walk in, because they didn't have all that security stuff then. Once we got inside it was a piece of piss to wander into an empty office and pick up anything that weren't screwed down. You know what I mean: typewriter, bits of knick-knacks, cash tin if there was one there, you name it. If we got questioned, we'd say we was looking for our dad, Mr Brown, or some bollocks. And if we was pushed, Tony could cry real tears and say he was looking for a toilet. Good earner, I tell you.

Still, we was young then, but as we got older we started to

think bigger. Told you about the lead with the firm, didn't I? I ain't ashamed to say it: we started doing break-ins. Not houses or nothing, because we had honest principles, but shops or warehouses, anywhere that held a bit of saleable gear. Problem we had was it was fucking hard to move stuff around, because we didn't have no motor; we was too young to drive anyway. There was one time we done over this little warehouse off Commercial Road. Electrical gear, washing machines, fridges, you know what I mean?

Can't be any nickings over this after all this time, can there?

I think the law have got enough to do without worrying about a break-in, in a place that's probably not there any more.

You know, don'cha.

Anyway, how the fuck we thought we was going to get the stuff away I dunno, but when you're keen for an earner you don't always look ahead. Times was different then – no security, nothing. Round the back of this place they had windows with no bars or nothing. Tone was a bit of a reader and he'd picked up this way of breaking glass without making a sound. He's pulled out a tin of syrup and a rolled-up newspaper. I'm thinking, 'What the fuck's he up to?' and he poured the syrup on the paper then stuck it all over this pane of glass. Bosh! And the glass has folded down quiet as a mouse. Clever that, innit?

We think we've got a right result. We're in and sweating our nuts off carrying big stuff out. The penny still ain't dropped about how we're gonna shift it all. It was dark and all of a sudden this voice said something like, 'What the fuck's going down 'ere?'

We're lifted.

I wanna thump whoever it is and run like fuck, 'cept I can't see 'im, then I get a torch shone on me and this voice goes, 'Lenny fuckin' McLean, chip off the old block.' Turns out an old mate of me dad's lives right across the alley – forget 'is name for a minute. Anyway, he's taken the piss for a bit, what with us not planning the job right, then he's offered to get the stuff moved for a decent cut; sweet. A week later, he give us a couple of ton for our cut, so we was well wedged-up for a bit. After that, we decided it's better if we stuck with small stuff, because it's a lot less agg.

You thought I was gonna say we was nicked that time, didn't you, Pete? But that bit come later.

How did you explain to your mum where all this money came from?

That was a problem. Gotta say, I told a few porkies to cover it. Really, we wasted most of the money we got because we couldn't buy nothing to take home, so mainly we ate it or pissed it up the wall. Sometimes I told her that I'd run a few errands for somebody and got a bit of wages, so then I could give her a few quid. I think she knew the truth, though, because I was too much like my dad.

You must have been about working age then. Couldn't you get a job?

I could get one, just couldn't keep it. When I come out of Borstal, Mum pulled a few strings and got me fixed up in the

77

print. I say pulled a few strings, because being a closed shop, bit like the docks, you had to have family already in it, so she says this husband of her mate was my uncle. What a fuckin' carry on that was. Mum got me kitted out in a suit from Burton's, so I'm looking the dog's plums, but the work wasn't up my street at all.

You know, I'm not stupid, Pete, but I never wasted too much time on reading, writing or spelling. So what do they get me doing? Filling in book stuff and filing and all that. Did I make a fucking mess or what? I was bored shitless and it didn't help when the manager dug me because I'd been in prison. Fucking idiot. I locked him in the bog one day for a laugh; tied the handle up and let 'im squeal and holler for ages. Somebody let 'im out eventually and he sacked me on the spot. I just give him two fingers and told him to fuck hisself. I got me cards but no wages but I'd nicked a load of paper and stuff anyway during the week, so when I fenced it through Tommy the Talker I got a few quid. Better than that, me and Tone went back a week later and lifted a load of lead they used for printing. Did you know they used to print books with lead letters?

Yeah I did, and that wasn't too long ago until they moved on to computers.

Well, once they used them they was scrap, and that's what we lifted. Our arms were six foot long by the time we carried it all down to Tommy's gaff.

Getting back to why me and Tone ended up in Borstal. Things had been a bit quiet and we were strapped for a bit of cash. We're sitting in a café down Hoxton Market, kicking around a few ideas, when in comes this fat geezer who I'll give the name Bill. So our nuts are going round and round thinking, 'How can we turn 'im over?' You know, chat 'im up and p'raps get round the shop and nick a few pairs of shoes, whatever.

We've slipped over and sat down at his table. He knows us, but he thinks we're brothers. I've gone, 'Whassup, Bill, you've got a face like a donkey's dangler.' Fuck me, we got 'is life story: turns out he's been nicking cash out the till so's he can do a bit of gambling and it's coming up time for his firm to send in people to check the stock and the books. We give him all the fucking 'tough luck, mate' bollocks, then Tony gives me the nod and we get up and go to the counter and order some grub. While we're there, Tone come up with an idea to get a bit of scratch together and help Bill out – not that we gave two fucks about him really.

This c**t's still sitting there too fucking miserable to get himself a cuppa, so we've got 'im one and sat down again. I've said, 'What happens to the cash in your shop?'

He looks stupid, then he says, 'I take it down the bank.'

'OK,' I says, 'give us the wink when you go on your next run and we'll nick it off you.' You'd think I'd grabbed 'im by the nuts, because 'is eyes opened up and his face went all red. I've said, 'Well, fuckin' say something then.'

He's choking away there until he says, 'You're having a laugh, I'm in enough trouble already.'

I've spoke to 'im like he was a kid: 'Listen, Bill, listen. Never mind shaking your fucking head, listen. You put the

79

takings in your briefcase and go to the bank as usual, got that? We snatch the bag and your firm's insurance covers it. We get a lump for our trouble, you get a sweetener and you're off the hook. There you go again,' I've said, 'pack in shaking your fucking head, what choice you got?'

He says, 'What I'd have in the bag wouldn't be worth it.'

'No,' I said, 'that's where you gotta be a bit cute. Tell your people you ain't been to the bank for a while because you had a bone in your leg or whatever. So you're banking a few weeks' dosh. Tell 'em there was a million pound in it, they'll never know.'

Took about an hour to convince this c**t, but in the end he went along with it.

As we're leaving, I said to 'im, 'Two things: when we do the business, I'm gonna have to give you a little slap to make it look kosher; and, second, don't pull a stroke like putting three half-crowns in the bag, because us gettin' rumped ain't good news.'

The next day we've slipped into Bill's shop and picked up some tasty boots each, 'So we can run faster,' we says.

It went off sweet as a nut. A week or so later he come waddling down the road, sweating like a c**t. I've stepped out and gone bosh! Right-hander on the forehead and he's gone down like bag of shit.

You can make that 'sand' if you want, Pete, in case they don't like all the bad language.

We'll square it up when we put it all together.

Good boy, I can rely on you.

So he's gone down, we've grabbed the bag and legged it.

Know what that silly bastard had done? Put the money in one of them security cases and no matter what we did we couldn't open the fucking thing. Took it to Tommy in the end and he opened it for a score. All in all, we had a great result. We sent somebody round with a few quid for Bill – not much, mind you, because we did all the work.

Lovely, we're wedged-up again – only and here's a lesson, we opened our mouths to the wrong people. Being flash, see. Some geezer by the name of Norton gets the whisper and blackmails Bill into giving him the keys to the shop or else he's on to Old Bill. He turned over the shop then he's only locked up after hisself.

Two minutes and Bill's lifted; three and Norton's pulled in; four and we join 'em in the nick.

Val! Val! Where the fuck is she? Go on, son, you're gonna have to make the tea. I'll have a little think while you're out there.

[Lenny sings] 'I thought I'd stop by a while and see you just once more before I leave town but his car's parked in your driveway, so I won't come in while he's there...'

[Lenny shouts] How's that, Pete, good or brilliant? You there?

Good boy, stick it on the table. No biscuits?

I'll shoot over the shop.

Nah, 'spect Val will bring some in.

I'll carry on. I was arrested at the flat about six in the

morning. They picked Tony up from Nan's at the same time, because he lived with her. We're given the works and bailed for a month to appear at the sessions.

Now, at that time, I'm older, bigger and I've got bundles of confidence and I ain't frightened of no fucker, don't matter how big they are, so going down like they said we could expect didn't bother me at all. Just as well, really, because Bill, being a sort of straight-goer or so they thought, got a fine and probation. Norton got 18 months, and we got three years' Borstal detention.

Like before, they don't even let you go home for a toothbrush – no, straight in the bus and off to the Scrubs.

That's Wormwood Scrubs, right?

Yeah, but we wasn't serving there, we was held while they sorted out sending us to Hollesley Bay, somewhere on the Norfolk coast.

Talking of Norton reminds of another story, and if I don't tell you I'll forget. Years later, me this one particular kid and another pal called Ronnie robbed a shop in the West End. This was a smash and grab, what they call ram-raiding now, and got ourselves bundles of suits and cashmere jumpers. Anyway, we had them in the motor and arranged to have a meet that afternoon. The kid got there first, then I come in and Ronnie got a bit tied up with law on a completely different matter, so he couldn't turn up. This kid says to me, 'Len, what we'll do, because that c**t can't be bothered to turn up, what we'll do is fence the gear and me and you cut it up and fuck Ronnie.'

I've gone, 'What did you say?' and he's said, 'Fuck Ronnie.' I said, 'You slag, you piece of shit, Ronnie ain't here because he's been lifted and you wanna rump him? No, I'll tell you what, fuck you,' and I belted him and broke his jaw. He got nothing 'cept a wired-up face and me and Ronnie cut the money up. I thought, 'What a slag.'

You tell me where I was while I'm rolling a fag.

On your way to Borstal with Tony.

Oh yeah. Well, it took all day to get there, then they banged us up about nine o'clock. Tony was allocated a room miles away from me, so I've slung out the kid in the next room and told 'im to swap places with my cousin. That was OK until they came looking for this kid in the middle of the night – poor sod's dad had died. 'Course, he ain't there, is he, so that caused a right ruckus. The three of us got taken in front of the head warden, given a right seeing-to and sent down the block for three days. Now, it weren't really the kid's fault that he'd been slung out of his room and he was just a little ordinary kid but he never squealed, never made no excuses, just took it like a man. Good stuff that boy, and he was under my wing until he got released even though I had enough to do, what with Tony under my wing, because like I said before he was a cocky little fuck. He was a nuisance to me and a nuisance to every kid in the place. With me behind him, he felt he could get away with murder and I had more fights over him than I had over myself.

Did he thank me? No, he took the piss, which reminds me, I used to spend all my money on tobacco, but Tony didn't smoke so instead he bought nice-smelling Palmolive so he didn't have to use the fucking shit carbolic the Borstal give us. Being on the work party, I used to finish about an hour before he did because it got dark, so what I used to do was nip in the showers and use his soap; I smelled like a whore's drawers, but I didn't give a fuck, because it was better than smelling like a hospital. He tumbled what I was up to, because it was shrinking every day, so what he done – and he didn't fucking tell me till after I used it – what he used to do was put it all round his arse, all round the top of his old man and soak it in the urinal – dirty bastard – and then I used to use it. When he eventually told me, I wanted to fucking strangle him. Didn't, though, because I loved him like a brother and knew he could get away with any shit.

Tell you what, if he said, 'I'm a lover, not a fighter' once, he said it a thousand times. The second day we was there, this big black kid nicked his baccy off 'im. I was out on a work party, so he don't tell me until late. I've shot down this black geezer's gaff and he's laying face down asleep on his bed. Don't matter: I've gripped the back of his neck, shoved his face into the pillow and give him four belts to the back of his head. Bet his brain rattled like peas in a bag. His roommate is trying to pretend he's not in the room, but he'd tell the black kid who done him soon enough. I've gone through his stuff and nicked his tobacco – or Tony's, I dunno – nicked a few other bits and said to his mate, 'My name's Lenny McLean if he asks.'

Don't get me wrong, Pete, it were nothing to do with him being black, because some of my best pals have been black and I would kill for them. Don't matter what colour a guy is, if he takes the piss he'll get bashed.

Talking of work party – fuck's sake, we worked like bastard slaves. There's a lot of fields in Norfolk and I spent months doing something or other in them. I remember we were digging taters and I said to this screw, 'Ain't they got a machine to do this?' and he said, 'You are our fucking machine, keep digging.'

In a way they tried to teach us different stuff, though I weren't all that interested. They stuck me in the pig sheds, because this was almost like a real farm, and there was hundreds of these smelly bastards and every one of 'em shit 20 times a day and I had to shovel it up. They had this breeding unit and when the little pigs get to a couple of weeks old they cut their nuts off; made me break out in sweat. What they did was pick them up, nick their bollocks with a sharp knife and pop out their balls. I've said to this sorta vet bloke, 'Don't that hurt?' and he said, 'Only if you nick yourself with the knife.' Funny c**t.

I'm a doer, Tony's a talker, and somehow he's talked himself into a job in the tailor's workshop, so, while I'm freezing my nuts off, doing me back in, getting blisters up to me arse, that crafty bugger's turning his uniform trousers into drainpipes and his jacket tailored at the waist. Talk about a fucking teddy boy. Me, I'm stuck in blue overalls like some swede farm boy. Had some laughs, though.

He come sauntering down one day like he owned the place, I'm emptying barrows of shit, and he looks like going on a night out. He said, ''Ere, boy, I put your name up and got us some smokes, let's have a drag somewhere.'

I've told one of the kids that if a screw comes along I've gone for a tomtit, then we slipped into one of the sheds. I said Tony was a livewire; well, he can never stand still. He's hopping from one foot to the other, he's chucking a pitchfork into the wall like he's playing darts, he's swinging on a chain. Next thing, he's climbing up this wooden partition that divided the barn up and he's sitting on top. Now, we've already heard noises from next door and we think its rats or something. Then he's burst out laughing and shouted down, ''Ere, Lenny, get up 'ere, there's two horses next door having a shag.' I've swung myself up, but it's all over and the biggest one's just standing there, puffing clouds of steam out of his nose. I ain't kidding, Pete; his old chap must've been five foot long.

Well, Tony's jumped down, grabbed a load of taters, then climbed back up and started chucking 'em at this horse. I mean, fucking cruel, really, but we didn't know any better at that age. He's hit everything in sight except the horse. Then, with one of them flukes you can get, he's caught the male one right on 'is bell-end. Fucking hell, you never saw nothing like it. This horse has gone crazy; it's run round, kicking, bucking and screaming like a girl. It's kicked the female horse, then it's kicking fuck out of the wooded walls. Lumps of wood are flying off and the whole place is shaking;

we're down like a shot and off. Trouble is, as we've opened the door two screws are waiting. So we're in front of the head warden again. Could've been worse – we got a month's loss of privileges and sent down the block for two weeks; didn't touch our remission, though.

While I was away, my uncle Jimmy Spinks died and I was gutted; it was like a piece of me died as well. I thought they might've let me out for his funeral, but unless it's really close family they don't wanna know. He had a brilliant send-off, so Mum told me. You know, proper East End do: carriage, black horses, the whole nine yards. The Dave Clark Five was there, because they was friends with his sons; Freddie and the Dreamers was there, the Twins went – the Kray Twins, they was up and coming then. It was the biggest funeral Hoxton has ever seen. It was big, it had about 50 black cars and about a hundred cars following, it was like an old gangster's funeral. Billy Hill come over and he went to it. Jack Spot didn't because, like I said, them two didn't get on. I only wish I'd been there to show my respect for him. He'd understand, though.

What with the hard work I done in the fields, a bit of training in the gym, plus regular stodgy grub, I filled out more than as much again as I'd done before. The trouble was, all those early years of being knocked about gave me loads of aggression inside me. And I really think it was then that people started to call me a fucking raving lunatic.

And were you?

What's that?

A lunatic.

That's a good question, son; I s'pose sometimes I looked like one and I acted like one, but almost all the time I knew what I was doing. If you know what I mean, sometimes it don't hurt if you get a rep for being a fucking nutcase. When it come to a bit of trouble, I gotta say I did flare up and go a bit wild, but inside I'm cool. Having said that, there was times when I completely lost it and I'll tell you why: drink, too much fucking drink, and that ain't good when you're a big guy like me with a lot of hate inside.

You know I don't drink, Pete. You've seen me in the pub with a cup of tea or a nice lemonade – well, there's a reason for that.

I've done a lot of damage over the years to a lot of people, but I can honestly put my hand on my heart and say I don't think I've took a liberty in my life. I've always fought for a reason, whether they were silly reasons or whatever, but they have always been for reasons and I don't think any of my fights was where I took a liberty, except probably a handful. Out of thousands of fights I might have been a liberty-taker of about five, or shall I say ten? Five or ten fights, don't matter, but the one that sticks in my mind the most, the reason why it sticks in my mind the most is because I done a lot of damage to the guy.

I told you about when I took Jimmy out to see his boy in Stamford House... No? Well, what happened was, there was a guy named Jimmy Briggs who was nicked on the Bank of Cyprus job with George Davis. Remember them slogans painted all over roofs and walls: 'George Davis Is Innocent'? I used to wonder how the fuck they managed to get in some of the places with their paintbrushes – still, that's neither here nor there. Jimmy was a good money-getter, but before all this happened he'd just come out of doing a ten for something he'd done with a few others. He was the only one nicked, but he kept his mouth shut and got a ten; everyone else got away. He was good stuff.

Anyway, one day I see him walking down the street, so I've pulled my motor over, put the window down and said, 'How you going, Jim, what's the matter? You look a bit down.'

He's gone, 'Yeah, I am because me boy's in Stamford House and I promised him a visit, but I've got no money to get down there.'

What am I gonna do when a pal's needs a favour, Pete? Same as you would, so I said, 'Get in the motor, I've got a few quid on the hip, I'm gonna take you there right now, because you can't let your son down.'

On the way we pulled up at a sweet shop, got forty fags and about a tenner's worth of sweets and told him to tell his boy they was from him. Know what I'm saying – I didn't want his son to think his dad was on his arse.

Anyway, we got to Stamford House, met up with young Jimmy and had a fantastic visit. Tell you what, didn't half take me back walking into that place. We come out and I said I would buy him a drink to cheer him up. We've gone to one pub, then another pub, gone to a club in the Angel, then ended up in the Green Man in Hoxton. At the time it was Lenny Gale's pub. We was having a drink in there and we'd had a marvellous day, everybody was singing, drinking, laughing and joking. Jimmy gets hisself up to the bar and starts chatting to this bird – can't remember her name, but that don't matter. I thought she was a bit flash, this bird, and I didn't take to her at all. I had nothing against her – I was having fun, I was with Jim and one or two other few people and I decided to go to Riley's in north London, so I said to Jim, 'Come on, we're going somewhere else.'

He's said, 'OK, Len.'

Then this bird said, 'No, he's staying with me, he ain't going nowhere.'

I said to Jim, 'Come on, what you gonna do, are you coming with me or staying with her?'

She said, 'Look, you big c**t, he's fucking staying with me.'

I said, 'Excuse me, who are you talking to, you saucy pratt, don't you fuckin' well swear at me or I'll smack your arse.'

Jim stuck up for her, saying, 'Don't have a go at her or I'll put one on yer.'

'Fuck's sake, Jim, what's this? We've had a good day, we see your boy, I've stood you a bit of scratch and now you wanna fight me.'

'Lenny,' he said, 'I'm just saying; don't have a go at my bird.'

'Your fucking bird? You've only met her two minutes ago. Tell you what, I think me and you better go outside.'

I'll give him his due, he was game. We walked outside and he's given me a belt, so I hit him straight on the chin. I knocked him on his arse. He's got up and taken another swing and I've gone, bosh!, and broke his jaw but then I was fuming to think I'd been with him all day and he's kicked off like he done, so I laid across him, and hit him hard a couple of times and broke my thumb so I couldn't hit him no more. I've lifted up his chin and bit a lump out of his throat.

You're looking at me like I was a beast, Pete, and I've gotta make you right: I was.

This is a pal and we've had a blinding day and there I was biting his throat out. He's kicking and trying to shove me off and I kept biting, even though I've got blood pumping on to me; I mean, I've really lost it. I could hear people screaming and shouting, 'He's dying, he's dying,' and I'm getting hit on the back, fuck knows who by, and they're all trying to get me off him and I'm pushing them away. The next thing is I'm spewing up. I've got all blood down me throat. I've got off Jimmy, knocked everybody out me way, got in my motor and fucked off.

I found out later that people rushed Jimmy over to Barts, because it was only 20 yards away, and he was dead on arrival. Lucky for him, and lucky for me, the doctors operated on him and brought him back to life. His jaw was broke in several places, he had a lump out of his throat and he was all wired up with a copper stood by his bed. Some slag had phoned the police and said Lenny McLean done it, so they come round me house next day, crashed through me door, nicked me and took me to Shepherd's Wharf station. I was there for about 24 hours; I kept denying it and denying it, but they wouldn't let me go. In the end I said, 'Who's in charge of the case?'

This detective said, 'I am,' so I've asked for a word just the two of us in private.

I said to him, 'Look, Jimmy's one of your own, he won't speak to you people. What will happen is, you'll charge me for attempted murder and Section 18, we'll go to court and then, once we get to the Bailey, Jimmy will stand up in the court and say it was not Len. You'll be fucked, the magistrate will say to your people, "What's your game wasting my time with this old bollocks?" and the case will be dismissed.'

Once Jimmy come round, they had a word with him and like I said he kept his mouth shut. They didn't believe him, but what they gonna do? So they've said, 'OK, we got the picture, Lenny can go home.'

Was that the end of it?

Well, right then it was and I lost a pal into the bargain. I hold my hands up, I was right out of order, because I hurt that man, I hurt him real bad and I took a diabolical liberty. But he had proper old values and years later when you'd think it was proper old news, Old Bill started digging around when they've nicked me on that murder charge. They wanted any old shit to show that I was capable of killing that Humphreys kid, so they've gone to Jimmy and tried to put the squeeze on him. Waste of time, because Jimmy stuck to his story and told them, 'Lenny's my pal and no way did he hurt me.' Hundred outta ten, Jimmy, wherever you are now.

Good story or what?

Yes, very good, but you started off talking about drinking...
Good boy, just you keep reminding me. Well, that's the point, after that I never touched alcohol ever again; not once, not even at Christmas or weddings. Make me right, Pete: have you seen me take a drink?
Not once, Len, not even the night you opened your pub. I always remember us walking round with a cup and saucer each.
Yeah, it's only a pity somebody had to suffer before I came to me senses.

[Doorbell rings]
Val! Get the door... Val!... Fuck's sake... Who is it?... That you, John?
[Maureen] **No, it's Maureen, Len.**
Come in, gel.
   This is my book man, Peter. I got the book man here, because I signed me book contract yesterday.
[Maureen] **Hallo, Len, you OK? Hallo, Peter, nice to meet you. Is that thing on? Does that mean I'm going to be in Lenny's book?**
You'd better be careful what you say, then.
[Maureen] **Is Val coming back in a little while? Because I've got a bit of stuff here; it should be £149, but to you it's 40 quid.**
Yeah, we'll have it. Oh, leave the lot, she'll have all that. Put that in the book, Pete, say that while I'm sitting here people are still coming selling hooky gear.

[Maureen] **Oi! This ain't hooky, it's quality merchandise.**

Whatever, Maureen.

[Maureen] **Look, Lenny, I've left them things on there with that 50 quid, but I will have to come back tonight.**

How much do you owe now, then?

[Maureen] **How much do I owe you? Three and a half I've give you; I owe you one and half. You tumbled, Pete? I borrowed a monkey off Len and he lets me give him 50 pounds a week back and, when it's paid back, I'll get Val a bottle of that snide perfume I'm selling.**

Snide? You told me it was pukka.

[Maureen] **No, it's pukka, Len.**

Why did you say it was snide, then? Didn't Maureen say it was snide, Pete?

Wasn't listening.

[Maureen] **I tell you what I done. Listen, I sold the perfume as the right gear but I also bought a dozen gross of tins of ointment, so, when you come out in a rash in a fortnight's time, just remember I've got it at a fiver a tin. It's a load of shit, but you can tell people that it's the right gear. I got it for a fiver a box and selling it for a tenner. I got people taking me fucking hands off for it; I got one girl who took me finger last time. She'll bring it back tonight, silly as arse'oles.**

Anyway, I got to go.

What's that geezer's name, because I'm gonna put him in the book. You know, that star who likes me, trains a lot and always says to you, 'How's Lenny'?

[Maureen] You mean Johnny Shannon, don't you, Len? Him that used to be in *Beryl's Lot*. He was in *EastEnders*, he was the rep in it, wasn't he, done loads of stuff. He was asking after you a couple of weeks ago, so I'll tell him you're busy on your book, shall I?

Yeah, I am, ain't hardly got time to have a piss.

[Maureen] I better go, then. Nice to meet you, Pete. Do you know, I used to live in Hackney and I live in Hornchurch now, and years ago I'd go out with boys that carried choppers and knives in their pockets. We'd go dancing down in Mare Street to a little place called Ma Johnson's and one night we was in there and suddenly the place emptied. These blokes have gone nutty and chopped a boy's ear off, then stabbed a load of people and the only way we could get out was to go in the boys' loo at the back and over the graveyard. Tough times in them days; I expect Len will tell you. I'm doing a tour thing at the moment with visitors from America and I am telling them that there was 2,000 American soldiers in our underground for 18 months waiting for the Germans – this in 1944 – with about 5,000 of our soldiers. No one knew they was there.

So what did they do all day?

[Maureen] I don't know, Len, probably played cards. How do I know?

Anyway, people say to me, 'Where can we go for a nice day out?' And I say, 'Just go into the underground, the foot tunnel.' They say, 'What foot tunnel?' Even English people don't know what's under London.

London's finished now, gel, that's why people are moving out.

[Maureen] **I moved out 30 years ago – best day's work I ever done.**

Know what you mean, Maureen. As soon as me film's out I'm going to either Hornchurch or Hertfordshire or Kent.

[Maureen] **Frank Bruno lives just up the road from me.**

Nice man Frank, nice man Frank. The only thing with Frank is, he don't hate enough. He's a man-of-passion fighter, but he got good money for it because he knows what to give the public.

[Maureen] **Well, I don't think he should fight again; I think he has done enough.**

See, he's sitting indoors with his wife and he knows he can get a million pound out of this coming fight. I mean, before he was getting, like, ten grand a week, but for this fight, if he does it, he'll get a million pound and he'll get knocked out in about three rounds. Everyone in the fight business knows it; I been in the fight business myself a long time and, take my word, Frank won't last more than three rounds.

Right then, you off, Maureen?

[Maureen] **Yeah, I'll see myself out. Ta-ra both of you.**

Good gel, see you later.

Nice to see you.

She gone, Pete?

I'll have a look... Yeah, just driven off.

Fuuuuucking hell! Can't she rabbit?

Seems a nice lady.

'Course she is, she's a diamond and the salt of the earth, but, fuck me, she never stops to breathe. I think we better have a nice cuppa tea after that, don't you?

Good idea, but I'll have to make it.

Fucking hell, well, make sure you put a teabag in this time. [Lenny sings] 'Maureen, Maureen; you are a queen... da da da da...'

Lovely, son, lovely, put it down and we'll have a smoke. OK, what do you want talk about now?

How were things when you and Tony came out of Borstal?

How do you mean?

Well, had things changed? Was life indoors different?

Well, it's funny, really. While I was away, it was like the outside was a million miles away. I hadn't seen very much of my family at all, because, what with not much money flying about, Mum couldn't afford to get up to Norfolk. I mean, today it's like two minutes in your motor, but then it was different. I think you could get an official bus up to the Borstal every now and then, but I know Mum hated that, because most of the families were out of the roughest places you could find and, though she weren't stuck up or nothing, her standards were a lot higher. End of the day, though, she still had a son who was banged up.

So I'm pretty excited to get back and see everybody. I might have been a big lump with a rep for being a bit tasty, but inside me I missed me mum very badly.

Tell me if I sound a bit soft, won't you?

Lenny, you're telling it how it is and people reading your

**book will think you're a bigger man than them that pretend
to be hard as nails inside and out.**

You really think so?

Believe me.

OK. Well, me and Tone done our time and what was almost
comical was how they turf you outta the gaff when it's all
over. On the way in you ain't got time to think – double,
double, double and screws all over you. Come the end of
your sentence, 'Here's a train pass from Ipswich, now fuck
off,' and bang goes the door. But, Pete, unless you've spent
years behind the door, you just can't imagine the sense of
freedom; I mean, it's like being pissed.

Talking of change, the pair of us soon noticed that skirts
were a lot shorter than when we'd gone away. Fucking stroll
on, our eyes was on stalks all the way to London.

So, Tone went his way and I went mine to see my family.
Everything was a lot smaller than I remembered – even the
flats seemed shorter. I've given our front door a good old bang
like it was the tally man or something. Mum opened the door
a little bit, screamed and flung it all the way open. I've picked
her up and swung her round and round and she was laughing
like a young gel; then I gave her a big hug and she was crying
fit to bust. A lovely, lovely moment after all them years. Didn't
last too long, because Irwin stepped out the sitting room as I
was walking up the hall and sort of barred me way – like he
was saying, 'You don't fuckin' well belong 'ere no more.' I give
him a look and he stepped out the way but couldn't stop
himself saying, 'Troublemaker's back.'

I felt like knocking him out, but Mum was right behind me and she said, 'Don't start, Jim, please don't start,' and he stepped back into the room and slammed the door. So, Pete, there weren't much change there.

Me and Mum went into the kitchen and she shut the door and that's when I said to her, 'Mum, it ain't going back to the way it was. If he starts, I'm gonna kill him stone dead.'

She said, 'Take no notice son, he's a little bit grumpy today.'

I'm thinking, 'A little bit grumpy! What a fucking laugh; little old ladies get grumpy, c**ts like him get evil,' but Mum either couldn't see it, or pretended not to see it. What she did, though, was make me promise I wouldn't hurt him. How could she ask me that after what he'd done over the years? She weren't a Christian or anything like that, but talk about turn the other cheek – she could've won medals for it. It choked me to say it, but in the end I promised I'd leave him alone. It's a pity he wasn't forced to make the same promise about us years ago.

Knowing him and knowing me, I knew things could only get worse until it kicked off big time and I broke me promise, so I started to spend more and more time away from the flat. Now, I've already been away from my family for a long time, especially Mum, and now I'm forced to keep away from her. I can't say I thought it at the time, but did it really matter? Your mum's gonna be around until she's knocking on a hundred, so plenty of time to catch up. Bad move, Pete, bad move. If I'd known how little time I had left with her, I would've cuddled that woman every single day.

Anyway, to keep out the way and earn a living, I got up to all sorts with the firm. We done the lot – bit like when I was younger, but a lot heavier stuff. I ain't talking shooters or shit like that – because we never robbed people, only places, if you know what I mean. Though there was one time when we broke into this big distribution place and I was given the job of making sure security didn't get in the way. I can be a bit intimidating when I wanna be, so there weren't no aggro; in fact, they was a cracking bunch of blokes and we had a good chat while we waiting for the lads to fill a lorry up.

What would you have done if security had fought back? Would you have hurt them?

Peter, Peter, Peter – it never happened, and the truth is, unless they got really leery, I could've kept them quiet without doing any damage. Now, we weren't Robin Hood or nothing like it but, while the tape's on, all I'll say is them lads got a nice drink afterwards because they didn't get in the way and did us a few favours.

Every Saturday we'd meet up in the West End in a club called The Tiles in Oxford Street – it's all shut down now, because we're talking about 1966, 28 years ago. Fuck me, we spent some time in that place, me and my pals. I don't want to mention their second names, because most of them kids that I did the break-ins with have gone straight now, so we'll just go Keith, Fred, John. We'll leave out their second names, is that all right? What we used to do is nick cashmere jumpers, roll-necks and coats because they sold well and were worth top dollar. I'm talking shop windows here all the way up Oxford Street, and, if we couldn't smash them with metal crates full of milk bottles, because they used to bounce off the windows sometimes, we'd get metal ramps. Lot of building work going on then, so we didn't have to look far for a site, then we'd nick them long girder things and use them as ramps to drive a car up. We'd balance them on milk crates or on the bottom rails of the windows, drive up them and smash right through the glass. The motor never used to go right in – just the front, then we'd jump out and clear all the stock.

Did you leave the motor in the window and have another one to take the gear away?

No, just the one. I mean, the front looked a fucking mess, but it drove and that was all that mattered. We'd back out, sling the stuff in the back seat and the boot and drive off. We did have another motor, but that was always parked up three or four turnings away. Once we fenced the clothes we had our bit of dough for the week, and Mum's wages, so we were doing very well for 17-year-olds.

The trouble is, in the West End I was getting a terrible reputation for fighting. I always used to fight in the clubs knocking people out, knocking the doormen out and I was getting a name as a right tearaway.

Were you picking the fights?

No, I wasn't so much picking fights as getting drawn into them by mugs who should've left me alone. I was a young man then and if someone bumped into me I would fight them, or I would fight if somebody gave me the old cross eye, whether they meant to or not. Truth is, I'd have a ruck over more or less nothing in them days. I was young and I suppose it was a bit of bravado looking for fights wanting to be a tough guy. When I see kids doing it today I say to myself, 'Where's the sense in it, they ain't getting a tanner,' but being young is being silly and we all done it. It wasn't until I got older that I realised fighting for nothing ain't worth nothing. I got known as a tough kid, the toughest guy on the block. I was at a 21st birthday party of a pal and I smashed up his dad's pub – was I a fucking idiot or what? As time went by, I began to realise I was going too strong and people had started leaving me out. They wouldn't invite me to parties, because I was making people's nerves bad, because I was guaranteed to fight. I thought it was clever, but it was only later on in life that I realised I must have been a complete pratt. I broke my hands dozens of times for nothing.

I don't really regret what I got up to back then, but there ain't no doubt I was running wild. I slept here, I slept there; anywhere so I didn't have to go home. Why I wasn't nicked for something or other, I dunno, because I was running wild. Sleep during the day; piss it up the wall at night, then on for a bit of business. Half the time we done jobs while we were out of our heads on beer or purple hearts. And fight! Fucking hell, every night somebody got a bashing. Like I said before, I wasn't taking liberties – anybody I took on was asking for it. Bouncers were a favourite: I took the piss and when they come at me I'd kick off. I must've been a complete fucking nuisance, because, when I took on minding myself, almost every night I'd come across youngsters just like I must've been.

I think if I'd carried on there ain't no doubt in my mind that me or all of us would've ended up doing a ten-stretch – no doubt at all. What saved me was a person that saved me tons of agg a thousand times in the years to come: my Val.

How it happened was this. I was working for a pal of mine's dad in the Standard pub up Kingsland Road. Do you know that drinker, Pete?

Yes I do. On the left going up. Bar at the front, not that big.
You got it, son. Well, I'm behind the bar and a fella walked into the pub with this girl. I looked and I looked at the fella's nose and it was flat as a pancake and I thought, 'Fuck me, I bet he's had some fights in his time.' Later on, I found out it was a girl who broke his nose. There was this beautiful, skinny blonde with him. I looked at her and she looked at me and she looked again and I said to my mate, his name was Jack, I said, 'Jack, I'm gonna give her a pull.'

I waited for the guy to go to the toilet and I went over and said, 'Hello, my name is Lenny McLean.'

She said, 'Yeah, I've heard all about you, you're always fighting.'

I've gone, 'Who said that? I'll knock 'em spark out.'

That made her laugh and I'm thinking I've cracked it.

Pete, I don't have to tell you about women, because you're on your tenth missus [laughs].

Only second, Len, haven't met number three yet.

I'll tell her when she phones up, you watch. No, what I was gonna say is, forget all the bollocks about being a film star and a stud, if you can make a woman laugh, you've got her forever. How's that? Blokes are gonna thank me for that advice once they've bought me book – worth the price of the book that is.

I've gotta move fast here, so I asked if she would like a drink.

She said, 'No, I'm with my boyfriend and he wouldn't be very happy if he came back and I was drinking with you. And, knowing about you, you'd probably hit him.'

I've gone, 'No way, I ain't a liberty-taker,' but inside I'm thinking, 'She's dead fucking right.' I said, 'Well at least you're a loyal girl, and that's nice, but if you fancy parking him up I'll be in here next Saturday night if you fancy a drink.'

She said, 'I might just do that.'

Now, she was such a beautiful kid, I was fidgeting about all week wondering if she would show up. I was 19 and acting like I was 14. Turned out, she give this guy the elbow during the week and come down the Standard on the Saturday. We had a quick drink then I took her to a party and I've been with her ever since; she's an angel.

I think I got off on the wrong foot straight away with her parents because that night I didn't get her home until really late. Either that or they'd heard about what I got up to – small place, the East End. Her mother and father just didn't take to me at all. Well, it weren't her real father, because she had a stepfather; her real father died at 23, so she was in the same boat as me.

When we was talking, I said, 'Bet your stepdad's a proper bastard,' and you'd have thought I'd slapped her. You know what women can be like.

She's saying, 'What a nasty, horrible thing to say.'

'Course, I'm backtracking like fuck because I don't wanna lose her, but why I said it was because I thought that's what stepdads were like. Turns out, hers was a proper diamond and a proper dad to her. In fact, he must've been good stuff, because he come out of a proper family. The Smiths of Bethnal Green was in the rag trade and been in the area for hundreds of years. You ask Reggie or Ronnie, Pete, they'll tell you.

Here's a tricky question for you: what was Val wearing that first night?

Well, son, good job you didn't bet money I couldn't answer that, because you'd have lost. That first night she walked in the Royal Standard she was wearing a beige suit, red shoes and carrying a red bag. She was about seven stone and I could've got her whole bum in my hand. Don't get me wrong, Pete: I didn't actually lay hands on her, because I had too much respect. I'm just trying to let you know how tiny she was. The following week, or the week after, I took her to a club called the City Club, in City Road, and then after, when I took her home, her parents let me stay over because it was pretty late. No nonsense – they chucked me in the spare room.

When I got up the next morning, I met her mother and father for the first time, but you got to understand, Pete, she's come from a straight family, good people, and I suppose they thought I was a wise bet. I was young and let me gob do too much flapping trying to impress – except I expect it come out all cocky. I've offered to get the ol' man a bit of hooky gear, told them I'd bashed up half the East End and on top of that told them I just come out of Borstal. So what they gonna think?

Obvious really, straight away they took a disliking to me and they didn't want their daughter to go with me, but my Val loved me and, well, what's love at 18? You don't really know, do you? All I know is that she liked me a lot and I liked her a lot. I've asked her if she wanted to pack me in and she said, 'No, I want to be with you.' So that was that.

We used to go to clubs and pubs, we used to have a laugh and giggle and I always ended up smashing the pub or club up. Whenever I walked into a pub, it would empty in about five minutes – there would be nobody there, only me and Val. And so the years went on and she's been a good un. She's been really good. I mean I've been a fucking nuisance, don't worry about that, I've been a bastard but she's always been there for me. She has always been by my side; she's my right hand, really.

I don't blame her parents for disliking me because now I'm a father I wouldn't let my daughter go with an absolute c**t; I wouldn't stand for it. I'll give you a clue as what sort of silly c**t I was, Pete. One day I took Val out to a party and when we left the party I took her home, but on the way I stopped off and picked up a Chinese meal. All right, I might've been sucking up to her parents a bit, but I was doing it for my Val's sake. We've got to her house, and then all of a sudden the door opened and her mum dragged Val in by the collar, she's gone flying up the passage, tripping over her high heels. Trying to quieten things down, I've said, 'Hold up, no need for that, I've bought us all Chinese.'

Her mum's screamed at me, 'We don't want your bloody Chinese, bugger off.'

Remember, I was a proper bastard then and what I done because I was young and wild – I wouldn't allow it now – but I've shouted, 'Well, fuck you' and slung the Chinese at her mum. It's hit the wall, burst open and Val's mum copped the lot; what a fucking mess. Her stepfather's come out and I threatened to bash 'im. How's that for a stupid prick, Pete? I'm young, I'm big and I'm tough and I'm offering to knock an old man's lights out. Disgusting, really; I ain't one bit proud of myself. But I haven't finished yet. I've grabbed whatever and smashed all their front windows. Val's crying, her mum's crying and her dad is giving me some verbal and that's winding me right up. Luckily, before I did something even more stupid like knocking her ol' man sparko, the law turned up and three of them jumped on me back. I've slung them off easy, then got one of them by the throat and told them if they jump me again I'm gonna tear this copper's head right off his fucking shoulders. That slowed 'em down. I honestly think I went a bit off me head. Then I heard Val begging me to stop and that done it for me, so I put me hands up and went quiet as a mouse.

I was locked up all night and that gave me a bit of time to weigh up what I'm gonna suffer for criminal damage and assault with a bag of Chinese. Then, fuck me, I'm released with no charge. Her parents, even though they must hate my guts, have decided not to press charges. Give them their due, they didn't nick me. The police escorted me back home in case I kicked off again, but there was no chance of that. I never spoke to her mum or father for a long time.

After about a year or 14 months, we got married and my mum was well pleased. Val's parents tolerated me but that's all, because if I went round there on a Sunday or a night-time I would be sitting in their front room and they would be in the kitchen; I could hear 'em eating their tea, eating their lunch and drinking tea, and they would never come and say do you want a cup of tea or do you want a sandwich or nothing. Val would be embarrassed, seeing that they was out there noshing and didn't offer me nothing, so she would go out there and make me a sandwich and bring it in to me. Funny really, and it's a horrible way to be; my Val was like my mum – you know, stuck in the middle, trying to keep both sides happy. What hurt me was me and Val got married at a register office, because really that girl deserved the full nine yards. You know what women are like, Pete, the posh dress and all the trimmings, something they've probably thought about since they was a little girl, and I never gave her that. My mum come to the wedding, my nan come, my uncle and my sisters come and Val's mum and dad. After, we went back to Val's and there was nothing; nothing at all. No, I tell a lie: her mum made a cup of tea and sent Val round the shop to get a tin of corned beef. It was embarrassing.

When I spoke to my mum, she said, 'Look, son, you can't have nothing because it's your big day, you just got married.' So what she done, she got hold of Jim and told him to buy a load of booze – only good thing he ever done – and my mum done a big spread and she had a party in the house, so she set me and my young girl up.

We started our life together in Georges Square at the back of Old Street. We rented the house – it was two rooms with a little cubby hole just big enough for a cooker – and it was just me and Val and she was my whole world.

When we took the place over, it was like a bombed house, an absolute tip. Well, I had a go at a bit of decorating, but after I painted everything in the toilet dark blue – and I mean everything: walls, ceiling, light switch, even the toilet seat – Val said, that's it!

I didn't think it looked too bad for a first attempt, but she wasn't happy with it and went and saw my uncle Fred. He come round, spent all his money on it and done it up for us and it was like a little doll's house. He's a nice man, Fred. Every year, without fail, when we was kids, he bought all our Christmas presents because he knew Mum didn't have no money to spare. Lovely, lovely man and I won't ever forget what he done.

Well, we ain't married five minutes and Val wants me to get a 'proper job'. 'Oh please, Lenny, go get a job and go straight.'

What can I say? Anybody else I would've told to fuck off, because I was fiddling and nicking enough to keep our heads above water, but I wanted to give that girl the moon, so I wiped me mouth and had a look round.

First off, I got a job in a clothes factory in Curtain Road packing clothes, and every night they used to give me a wheelbarrow with parcels of clothes like woman's coats and dresses and I had to take 'em to the post office. I mean, basically it was like getting a wolf to look after a bunch of chickens, because I'd wheel 'em round to our house, nick half the stuff and sell it on. Some days our house was like Bethnal Green Market. Didn't take long before I got the sack. I got another job in another clothes place, packing woman's clothes. I'd work weekends on my own, so I'd open the window and pass them out to my mate and flog the stuff off; I soon got tumbled and got the sack. I'm beginning to think, 'Fuck this working for a living, it's too hard.'

My reputation as a fighter was starting to creep out from just Hoxton, so I become well known all over the East End. A guy from north London came to see me who had a contract with a big firm of decorators. He was the main contract man and he come round and see me – I must've been in me early twenties about then. He's said, 'Len, I'd like you to mind me, because what happens in all these places I have to get done up painted and decorated, well, sometimes the painters get all aggressive because their money's a bit short or a bit late. So I'd like you to mind me and make sure no one has a go at me.'

So I took on the job of minding him and I used to drive him about to his jobs. And this went on for months and months. I don't like bullies and liberty-takers, I fucking hate 'em, so I felt a bit choked when he used to tell me about these painters. All week they was painting and they worked very hard, come Friday or Saturday when they were due their wages, this bloke would tell 'em, 'No, that ain't right, you're not getting paid 'til it's done proper.' From where I was standing, I thought these fellas did a really nice job; fucking hell, they was all tradesmen and proud of it, so I did wonder why he was saying their work weren't no good. Then the penny dropped: he was rumping them. They stood there and took his shit because I was standing behind him. I didn't like it one bit, because these were family men trying to put steam on the table.

One day, he said, 'Lenny, I want you to learn the painting and decorating game.'

I said, 'Go on, then,' and he give me a big bucket and a wet sponge and said, 'Get up there and wash them walls and ceilings.'

As I put the sponge to the ceiling, all this black shitty water went down me arm, all over me shirt, round me niagras and ended up in me plimmys. I thought, 'Fuck this, he's taking me for a c**t.' I've chucked the sponge as far as I could throw it just as he's walked in the room.

He's gone, 'Oi! I ain't paying you to make a fucking mess.'

111

I'm already pissed off, so he done a wrong un. So I picked up the bucket and tipped the lot over his head. I got off the ladder and knocked him on his arse. He ain't so tough now, the c**t. I've said, 'Oh yeah, while I'm at it, here's a few digs for them lads you been ripping off,' and belted the life out of him. He's laying on his back, so I reached into his pocket, nicked what was owed me, plus a few quid for dry cleaning, and that was it. Out of work again.

Fucking hell, Pete, I ain't ever talked as much in my whole life; it's knackering. Shall we have a brew – that's what you say up your way, innit?

Well, they do, but I'm not from up that way, remember?
I just happen to live there.

Oh yeah. Still, we'll have a brew anyway.

Val! Pete said he could do with a sandwich and a cuppa.

You know, my son, we used to use one teabag a week, now she buys four boxes.

Where was we? Or shall we wait for a sandwich?

We'll have a break.

Yeah, lovely, I'm feeling a bit tired anyway. [Lenny sings] 'I'm tired of living but I'm afraid of dying, da, da, da.'

Now, I'm quite happy to do a bit of ducking and diving, but my lovely wife Valerie had other ideas and she went out and got me a job as a window cleaner. Well, she didn't get it as such, she saw an advert in a shop window and took down the phone number. We didn't have a phone indoors then, so she made sure she dragged me down the road to give 'em a ring.

I don't like fucking heights anyway, but it wasn't a bad job because you started at six and finished at twelve. It was a little firm in Essex Road and after about two months they made me the foreman. I wasn't too bad at the job, but I think they knew I nearly shit myself every time I climbed a ladder and that got even worse when one of the guys fell and killed hisself. What I used to have to do is go in early morning, get all the sheets for work that had to be done, give 'em all to the window cleaners then send 'em out. After that was done I used to fuck off home. At the weekend I had to do all the time sheets, get 'em sorted and pay the lads out. Absolute doddle.

If they had days out of work, I'd still book 'em in, but, being a bit crafty, I went and bought a load of wage packets from Smiths and make new wage packets. I used to be on like a monkey a week. Then, like always, somebody cottoned on to what I was doing and grassed me up to one of the guv'nors. He was too frightened to sack me, so what he done, he had two friends who was Old Bill, and one Saturday morning him and these coppers have come banging on my door. I know and you know that the police ain't allowed to use their job to put the frighteners on people and they ain't allowed to sack people. That gutless c**t has given these two a bung so they'll stand behind 'im thinking I'll roll over; some hope, I wouldn't have given a monkey's toss if he'd brought a chief inspector with 'im – no offence to your sister's husband, Pete. Old Bill was right out of order, so I had a licence to knock the three of 'em spark out.

As I've opened the door, this guv'nor stood up on his tiptoes and said, 'McLean, you're sacked!'

I growled at him and he jumped back and the two coppers stepped forward and held their card in front of my nose saying, 'We are police officers.'

I said, 'Put them away before I stick 'em up your arris, what sort of thick c**t do you think I am? You're both wearing uniforms, I know you're police.' I said, 'Hold on a minute,' and I went indoors to put some pants on, then I've gone out and said, 'Right, you muggy c**ts, let's have some.' No, they ain't up for that, because the three of them run off. I chased them down the stairs in just me pants, but they jumped in their motors and screamed off. I could've had them coppers nicked, but that ain't my way. I thought, 'Fuck it, I've had a good run with the job anyway; another job down the pan.'

[Val] **How were them sandwiches?**
Well, Val, I had three, Pete, had one, so I think what he's saying is they was fucking horrible.
[Val] **Take no notice, Peter.**
I don't, I'm getting used to it now.
Thanks, babe. Ain't she lovely, son? Hang on while I roll up...

OK, so after that little business, I've decided to tear my cards up and make me own living. It ain't gonna be too legal, but how else am I gonna look after our baby Jamie and my Val? She weren't too pleased, because I think if she'd had her way I would've gone to work at seven and come home at five – you know, like straight-goers do. I loved that girl to bits, and I still do after all these years, but I'd given her way a try and it didn't work out. I had to tell her, I'm not working all my life for the system then when I'm 65 and we ain't got two bob they put me in the ground; fuck the system, I've always fought against the system, I've always been against the system and I always got a good living. My wife don't say nothing about what I do, I'm the go-getter and she's the housewife and I love her to death. She's my friend, my wife and my lover.

I just couldn't hold down a job – not because I'm stupid or nothing. I do believe if I'd been born in St John's Wood or somewhere like, I could've turned out to be anything I wanted, but I was born in the East End and had the shit kicked outta me every day while I was a kid. My record wasn't too good either and that can be a big handicap, like any ex-con would tell you.

So I decided I was gonna work on the other side of the line, got a few bits and pieces lined up and got stuck into that. Mainly I got invited into jobs because, although I had muscle and I could be intimidating, I was invited because I had a brain as well. Anybody thinking I'm a thick, punch-drunk thug would be making a very serious mistake. I got a really good earner not too long after that. You got to change the names though, Pete, because the people are still walking around. Let's call 'em Danny and Bill, what do you think?

I'll change it later on, doesn't matter for now.

OK, son, you're the writer.

Well, Danny phoned me and said, 'Len, got a job for you, mate.'

I said, 'OK, let's have a meet in the Green Man in Hoxton.' So we've met up and I said, 'What's the work, Dan?'

And he said, 'We've got the word on nicking a 20-ton lorry load of chocolate bars and we want you in on it.'

I was well up for it 'cos it seemed like a good earner and easy money. Dan had already sorted a slaughter over Kent way – that's what we call a safe house for unloading or sorting out stolen gear. The nicking was a piece of piss, because the driver was in on it, but then we had to transfer the load into another lorry because it had the name of the company all over it. We done the swap in a disused garage, then me and Bill followed behind in case there was trouble. We get to this farm and it's owned by an actor – another fucking actor – and he was away. When we opened the big container, I've never seen so many chocolate bars in my fucking life. Me and Bill and Danny and his younger brother starts unloading. And you know what it's like when you start any bit of hard work, you're laughing and you're eager and you're spending the money you're gonna get, but after four hours of sweating our nuts off, none of us was laughing. I said to Bill, 'Fuck me, I hope we get a raid.'

He went, 'Why?'

I said, 'I want to get fucking nicked because I'm absolutely bolloxed.'

'So am I, Len,' he's gone, 'but I don't want to get nicked.'

I said, 'I don't give a fuck; if they walked in here now, I'm so fucking tired I'd fall asleep.'

Know what? I don't think I've eaten one of those chocolate bars since that day because I ate so many I felt sick to the stomach. Good result, though, we came away with about three grand each and back then you could dig holes all day long and never earn that sort of money.

We gotta box a bit clever here, because they might still have that job file.

Can do, but after ten years it's chucked out.

Is it really?

Anyway, I started getting a reputation because I was always fighting and in them days I used to drink, and I used to go round the clubs and pubs and get a bit worse for wear and then end up smashing clubs and pubs up and fucking fighting, always fighting and rowing. I've told you why I gave up drinking and I haven't had a drink for 15 years, because I grew up and woke up and realised it was no good smashing pubs up and fighting people, because you get into too much trouble.

[Val's voice calling from kitchen] **You ask me, Peter, I'll tell you about trouble.**

So when did you start fighting – for money, that is.

For money? Yeah. Because really I've been fighting all my

life. Funny story there, Pete. A kid from downstairs give Barry a bang round the ear'ole, and knowing Barry he probably deserved it, but, with 'im bawling to Mum, she sent me downstairs to sort this Brian out; Brian Hyams, where did that name come from? Forty years and it just popped into my head. Mum shouldn't have done it really – you know, encouraging kids to fight – but who knows why she did? I ain't no age myself, but I've gone down and given 'im a couple of bangs. That's it, he's bawling up the stairs then. He was bigger than we were, so that made me a bit of a hero with the smaller kids. On top of that, Mum give me a couple of coppers to spend in Morgan's. So you could say that was my first paid fight.

Sorry, Pete, I know what you meant: when did I get into the bare-knuckle game? Well, I dunno why I wasn't approached before, really, because I had this rep as an unbeatable fighter. Still, what happened was, I was driving through Blackwall Tunnel one day and the fucking motor blew up in cloud of smoke. I'm bolloxed: no tax, no insurance and no licence and probably Old Bill turning up next minute. I've jumped out, give the 'I'm gonna make a phone call' sign to the cars behind and fucked off. I couldn't get run over in the tunnel, because no fucker could get past. Complete chaos; backed up for miles and ended up on the news and everything.

Anyway, after I've gone home for a cuppa I got my mate to run me round to a car dealer in Kingsland Road; didn't know 'im, just heard he knocked out some cheap motors.

118

Anyway, this funny little fucker has flogged me a motor and guaranteed it to the end of the road. I've given him a look and he's said, 'Trade joke, pal!'

I never even got to the Roman Road before this thing run outta steam; no, I tell a lie, it had loads of steam and it was pissing out the bonnet. Now I'm steaming. I've got me pal to tow me back to the car lot and I ain't happy. The little fella that sold me the motor seen me coming in and disappeared behind some old caravans. I've shouted, 'You got one minute then I'm gonna tip this fucking caravan on top of you.'

After a bit he comes out looking all surprised – 'Sorry, mate, didn't see you there, I was having a piss.'

I've gone, 'Taking the piss more like – you've taken a diabolical liberty with this motor, it's a bag of shit.'

He's looked like I've just insulted his mum, saying, 'Well it was all right when you drove it out.'

'Well, pal,' I've said, 'I ain't gonna argue with you, I want my money back; I give top dollar for that motor and I ain't chucking that down the pan.'

Give 'im his due, Pete, he was a brave little fucker. He's stood up on toes and he's giving it a load of front: 'Money back? Top dollar? Forty-five nicker you gimme, but up the ante a bit and I'll sort you out something tasty.'

I've gone, 'Listen, short stuff, I don't need fucking tasty, I just need a motor that goes and I'm brassic so you better sort it before I get the hump.'

He says, 'I know who you are now. Why don't you have a fight and then you could go a bit upmarket?'

I can't believe this guy: he just about comes up to my tit and he's offering me out. He might've been a little fat guy, but he could move. He's shot backwards about ten feet, saying, 'Hold up! Hold up, you c**t, not with me.'

Now, there ain't many people can call me that and keep standing, but this guy's got balls, so I wiped me mouth.

He's put his hands up – like that was gonna stop me – and says, 'No, what I'm saying is, I know who you are now and I've heard you're a bit clever with your hands.'

I've gone, 'Yeah?'

And he says, 'Well, I arrange a few fights in this yard and I reckon you could earn a few quid from the gippos or whoever comes along. You can use my sports facilities if you wanna shape up a bit.'

I ain't completely sure what this guy's on about, so I don't say nothing and I'm still giving him the look. I let him rabbit on for a bit then said, 'So how does this work, then?'

'Well, all you gotta do is turn up, bang a few heads and it's winner-takes-all less a bit of exes. Good money most nights. Follow me and I'll show you my gym.'

I'm acting a bit dumb, Pete, because you don't wanna give too much away, but I ain't stupid, I know what the bare-knuckle game's all about – just never got into it up 'til then.

Anyway, I've followed him through these caravans and he stood there holding his arm out like he was showing off a new baby. 'There you go,' he said, 'whad'ya think?'

What did I think? I think we're looking at fucking old

lean-to, a bag of sand strung up on a bit of rope and a couple of bales of straw as benches. I couldn't think of nothing to say, so I didn't say nothing. Dunno if you've noticed, son, but, if you keep your mouth shut, it makes the other person talk more than they want to.

That's what I do when I'm interviewing people.

Is that what you're doing with me, then?

Well, it's working, isn't it?

Crafty fucker, ain't you? I'll finish this story and we'll shoot out because I've gotta get a haircut. Is that OK with you?

No problem, we can still talk in the car.

Good boy, and on the way back I'll introduce you to Kenny, because his showroom's only up the Roman.

Kenny?

Yeah, Kenny Mac, the geezer I'm telling you about. His name ain't Mac, it's a bit more, but I can't remember what it is. Make sure you ask him when we get round there. Put it in your notebook.

Anyway, this Kenny says, 'Tell you what, Lenny, if you're up for it I'll sort you out a decent motor and we'll talk money later. Whad'ya say?'

Now I'm thinking, 'I can blag an expensive motor off this mug and then he can fuck hisself,' so we've shook hands and I drove out in a very tidy Escort. I thought I've got a right result for 40 quid.

Let's go out, Pete...

* * * * *

Right, you OK, son?

Yeah, I'm fine, Len, ta.

Good boy, drink that tea up, then, and tell me what we was talking about yesterday.

Getting into the fight game and you'd just driven away from the car lot with a new Escort.

You're right. Well, almost, because it wasn't a new motor – but good nick, though. What did you make of Kenny?

Decent sort of man. Doesn't say a lot, but seemed to think a lot of you. His surname is McCarthy by the way.

Yeah, I remember now. Well, he would think a lot of me, because he earned fortunes outta me. No, I'm joking with you, Pete, he's a diamond and stuck with me all the way.

Anyway, I've got myself a nice motor for practically fuck all and, as far as the bare-knuckle fighting goes, I never expected to hear another word and I've carried on as normal with a bit of this and that. Must've been two or three weeks later, I come in and my Val said that some bloke had rung up and told her that he'd set a fight up for the following Thursday – this was on the Saturday – and would I give him a call. Straight away she wants to know the ins and outs of a duck's arse; I never liked lying to her, so I said, 'I'd been invited to a boxing match,' and that weren't really a lie, was it? There *was* gonna be a fight and I *was* gonna be there. Val give me the old cross eye, but didn't say no more.

Come the Thursday and I've turned up at the yard gates; some kid opened the gates then banged them shut behind me. Now, I ain't too sure about this, because I've never gone into a fight cold. You know what I mean, usually something's kicked off and I've flared up; adrenalin rush, see. Kenny's got things set up, like a ring made out of rope and gas cans set up on the dirt, and there's a load of pikeys standing round giving me the eye.

Talk about world-class ref, Kenny's walking up and down in a white shirt with the sleeves held up with them stretchy things and he's carrying a stopwatch in one hand and an iron bar in the other. He's come flying over to me, shouting, 'You're late, we're all waiting.'

I've just said, 'Oi, you cheeky c**t, I didn't expect to have to clock in,' and he shut up moaning and said, 'That's the geezer you're fighting over there.'

I looked over where he was pointing and this big lump put his hand up to me sort of friendly, then turned it into the finger. I didn't even take me coat off, just jumped over the rope, met him halfway and hit him a blinder on the side of the chin. Fucking hell, Pete, you could've heard his jaw break half-mile away. His feet come off the ground and down he went and it was all over.

Was Kenny chuffed to fuck? No, he complained that I hadn't waited for the bell. I said, 'There ain't a bell,' and he gives one of these gas things a whack with the iron bar to prove a point.

Bit long-winded, but that was the start of fighting for money, like you asked.

So how much did you earn and was there trouble because you knocked their man out?

Trouble? No, they was as good as gold and paid Kenny on the nail, though it wasn't always like that, I found as time went on. Kenny slipped me 200 notes and said the motor was covered, so I'm well chuffed. I can't believe I asked him if he was sure, because it was good bunce for 30 seconds' work, but he said he'd made a couple of shillings, so that was OK. I had a lot to learn about side bets.

What did Val have to say about you taking on something like that?

Ah, well, when she asked me how it went – like, this boxing match I was invited to – I just said, 'It was a straight knockout, love,' and changed the subject. I didn't mention the money, just slipped it to her over a couple of weeks like I'd earned it working straight.

Don't tell me you were frightened of her?

'Course I weren't, but what they don't know they can't moan about and I've said already she never was happy with me fighting; it's a woman thing.

So you carried on bare-knuckle fighting without her knowing?

For a bit I did and got away with it, because I never got marked, and by the time I did tell her I think she was relieved because I was getting into some heavy stuff and she looked at it as 'What can I say?'

The lesser of two evils?

Exactly, Mr Writer. See, I've done it and you've got the words. Good team, eh?

Anyway, after a bit, this fighting got regular. Pikeys are a funny breed, they can't live without drinking, fighting and betting, and 'course they all go together. Don't get me wrong, Pete, like black geezers I ain't got no problem with them and loads of my mates are gypsies or pikeys. So, when they get a sniff that there's a bloke doing the business round Kenny's yard, they're queuing up to have a pop and prove their brother or cousin or son can belt the shit outta this new guy – that's me. I done them all double quick, so then Kenny's got the idea to start spreading ourselves around a bit. We started to go to fairgrounds and race days – anywhere for a fight and a good earner. I've taken on big ugly bastards and they couldn't touch me. Know why? Because they might've been big but they were slow and I don't wanna give myself too much of a gee but I've always been very fast and got a right that could tear your head off. No messing, in the ring or whatever: straight in, bosh, all over.

What about minding?

Well, that comes a bit later, when my name got spoke about a bit more. I think the first job was from a man named John Smith. Yeah, you're laughing because you know I've changed his name.

I had a phone call from this John Smith saying, 'Can I come round and see you, it's very important.'

I said, 'You certainly can.'

Anyway, a couple of hours later, a motor pulled up and it was this geezer and his father; they come in, I shook hands with them both and said, 'What's the problem?'

The father said, 'Well, I'm in the car game,' and I said, 'Yes I know, Rolls-Royces and bits and pieces.'

Anyway, he was involved in moving Rollers to Spain and working through a team in the UK. Turns out they've decided to rump him for close on 400 long ones and would I have a quick word with them and get it back. He told me he's already got a meet with these people and I said, 'You've been a bit quick, ain't ya? Why didn't you tell me yesterday?'

Don't matter, I've gone out and jumped in the car with both of them. We pulled up in the West End and parked up. As we walked to the hotel, we see a car outside with four geezers in it that would have been with the man. We went into the restaurant and there was a man sitting there, so I shook his hand and the others introduced me. He said he'd heard of me, so that cut down a lot of growling time. I said, 'Basically, you owe my pals 400 large. And it ain't only them, it's me an' all because I'm well involved, what with them investing some of my dough in this little bit of business.'

That was all bollocks, Pete, but it makes them keen to get it settled.

He's said, 'Lenny, it went wrong, we got robbed for the motors over there.'

I've gone, 'Leave it out, we ain't interested. That was your side of the deal and that's your problem. If it's all gone pear-shaped, it's down to you.' I growled at him and got hold of him and this was in the fucking restaurant.

Two of the guys that was sitting in the car outside come in and headed over to where we was talking to the main man.

I'm ready for the off, but before they could open their mouths I've warned them: one move and I'll unload them both then tear their boss's face off. They must've known me as well, because they stepped back and wouldn't look me in the eye. Anyway, he agreed on everything, so I've gone outside, tapped on the window of the motor and told the two guys inside to fuck off and crawl away.

They drove me back home and before they left the father said, 'Thank you very much, friend, we'll send you some cash as soon as our money comes back.'

The following day, a big envelope was delivered by hand with ten grand in it, so I was set up for a good while.

Let's have a nice cuppa tea and a biscuit, son. Turn that off for a bit because I wanna tell you a few things...

* * * * *

So you see, Pete, there's still nickings going on, so we have to box clever, if you know what I mean.

Anything you say stops right here – you know that, Len.

'Course I know it, or I wouldn't be telling you.

Did I tell you Joey Pyle's getting out soon? 'Bout fucking time, because they took a right liberty with him. He was in Whitemoor over the Christmas when they had them riots. I've got a letter where he told me it was stinking after the fires and the place was flooded and they expected them to eat Christmas dinner amongst all that shit.

How long did he go down for?

Joe got 14 years, but it was the newspapers, the fucking media, that got him 14 years. I mean, when Joe was a young man he was a bit wild and he had a few connections with one or two people. What happened was, as he got a bit older he had offices at Pinewood Studios and he become a film producer and he was involved in putting this project together and, if it had've come off, Joe would have been a millionaire twice over. But, because of his reputation when he was younger, the police wouldn't leave him alone. And you know, he was jailed for murder but was found not guilty. I know Joe well, and I'm telling you he was a film producer and involved in movies. Did anybody mention that at his trial? Did they fuck, all they kept saying was this guy is mafia connected, mafia this mafia that, why didn't they turn round and say he was a businessman and film producer? Don't matter what he done when he was a young man, the man was banging on 60 – he is over 60 now. We were all wild when we were younger and I think that's what the jury thought: he still was. What they should have put in the fucking paper was that Joe has been fitted up by a grass to get Joe maybe 14 to 15 or even 20 years in prison. They don't like anybody getting away with anything, because they think it makes them look mugs. Don't matter how long ago it was, they never let go. Anyway, the law got their way and they got hold of a grass that went to Joe and said, 'Joe, can you get us a certain thing?'

Joe said, 'I'm not interested, I'm in the film world.'

'Can you? Can you? Can you?'

Drove Joe up the fucking wall. So in the end, to shut this fucking nuisance up, he made himself busy, went to somebody else, got what this person wanted then, and met her at a hotel; Old Bill was waiting for him and he was nicked. In any other country, it would be against the law.

A well-liked man, Joe, a very respected man, and I've got all the time in the world for him.

There's another one: Charlie Richardson, a good friend of mine, 25 years, he got. He was like the opposite of the Krays: on the same level, but a rival. Charlie's another well-respected man; I've got a lot of time for him. When you think Charlie was actually in the *Guinness Book of Records* for the man with the longest sentence for GBH. That's all he has gone away for. He was given 25 years. They took a diabolical liberty.

You know, the use of violence on other violent men is not anything to do with anyone else. When you think about it, how can you give a man 25 years for GBH? But that's what they done.

Every time Charlie opens his mouth, a lot of sense comes out and I think, if he had've been born somewhere else, or put his brains into business in the sixties instead of violence, I think he would have been one of the first yuppies. The man has got a business brain like a professor, he's business-minded, because, you know, in the sixties he had a gold mine going but, as soon as he got that sentence, the government nicked everything off him. The South African government took everything off him, so if he hadn't got that sentence he would've been a multimillionaire today. If he

129

has one or two problems, he will always phone me and I've helped him out several times. Good stuff, Charlie, I've got time for him, they never broke him; he is a perfect gentleman and I will always be there for him. I'm a phone call away for Charlie, whenever he wants me.

Sorry, Pete, getting away from what we was talking about. What was we talking about?

Well, you finished talking about a bit of minding, so it's up to you where you go from here.

Did I? Well there's more to that, but I was thinking of something else to tell you. Does it matter if I jump ahead?

No, not at all. If it's in your head, just tell it and we'll chop it around when we're ready.

Good stuff, because I already said if I don't say when I think of something it goes right outta my head. This bit I'm gonna tell you I can honestly say changed my life. You ready? Put that thing on, then.

It is on. It's always on.

Anyway, what happened was, I had a lovely fortnight in Fuengirola with my Val. I come back off holiday and I've slipped down the Hippodrome to get wages that I was owed; I thought I'd have a quick coffee, because I don't drink beer or spirits, and as I was sitting there a young girl come up crying. I'm thinking, 'Fuck me, I'm still on holiday and I can't sit down for five minutes.' I've said to her, 'What's the matter, tiny bum,' and she said, 'There's a man downstairs, he's hit the DJ and now he's on the bar naked and playing with his, you know.'

I said, 'What? The dirty c**t,' and flew down the stairs.

The rest of the minders were following me, because I was always the leader – wherever I worked, I was always the leader. She was right, turns out some guy is making a nuisance of hisself: he's taken his clothes off and he's pissing and wanking in front of all the young girls, dirty bastard. Now, this might not be a big deal at a private party, but we have a responsibility to look after people and make sure they have a good time without any aggro. A lot of people think doormen and bouncers are on the job to be bullies, keep people outta the club for no reason and to punch a few heads when they feel like it. That ain't so. We're there to look after these kids. You know, you have to think they could be your own, so you'd like to know somebody's looking out for them.

By the time I got down, he's disappeared and so have the other minders, except Robert, who was just coming down the other stairs, I was told that this silly drunk has already had a slap from the DJ because he was trying to climb up on the stage; now I can't find him. Some girls told me he was in the foyer and still got his dick in his hand; I'm getting the hump.

By the time I've caught up with him, my mate John was just coming down the other stairs. I've said, 'John, keep an eye on this door because I'm gonna pull him into the little locker room, have a word and get some clothes on him.'

I've grabbed this guy by the shoulders and pushed him into the room – well, it wasn't really a room, more a cupboard where they kept the brooms and mops. He's gone for me and tried to throw a punch. I went, 'Oi! That's my game!' and shut the door. He's gone fucking mental, kicking, punching and making a right nuisance of hisself.

What am I gonna do? What else but give him a little slap to quieten him down? I've give him a tap with the back of my hand and said, 'Now, you dirty slag, calm yourself down or you'll get some more.'

That done it and he's gone all the other way. I thought he was gonna pass out, so I've held him up against the wall and shouted for John to find his clothes so I could cover him up and get rid of him. I hadn't hit him that hard – one slap then pushed him up against the wire rails where they hang things up. John's slung a T-shirt and some jeans in, no pants and no shoes but, fuck it, as long as he's decent, it ain't my problem. I can talk to him now and I've told him, 'Son, you're drunk as a sack and in the morning you're gonna feel an absolute c**t. Get some strides on then get outta this club and only show your face here again if you can behave yourself.'

He's nodding his head, so he knows what I'm telling him.

Robert stuck his head in the door and I've said, 'Come in, Rob, and put some clothes on this guy, then I want you to make sure he leaves the place nice and quiet,' so he's took him by the arm and led him away and that's the last time I saw him. Remember this, Pete: Robert only stepped in that cupboard for one minute. It'll make sense later on.

I went back to the office, because really this is a normal night for me: bit of aggro, little flare-up, nothing out of the ordinary. I was talking to one of the other minders and I said, 'Where was you when this was all going on?'

He said, 'I was coming down the back stairs.'

I went, 'Yeah, OK, fucking long way, innit?'

That was me then; I picked up my bit of scratch and went home.

Next morning, a pal of mine called Mickey phoned me about seven. He said, 'Len, you know that guy you had a bit of trouble with last night, the one you had to slap?'

I went, 'Yeah?'

'Well,' he said, 'he was found in Tottenham Court Road.'

'Well,' I said, 'so he was found? Makes sense, because he looked a bit lost when I saw him last.'

'No,' Mickey said, 'he's dead – they found him dead.'

It ain't down to me; I didn't hit him that fucking hard.

Mickey said, 'Len, you proper awake? The guy is stone dead; I got it from a pal of mine in the fire service.'

I went, 'God, I'll have bundles of agg now, thanks for marking me card, mate, come round and see me.'

I woke my Val up and said, 'Val, I'm in a lot of trouble. I hit a guy last night for pissing and wanking over girls and Mickey tells me they found him dead.'

She's starting crying, saying, 'Oh, God! Oh, God!'

I give her a cuddle and told her not to worry, it's probably all a mistake and it ain't the same guy at all – though inside I've got this dodgy feeling that it ain't looking good. I said, 'Look, I'm too old and too well known to do a runner so I'll have to face it if it's true, but we've got about 20 grand in the

Abbey Nash, so you won't have to worry about money if I get lifted.' That didn't cheer her up none.

Anyway, I went to work on the Monday and Old Bill are crawling all over the place. Evidently, what they done, they tracked back to see where this guy's been and somehow or other it's led them right back to the Hippodrome in Leicester Square. You've walked the streets with me son, ain'cha. How many people, including coppers, say, 'Hello Lenny'? Go on. How many?

Shit, that's a question. It seems like everyone we pass seems to know you.

Bang on. So, once the law have started checking out clubs, they've only got one name on their minds: Lenny McLean; the beast, the animal, that very dangerous man.

So what's happened, they've interviewed me for an hour and they interviewed all the other guys. And what they more or less all said is like this guy was making a load of trouble with his dick in his hand and frightening all the girls. Now, most of the minders are big guys, but they're straight kids, they ain't got a clue, so, with Old Bill giving them the old cross eye, their tongues run away with them. Lenny got hold of him; Lenny took him in a room to quieten him down; Lenny had to give him a clout. Lenny, Lenny, Lenny, like a fucking broken record, instead of what they should have said is, 'We got nothing to say.' Anyway, they questioned me again and all I could say was I'd taken him in a room, straightened him up, dressed him and that's the end of it.

About a week after, bang-bang at the door, I looked out the

window. There's DI Cater, another plain-clothes guy and loads of uniforms in the street, plus motors parked up all blocking the road. I woke Val and said, 'This is it, Val,' but in the meantime there was a guy in my kitchen. Oh no, no, I was already up – sorry – Val was asleep; I was in the kitchen with a guy.

Val! Val! What's Ronnie's second name? You know, Ronnie, Ritchie's mate. What's his name?
[Val] **Joyce, love. Ronnie Joyce.**

Oh yeah. So what happened was, that day, my friend Ritchie Anderson was in Wormwood Scrubs on remand for Section 18 – attempted murder – so Ronnie had come round to talk to me about slipping up to the Scrubs for a visit. I just got out the chair to make a cup of tea when all of a sudden: bang-bang at the door. I stood up, looked out the window and two plain-clothes were on my doorstep; then, like I said, police cars with lights flashing blocking the road off. One of them's banging on the door, saying, 'Open the door. Police. Will you open the door?'

I've said to Ron, 'I think I'm gonna be lifted in about two minutes, because that's Old Bill.'

He went, 'Cor, what you done, Len? Is it that wages-van business?'

I said, 'Leave it out, that was fucking months ago,' though to myself I'm thinking, 'I wish it was that job.' 'No, mate, I hit someone a bit ago and he's died.'

135

Straight off, Cater said, 'Leonard McLean, you have the right to remain silent but I'm charging you with the murder of Gary Humphreys.'

I said, 'Do what?'

And he said, 'I'm charging you with the murder of...'

'Yeah, yeah,' I said, 'got that bit first time, Gary who? I don't know what you're fuckin' well talking about.'

He said, 'We better talk inside,' so I let the two of them in and four muggy uniforms come piling in behind them.

Cater went, 'Can you get your clothes? An officer will go with you.'

I said, 'No fucking officer's going in my bedroom while my wife's in bed, you can wait there.'

He said, 'We can't, you are under arrest and have to be observed from this moment.'

I said, 'You can wait outside – and, don't worry, I ain't gonna jump out the fucking window, am I?'

Sergeant Prunty said, 'Come on, Mr McLean, don't start playing up.'

I said, 'Playing up? Fucking playing up? You're nicking me for murder, but that don't give you no right to come into a lady's bedroom. Just remember, there's only six of you. Step outta line and I'll fucking unload all six of you.'

Pete, listen, I wasn't doing myself no favours, I know, but you can't let these c**ts get the better of you.

I went upstairs and give Val a kiss; she'd heard what was going on and was laying there with the duvet over her mouth so them mugs couldn't hear her crying. I wasn't too

136

worried about myself right then, but to see my wife all upset tore my heart out. I said, 'It's gonna be OK, babe. Get hold of Ralph the brief a bit lively and tell him I've been taken to Vine Street nick; he'll know what to do.'

I went back downstairs, shook Ronnie's hand and I walked out the front door. I didn't know it then, but I wouldn't be doing that again for the next 18 months.

Were you cuffed up?

No I wasn't, because as I said there was only six of them indoors and none of them had the bottle to suggest it. I went without a fuss, though, because there weren't no point in having a ruck.

Talk about make a show. I bet they didn't make this fuss when they arrested the Yorkshire Ripper. Cars in front, cars behind and they've got lights flashing and sirens going. Fuck's sake, I haven't even got a guilty yet. While we're on the road, my nut's doing a hundred miles an hour. How could that guy have died? Honest, Pete, I only give him a tap; I'm thinking p'raps he's one of them people who have some sort of illness where they can die over nothing – I mean, you read about it all the time. Whatever, the law is gonna make as much out of it as they can, because it ain't no secret they want me off the streets. I think that's when it hit me: with my rep, they're gonna be screaming for a long recommendation, and that could be 25 years. Twenty-five fucking years, I'd be shuffling up the Roman to pick up me pension on one of them metal frames the day I get out.

We got to Vine Street; they stuck me in an interview room and made a start. Cater and Prunty didn't even try to play good cop, bad cop; they both was bad. They said, 'Len, we know you struck Gary Humphreys on the chin and shortly afterwards he was dead, so you could save us a lot of time and expense by admitting your guilt; it would help you in court.'

I said, 'Look, between me and you and off the fucking record – we're not making statements, are we?'

He went, 'No.'

So I said, 'What would you do if you see a man naked, pissing and wanking over young girls?'

He went, 'Well, you know, we can't answer that.'

I said, ''Course you can't, you muggy c**ts, because all you're interested in is getting a gee for yourselves by wrapping this up double quick; well, fuck the pair of you. Stick me back in the cells.'

They put me straight in a cell; then after about an hour they come for me and took me back to the interview room, where there was Sergeant Prunty and DI Cater – his father was involved in arresting the Krays. Anyway, when you get interviewed by the police they have to have it on tape, everything has to be taped. They put the tape on, so I thought, 'Bollocks to them, they're not having me for a murder, because that is the sort of crime that's the end of you – you know when you're in your forties it's goodbye, God bless, end of.'

I thought no way they were gonna have me, so, when

Cater said, 'Can you tell us what happened with Gary Humphreys,' I said, 'No, I can't, but what I will tell you is that I'm John Wayne and Michael Caine.' They've looked at me like I've lost the plot. I said in Michael Caine's voice – you know, like an impression, 'Not many people know this, so fuck off.' Then I did John Wayne: 'So get on your horse and drink your milk.'

Cater's flung down the folder he had, shouted, 'Interview suspended at 12.42,' and stormed out. First round to Lenny.

Two days I did Michael Caine and John Wayne and then every now and then I flared up at 'em and growled at 'em and done me nut, because I noticed every time I done me nut DI Cater kept sending uniforms out to get me tea. Anyway, after two days' questions and questions, they got sick of it and they got nothing out of me because there was no way I was gonna put my hand up to giving a guy a right-hander, because it's murder and that means life imprisonment. So what they done, the bastards, how they got me was this. DI Cater said, 'OK, Mr McLean, we have just arrested Robert Lopez.'

That give me a knock back, so I went, 'Why, what the fuck has Rob gotta do with this?'

He said, 'Well it's pretty obvious, he was in the room with you.'

I went, 'Yeah, for about ten seconds.'

'Well, you categorically deny that you struck the blow that killed Humphreys, so it can only have been Robert Lopez.'

I thought to myself, 'Fucking hell, you got to think here.

It's all right sitting in the pub with your mates and saying what you would do and what you wouldn't do in a situation – that's all right when you got a pint in your hand, but now we're talking about the real thing. Your back's against the wall, you're looking at a life sentence – murder can only mean one sentence: life.'

They've got my nuts in the grinder and they both know it. They know it's gonna be hard work making that charge stick on Robert, but I think they would go all the way, and all the time it takes that nice young kid is gonna go through the worst hell he's ever known and probably ruin his life. I wanna jump up and bang their fucking heads together, the pair of c**ts, but that wouldn't help. I've gotta think.

I thought to myself, 'Come on, Len, you're always handy when the chips are down and you're the best, so let's see how big your heart is.' I went, 'Hold up, I got something to say.' They looked at each other and I've got a feeling they're trying not to put the big grin on. I had a quick flash in my head of my Val, Jamie and my little Kelly and what they're gonna do without me and said, 'It was me. I put my hands up. Charge me and let Rob go.'

Sorry, Val, I've just put myself away for life but I couldn't live with myself if a kid took the blame for something it looks like I done, intentionally or not.

Shall we stop for a bit, Pete? I'm as dry as fuck.
Yeah, me too and I'm not talking.
No, you don't say a lot, do you? But you listen, and that's

good. Ain't nothing worse than talking to somebody and their eyes are rolling in their head and they won't look you in the eye.

I ain't half jumped a long way ahead. I'm going backwards and forwards, does it matter?

Val! Nice cuppa tea, Val.

Tell you what, Pete, I'll leave that bit of a story and come back to it, is that OK?
Bit of a cliff-hanger.
What's that?
Keep me in suspense wondering what happened next.
Well, I'm sitting here, so I didn't get lifed off, but it was a very bad time and it affected me and Val for a long time – and still does a bit.

Good gel, stick it on the table. Pete said have you got any of them chocolate digestives? Because if you ain't he's gonna start bringing his own.
[Val] **It's all right, Peter, I let what he says go in one ear and out the other. Did you want a biscuit or a sandwich?**
Sandwich would be great, thanks.
[Val] **Don't have to ask you, do I, Len?**
No you don't, babe.

Ain't she lovely, Pete? She ain't 'alf suffered some agg with me, but she never complains, never says a word.

OK then, later I'll come back to when I was lifted – you remind me not to forget.

When I was a younger man, I remember always fighting, but fighting don't earn a crust, so if you're gonna fight, turn it into a few quid. One night an old pal of mine come to see me – what's his name, you know, the one I smashed the pub up with. You got to help me here, Pete. Have a roll-up.

You sure you told me about that?

Well, I thought I did. When I was trying to build up a bit of minding work.

No, I'm sure you haven't.

OK, then, here I go again, off on another angle. I'd done a bit of looking after a local pub, but it weren't enough to make a living. So what I done was get myself stuck in the corner with a pint and then all of a sudden a gang of likely lads would come in looking for trouble; proper leery bunch. They're annoying the customers, bawling and shouting, then drinks are spilled and a table goes over. That's when I step in like fucking John Wayne. I hand out a couple of slaps and do a bit of growling and they all fuck off. That's when the guv'nor wants to buy me a drink and ask if I wanna go on the payroll; sweet. What he don't know is the lads are all pals of mine. OK, it cost me a few rounds for them to kick off, but I'd got myself a nice pension.

That worked for a long while and I was earning some good dough for doing nothing, really. I'd show my face every now and then and word went out this pub or that pub was under Lenny's wing and everybody was happy; except one c**t. I mean, this landlord had had trouble from tearaways without me even pulling that scam, but once I quieted it all down he wants to cut my little retainer in half. We had a few words and next thing I get a tug from the law for demanding money with menaces; like I was pulling the old protection racket and that wasn't the way it was at all. Luckily, all that happened there was I was warned to get my arse out the manor. I could've got serious time for that, but the detectives that come after me was old school and I think they knew the score, so they gave me a chance.

That was the time me and Val moved over to Bethnal Green; I was ready for a move and it saved a lot of grief. But before we took off I had a bit of business with that landlord because off the record the DS had told me who'd grassed me up. Take it away, my friend, wherever you are now, you're a credit to the force. I got my mate to give me a hand and about three in the morning between the two of us we trashed his pub. Smashed every window by chucking dustbins through them, smashed hanging baskets, the pub signs and even the wooden tables outside. Amazing the damage you can do in a few minutes, especially if you're a bit wound up.

But that ain't what I was gonna tell you, Pete.

You started off looking for the name of a friend of yours.

Fuck's sake! You'll have to keep me on track, else I'll be all over the place. Danny, that was it. Just come to me; yeah, got it now.

Well, Danny come to see me one night because he had a problem. I said, 'What's up, pal?'

And he said, 'My dad's just took over a club up Commercial Road called the White Swan and it's a fucking nuthouse. There's murders over there, stabbings, riots the whole nine yards, and I'm a bit worried about my dad, so would you come over and look after him?'

'For you, Dan,' I said, 'You've only gotta ask.'

I went over there and had a word with Bill, his dad, and told him I'd be pleased to help out as a favour to my pal. He wouldn't hear of it, but insisted I kept the door money or no deal – and that was good money back then. I started minding that gaff, and, because I was a new face on the manor, the likely lads were queuing up to try me out.

I bashed 'em all up then I got a reputation – that the man's a fucking lunatic, Lenny's a crank. I fought everybody that had a name over that way, bashed them all up and then there was no trouble. Bill was well pleased and I told him to keep my name up for as long as he liked, even though I wasn't gonna be picking up no wages. He gave me a nice bonus when I gave it up, more than enough for a little holiday.

I suppose it was a couple of months later when he phoned me up again and sounded a bit worried. He said, 'Can you get yourself over here double quick, because I've got a bit of trouble.'

I'm thinking, 'Hallo, it's all kicked off again now that I'm out the picture.'

I got over there about five in the afternoon. I said, 'What's the matter, Bill?'

He said, 'Len, I've just had a Scotch guy in here with three

144

guys looking to take a pension outta this place; looked a pretty heavy mob.'

I said, 'Bill there's only two people that get money out of this place – that's you and me.'

He said, 'That's right, Len, but this guy is going round the East End giving it the big un with his firm behind him; I heard he stuck a hatchet in someone's head.'

I said, 'I'll shove it up his fucking arse. What time they coming in?'

He said, 'About nine, I think.'

'OK then, I'll be here at half-past eight.'

I was on the door of the White Swan at half-past eight, clocking everybody who came in. I spotted these mugs a mile away, but I didn't let them see I was even looking at them, just let them go over to the bar and start talking to Bill.

After a bit, Bill called me over and said, 'Len, I think you should talk to these people. I've told them you're my partner.'

That was old bollocks, Pete, but good on Bill, it don't hurt to spraunce a bit when you have to.

Straight off I've said to the main man, 'What's the fucking score?'

He's looked me up and down and said, 'I think you need some protection here, otherwise you could leave yourselves open to a lot of trouble.'

I've give him the look and asked him, 'Do I look like I need protecting?'

He's still looking at me like I'm some sort of c**t, but I let it go.

'You're a big fella,' he said, 'but when there's guns flying about it doesn't matter how big you are.'

'OK,' I said, 'what you offering?'

He looked at his little firm like he'd just got a result and said, 'Full protection? Let's say a monkey a week.'

I said, 'That's good dough every week, how do I know these boys of yours can deliver when it gets a bit rough?'

Now he really thinks he's cracked it, because he looks at these three fellas and they all laugh. I let them have their laugh, then I said, 'OK, pal, let's give 'em a test run.'

With that, I've grabbed the nearest two and smashed their heads together and they dropped spark out. Now, you've seen me move, Pete. Am I fast or am I fucking fast?

The last one.

It's all right, Val's gone out. Yes, fucking fast.

Before these two have hit the deck I've swung a left and hit the third guy on the point of the chin and his head bent back enough to break his neck; didn't, but definitely broke his jaw. That left the mouthy c**t, who just stood there with his mouth open. I got him by the face, pulled him towards me, then turned him towards the bar. I've pulled his arms right up his back and said to Bill, 'Go on, son, your shout.' Now, Bill was a bit tasty when he was a younger man, but when you get older you leave all that behind, that's why he called me in. He ain't shy of dealing out a bit of violence, though, so while I'm holding the man Bill's hit him across the side of the head with a full bottle of Jack Daniel's. Didn't break the bottle, but this guy's head looked like he'd had a hatchet stuck in it; fucking blood all over.

We tidied up by slinging the four of them on the pavement outside and somebody must've phoned an ambulance, because one come screaming up within about five minutes. That was the end of that bit of work.

Anyway, word got around what I'd done and the local coppers came round and said, 'Lenny, you hurt these four guys. We won't nick either of you, because we know what they was at, but we're warning you: don't go too strong or our guv'nor's gonna get the hump.'

The next message we got was Jimmy Boyle was coming down from Scotland with a bunch of his firm. I said to a young lad who let's say I'll just call Tommy, 'I've heard a rumour that Jimmy is coming down.'

He said, 'Yeah, I've heard the same, what we gonna do about it? How do you want to play it?'

I said, 'Fuck it, let 'em 'ave it.'

So Tommy went out and came back with a twenty-bore shotgun, a twelve bore and a handgun.

'Fuck me,' I said, 'I didn't know they made a twenty bore. You could bring an elephant down with that.'

By the pub door there was a cubbyhole, so we put the guns in there and waited for this mob, who was supposed to be coming down in the week.

I've said to Tommy, 'As soon as they come in, we won't do no talking – just let 'em have it, no messing.'

After getting all set up for a fucking war, they didn't come down that week, they didn't come down the following week, and the Scotch men were still in hospital. Never mind, we thought, we're ready when they do show.

In the meantime, there was this young kid hanging around and he was a fucking nuisance. He was a nice kid but a bit wild and always getting into trouble, always getting into fights, so I barred him from the club and the furthest he could get inside the place was the coconut mat, because I let him stand there. He was a pleasant kid, a nice kid, and I used to like talking to him, but I had to keep an eye on him, because he was a bit slippery. He never fuckin' well stood still, so I used to have to watch him because he'd be fiddling with this, touching that, and as I'm talking to him he's opened the cupboard door and seen these guns. Naturally, kid like that wants to know what they're all about, so against my better judgement I've told him we've got a firm coming down from Scotland to shoot the place up because we'd had a run-in with some of Jimmy Boyle's mob.

Anyway, he's told his stepfather and he's had a word with a guy I hadn't met but came good pals with later on. This was Ritchie, who I mentioned was banged up the day I got lifted for that murder. Ritchie was friends with Arthur Thomson, the top man in Scotland. Cut a long story short again, Ritchie's blown down Boyle's ear'ole and it turned out that the firm we'd put in hospital was nothing to do with him; they were putting his name up without his permission – bad move. I dunno about the other three guys, but the front man, the Scotchman doing all the talking, had got out of hospital by the time this come to light. I heard Jimmy Boyle sent a man down to sort the situation out.

Talking of guns, I remember a fella I knew coming to me one day with the offer of a bit of work. I've said, 'That'll do for me, what's the SP?'

He said, 'Not too much work, Len, but some good money involved and all you will have to do is mind our backs while we do a little transfer job.'

'Up my street, then,' I said, 'gimme the nod and I'll be there whenever you like.'

A couple of days later, Ritchie phoned and said he'd pick me up in an hour and we'd run up to the City. The motor turns up and there's my pal and three other guys who I don't know.

'OK,' I thought, 'he ain't ever let me down.'

Now, it was a scorching hot day, and what struck me was these three guys are wearing overcoats. I puzzled over that and in the end I've turned round – I was sitting in the front – and said, 'What's with coats, fellas?' and they opened them all at the same time and they're all fully tooled up; they all had a couple of guns each.

I said, 'Fucking hell, who we dealing with here, the mafia?'

He said, 'Sort of, it's a deal with the IRA and just in case it kicks off we've brought along a wee bit of insurance.'

'Well, don't that make me look like a spare prick?' I went.

'No, Lenny,' he said, 'I don't think things will get out of hand, but if they do I'm sure you'll calm things down without guns blazing away.'

149

I thought, 'Thanks for the gee, but if it goes tits up the first one to get it is the big fella. Fuck 'em, let them try.'

We ended up in a restaurant up West – but not in the actual restaurant, in a little room out the back. There was a couple of black Mercs out the front parked double yellows, and my pal said, 'Our man's here, away in you go.'

As we've got out, a guy got out of one the Mercs, gives us a nod and walked into the place and we followed him. My pal stayed in the motor.

We got in the room and sitting at a card table was a tough-looking guy and against the wall right behind him was three hard-looking fuckers. Our bloke pulled a chair up and sat down and both of them stuck briefcases on the table. I thought, 'Well this is a nice easy number, swap the cases and were ready for the off.' But no, these two started fucking arguing and it went on for ever. It was all down to who was paying what and who was accepting what. I wanted to bang their heads together, because I was sweating, dying of thirst and getting more pissed off every minute.

All of a sudden, our man jumps up, kicks his chair over and pulls a gun out shouting, 'Fucking Irish c**ts, you can't be dealt with.'

Then all the guns come out, so I've grabbed hold of one the Irish guys, knocked his gun out on to the floor, got hold of the skin on his face and smashed him up the wall. I said, 'Any of you move and your pal's gonna lose his eyes and his face.'

Funny, really, it was like everything froze for ages, then

Above: Lenny with his 'book man', Peter Gerrard.

Below: Lenny was only able to attend one book signing before he passed away. Tragically, he never knew that his book stormed into the number one spot in the bestseller charts.

Illustrator Ian Whetstone draws celebrities in the style of comic-book heroes. He chose
The Thing from the Fantastic Four to represent Lenny's strength and size.

Above: Lenny's parents' wedding day. This was a happy time, before life became traumatic for the family.

Below left: Lenny's great uncle, the legendary Jimmy Spinks.

Below right: Young Lenny with Bill Boy, outside Godwin House in the East End.

BOXING

at the

RAINBOW THEATRE
FINSBURY PARK LONDON

on

11th September 1978

In aid of CHILDRENS MUSCULAR DYSTROPHY & AUTISTIC CHILDREN

Featuring a 10 x 3m

CLOSE ENCOUNTER FOR A THIRD TIME for the UNOFFICIAL

HEAVYWEIGHT CHAMPIONSHIP of GREAT BRITAIN

Lennie 'Boy' McLean
THE COOLEST DADDY OF THEM ALL

Roy 'Pretty Boy' Shaw
WILL THE MEAN MACHINE REGAIN THE TITLE

Steve 'Columbo' Richards	Tommy Adams	John McDade
v	v	v
Steve Armstrong	Micky May	Danny Woods
Ralph Harris	Terry Scrutton	Micky Davison
v	v	v
Danny Chippendaie	John Ricky	To be announced

Doors open at 7.00 p.m.   Boxing commences 8.00 p.m.

Tickets £12.50 £10.00 £7.50 £5.00 £2.50

AVAILABLE FROM

C. PINI 01 837 6891

DIXIE DEAN 01 253 8072

RAINBOW BOX OFFICE

HENRY BROWN 01 739 7582

The poster advertising Lenny's third and final fight with Roy 'Pretty Boy' Shaw.

Above: Family matters. Val and the kids meant everything to Lenny.

Below: Jamie and Kelly celebrate having their dad back home after his twelve months inside on a murder charge.

Above: Lenny in action against Roy Shaw.

Below: With close friends, Richie Anderson (left) and Arthur Thompson (middle).

Lenny will always be remembered for his role in hit film *Lock, Stock and Two Smoking Barrels*, in which he played Barry the Baptist.

Just two of the many floral tributes at Lenny's funeral. He is still much missed.

the guns went down. It was all bollocks anyway – how did any of them expect to get away with having a shoot-out right next to a busy restaurant? The two main men had a whispered conversation, they swapped the cases and it was all over.

Funny, though.

When I got home, Val said, 'Been up to much today?'

And I've gone, 'No, not too much, babe.' No point in frightening her after it all happened, or didn't happen.

Go on, son, ask me something, because it ain't always easy coming up with things.

You know, Len, when I first met you, you were always saying you were a raving lunatic, but actually you seem the very opposite.

You think so? Well, like I've been telling you, Pete, the only thing I don't like is I'm getting older and I'm mellowing and I'm fighting against it.

Why do you want to fight against it?

That's a good question, son, and I haven't really got an answer to it. I suppose what it is, it might change me from the man I am. Really, though, I've got nothing to prove. I've been the toughest guy in the country on the cobbles until nobody would have it with me. I'm a ten-man job, but now I'm getting a bit older I should put my feet up. I might be mellowing, and I like the idea of mellowing, but any youngsters out there don't get any illusions of thinking I'm over the hill just because I like to sit and relax with my slippers on. If they fancy it, I would tear their heart out, because that's the way I am. I want to be nice and calm, but I can turn on a sixpence. How's that sound, son?

I hate violence. I've known violence all my life, you know, from when my stepfather moved in – you know, we're talking about five years old, five-and-a-half onwards, was just violence. Now I'm 45 years old and I think it's time I moved on to something a bit better. When I'm with nice people I love it, I love this relaxed feeling. You're a nice man, Pete, and very pleasant to sit with. Have I flared up? Have I raised my voice to you?

Not once, mate.

Speaks for itself, then. But if I'm with some youngsters and they want to try me out I lose all that mellow feeling and I get the aggression back inside me and I get the raging bull, the raging lunatic. That's why I like nice people around me, 'cos that makes me nice and that's what I want in life now. I mean, I'm 45 years old. I've done everything anyone could ever want to do. I've fought everyone with my hands, I've had people shoot me in the back, stab me, nick me for murder. I've had everything anyone could possibly want. I've got my lovely Val, I've got my two smashing kids and we've all got that bowl of cherries; all I want now is the cream to put on the top.

You've seen me perform, Pete. What did you tell your pals?

That business down the gym? I couldn't believe it and it was difficult to describe. Awesome didn't seem enough somehow.

Did you say I'm a decent fella and all?

I tell everybody that, because it's true, but if they've

seen those video clips they're thinking, 'Has he got the right Lenny?' and find it very hard to believe.

Do they?

Was I right or wrong to dig that c**t out down the gym?

You felt you had to straighten him out.

Yeah, I did, and you know why? I don't let anybody disrespect my pal, whether I'm around or not...

Transcript of Lenny's tirade at the gym

[Lenny talking to gym barman who is standing beside alleged grass]

You! What's your game? I told you to talk to my book man and when I turn my fucking back you're ignoring him and talking to this piece of shit. Don't talk to him, he's a bastard, I want to hurt him every time I see him, he's a slag. I want to kill him but he'll grass me up, he won't fight me, he's a c**t and a coward. Do you want a fight? Do you want to fight? Do you want to fight? You gutless c**t, do you want to fight? No, because you're a gutless c**t. Get out of this club – go on, get out of this club before I do you some damage, you muggy grassing fucker.

Sorry about that, son. Fuck his gym, let's go home. I don't wanna be here.

Shall I put that story on tape?

Sure, it helps later if I forget.

OK. I was working the doors when this famous boxer turned

up; I'll think of his name later. One of the minders come up to my office and told me he was downstairs. Now, I'd heard this guy had made a comment to someone I knew. They was talking about Roy Shaw and myself and he'd said, 'They're both fucking lunatics; Roy's been in Broadmoor and Lenny's on the way there.' I thought that was funny, but when I've gone downstairs I've put me look on and walked up to him all menacing like. He was a bit tasty as a boxer, but he looked like he was ready to shit hisself. I've glared at him and said, 'So I'm heading for Broadmoor, am I?' He's gone all red in the face and started stuttering, so I've burst out laughing and said, 'I've gotta make you right, son, and you ain't the first one to say it.' Tell you what, he looked fucking relieved I didn't have the hump.

What he'd come to see me about was he was down on his luck and needed a bit of work. OK, we all have a run of bad luck, no matter how much money we might've earned at the top. Anyway, I fixed him up on the door and put him with Basil, one of my doormen, until he learned the ropes. Everything was good for a week, then one night a bit of trouble kicked off and they both got stabbed by these two young mugs. By the time I got down to the doors, this boxer is holding his side with blood pouring through his fingers; he ain't making a sound. Basil, on the other hand, is laying on the ground and crying like a fucking baby that he was gonna die. This is a guy that's been in the business for years and ain't no stranger to giving or getting violence. The two kids have fucked off and somebody's already called an ambulance, so all I could do right then was pick up these couple of knives and get rid of them. Basil's still moaning, so I've told him straighten his mug and act like a man.

They got hold of those kids eventually and dragged them into court. Now, the boxer was a straight-goer, so he has every right to point the finger – after all, they'd done him a bit of damage. Basil, on the other hand, should have kept his mouth shut, 'cos, if you live and work on the other side of the fence, you never, ever talk to the law, no matter what. But, no, he's acted the grass and put the finger on these kids and they got banged up for a good few years – and that's not what we do. We could've found them, given them the bashing of their lives, a bashing they'd never forget, and all forgotten. Instead, they ended up behind the door.

You're giving me that look again, Pete, but what would you prefer? Arm, leg, jaw, ribs, they're all mended in six or eight weeks, as against losing your liberty for five years – and if you're a youngster, that can fuck you up for the rest of your life. That's why I can't bear that Basil anywhere near me, because I hate grasses, they're scum and that's why I had that go at him. Tidy that up how you like and I'll get them names for you before we do the book.

How was that?

Good, Len, good.

'Ere, Pete, when Reggie or Ronnie talk about stories, do they talk about it like me, you know, all jumbled up and all over the place?

Everyone does. It would be very difficult for someone to speak a readable book straight out of their head.

I suppose the book writer puts it down and cuts it up and puts a bit of colour in, am I right? I mean they must talk like me; there's not a lot of books where the blokes have done it themselves, is there?

No, when you're talking biography, it's almost always done like this and, yes, the ghost writer fiddles about with it but usually with the person they're writing with.

OK, son, well fire away with your questions, Pete, I'm on a roll. Let's spark up first, though.

You mentioned last week that you took on 18 guys and saw them all off.

Oh, yeah, I did, good boy remembering that. You don't forget nothing, do you?

What happened was, Dennis McCarthy had a club in Smithfield meat market, just off the market, called the Barbican. The geezer who owned it first bought it for about 80 grand and kept it a bit select, you know: only celebrities and stars were allowed in, so he didn't have a lot of aggro. When Dennis bought it and took over he had an ex-copper as a partner and they had a guy on the door named Billy. This Bill was just a nice guy, wanted to be everybody's friend, and what happens when you take that attitude is people take advantage, and he used to get a lot of trouble. He couldn't handle the trouble and he was getting it from south, north, east and it all got too much for him. Dennis and the ex-copper came round to see me and said,

'Len, we're having a lot of trouble down the club and it's keeping away decent customers, will you come and look after the place?'

I played it a bit crafty and said, 'I'm already fixed up, but if you want to give me a bit more dough I'll come and mind it,' so what they done, they give me hundred pound a night, which weren't bad.

I was doing five nights down there, and it was fucking hard work at first, because all the troublemakers treated the place like it was their own. I mean, one night I turned this mug away because he was too scruffy and an hour later he come back and stuck a gun under my nose – and I do mean right under my nose. I've looked over the top of the barrel and said, 'If you're gonna shoot me, do it and stop playing cowboy.'

He's hesitated, so I knew his bottle's gone, so I took the gun out of his hand and smashed it across the bridge of his nose and slung him across the pavement. All these years later, every time he combs his hair in the mirror he's gonna see this flat nose and remember Lenny McLean.

After a while, I straightened up all the aggravation and there was no trouble and Dennis and his partner loved it.

There's always a little big of agg even in the best clubs, no matter who's on the door; if flogging drink is your game, that's what you have to expect. A lesson you learn is that you never ever let stag nights in, because they get very boisterous at the end of the night. They're aggravation. This particular night, this mob of young guys must've put their

157

heads together to get past the door, because what they did was walk in, in twos and threes, over a period of time.

By the time they're downstairs, they're 18-handed and well on the way to being a fucking nuisance. There was a nice young girl behind the bar, about 18 she was, and she's given them their drinks and asked for 40 or 50 quid, whatever. Suddenly they don't like the prices and they've told her to fuck off because they ain't gonna pay. They said a few other things and this girl has got proper upset. Next thing, I get the word these guys won't pay their bill and they've been abusive to a young barmaid. This is right up my street and what I'm paid for.

First thing I've done is told the DJ to turn the music off. Now, most times we can nip a bit of trouble in the bud by being nice and calm and polite; upsetting that little girl, they don't fuckin' well deserve polite. I've gone, 'Right, you bunch of wankers, pay the bill then get out or I'll fucking do every one of you.'

Just like I expect, I get a load of abuse, like, 'No, fuck you, fat bastard, fat c**t.'

I ain't concerned, names don't hurt me like I'm gonna hurt them. I went, 'OK, you're all brave, you're all tough and you're all very drunk and you're 18-handed; you wanna fight, let's go upstairs. There's plenty of room outside on the cobbles.'

They put their glasses down, but I noticed more than a few of them tucking bottles and ashtrays inside their jackets. I'd already noticed that Eddie Richardson was in the house, and as I've gone past near his table I heard the woman with him say, 'Are you going to give Lenny some help?'

Eddie's laughed and said, 'You're joking, Lenny don't need no help.'

Overhearing that, I thought to myself, 'He's giving me bundles of credit there, but I think a little bit of help would go down better,' though I never said nothing. I was like one of them sheepdogs keeping them moving and giving stragglers a shove, but I got them upstairs and I got them outside. That's when they all kicked off, throwing bottles and glasses at the front of the club. I said to Dennis, 'Come on, we got to go out and hurt them.'

'We?' he said. 'Fucking *we*? I ain't going out there.'

I said, 'But it's your club.'

He said, 'I don't care; it's your job, Len, I ain't going out there.'

I've got bundles of pride, so I walked out the door and Dennis locked it behind me. I've faced this lot and they're all jeering and giving it large, so I shouted over all this noise, 'Calm down, calm yourselves down and listen,' and I've waved my arms like a teacher does, for them to gather round me. Now they're puzzled, because they ain't sure what's going on now, but they got closer and went a bit quieter. 'Now, you bunch of c**ts,' I thought, 'now you can have it.' I've pulled a cosh out of my jacket and quick as you like, bang!, I've slipped through the lot of them. I'm hurting them and their bodies are falling here and there. In a few minutes, there was nine laying on the floor and nine ran away.

I heard a voice, looked round and there was a mate of mine who'd come up the back way to give me a hand. He just stood there going, 'Fucking hell, Len, I thought I was gonna mix it beside you, but it's all over.'

I said, 'Thanks for turning out, but you better slip away, because Old Bill will be here double quick.' I could hear the sirens.

He's gone, 'You sure you're OK?'

I said, 'Lovely, mate,' and he fucked off.

Half a minute before the law turned up, I've slung the cosh up on the roof and waited to be nicked. You'd think I'd be the victim, but I know how their minds work.

I was taken to Snow Hill station and banged up in a cell. Not long after, they started bringing in the nine that had run off; the other nine were getting hospital treatment by then. They put them in the big holding cell right opposite mine and they're still drunk, screaming and hollering. In a few hours, all their booze and piss will wear off and they won't be brave no more. I don't drink, so I'm cranky anyway; I'm a natural crank. They escorted me into the interview room and said, 'Lenny, where's the stick?'

I said, 'I don't know what you talking about, there ain't no stick, I used my hands.'

They said, 'No way, Lenny you used a stick.'

'Listen to what I'm saying,' I said, 'would you go out with a stick in your hand against 18 men?'

They said, 'We wouldn't have gone out there and you were very foolish to have gone out.'

'No,' I've gone, 'I ain't foolish and I ain't stupid. What I am is very proud. I'm paid to mind the gaff and make sure that your sons and daughters can have a nice time with their friends without getting hurt. Pride and reputation – that's why I went outside.'

I was put back in the cell, so I got my head down and waited. Not many hours later, these kids are coming to their senses. All the piss has worn off and now they want to be nice kids, but I've been sober all night and now I'm glaring at them through my cell door and I'm growling at 'em and they can't look at me, they keep turning away. I'm screaming through the cell grille, 'You gutless bastards, all the piss has wore off you now, you fucking mugs. I wanna fucking kill you, and do you know why? Because you was brave last night, spoiling the night for decent people and digging out a little girl, but look at you now, you bunch of wankers.'

They can't look at me and every now and then I heard another one spewing up and taken out in case they had concussion. Eventually, an officer took me back to the room, got me to sign a bit of paper and said, 'We have got to put this before the DPP, you are bailed to appear here in two weeks when we will let you know what you will be charged with. I can tell you now it will most likely be Section 18.'

Two weeks later, when I went back, I found out that the DPP had written, 'We cannot proceed with a charge of grievous bodily harm against 18 men by Mr McLean as in our opinion it would be thrown out of court.' So I got out of that.

Good story that, weren't it? I've got another one, then we'll get a bit of seafood. You up for that, son? It's only next door.

I got a call from a well-known man in the demolition game, a guy who at one time in the late seventies was big in demolition – I'll call him Fred. He's asked me to go over and see him because he's got a problem. I got over there, went in his office and he made me a cup of tea.

I said, 'What's the matter?'

He said, 'I'm getting a lot of people buying bricks off me, so I'm getting a lot of money. I'm doing very well, but I'm getting a lot of people coming on the site threatening me and demanding this and demanding that. They want the bricks at this price, they want this at this price,' and he told me one guy in particular was taking a diabolical liberty, chucking his weight around and practically nicking bricks and wood off Fred.

I said, 'When's he due?'

He said, 'He's coming back in today, that's why I rung you.'

I said, 'OK, I'll wait here in the office.'

This guy's turned up in a tipper lorry, big muddy boots, a proper fucking Jack the lad with no brains. I could hear him shouting at Fred that he wants this, he wants that, so Fred said there's someone in the office wants to see you. He thinks Fred's rolled over and giving him an order sheet for a tanner, so he's come swaggering over to the caravan that was used as an office. As he's flung the door open and walked in all cocky like, I've hit him on the chin, picked him up, hit him on the chin, picked him up and hit him again and he's fell out the doorway; he's fell headfirst on to the concrete and he's well out of it. But by this time I've gone off my head. I've picked up a lump of concrete and, on my two kids' lives, I was gonna smash it on his nut. Fred's grabbed me by the arm just before I murdered this guy, saying, 'Enough, Len; don't kill him,' so I've put it down.

We chucked some water on him and eventually he come round and I give him a strong warning for him or any of his mates to keep well away from the site. He ain't so tough now and he won't look at me, just mumbled something and it was all sorted. Though just in case he thought he'd got away a bit light, I've given him a quick right and left and he collapsed on the ground. I got a couple of yard blokes to load him in his lorry and told them to drive it round the back streets, smash the windscreen, slash the tyres and leave him there. Fred never, ever heard from him again.

A couple of days later, I noticed some c**t with a sense of humour had changed the 'Beware of the dog' sign to 'Beware of Lenny'. Too fucking right.

Fred was well happy and offered to put me on a retainer at one and a half a week. That was a nice little result for me but, as often happens after a while when all the agg is forgot about, people think they're paying out good dough for nothing and excuses are made to cut down the wages. Suddenly there's a cash-flow problem with Fred and can he leave it until next week? 'Course he can – I ain't skint, because I've got plenty going on – but, after weeks have gone by and my back wages are mounting up, I think I'm being taken for a c**t.

So one day I was over his yard; nobody was around except a couple of old fellas, so I've had a good look round. I opened the door to this warehouse and clocked about ten ton of copper and lead; I thought to myself, 'I'll have that away.' I went home and I phoned my pal Ronnie Norris – I knew he had a big lorry, because he was in the scrap game for years and used to do a lot of exporting of engines to Gibraltar. I'd done him a favour a while back, when I got wind of tons of copper piping somewhere just waiting to be lifted. I got a drink, but didn't have nothing to do with the job. I've no idea what this particular copper was for, but it was all wrapped up in asbestos and I can remember going round his place and seeing him cutting it all up in a big cloud of white dust – that's another story.

Back to the other thing: after I phoned Ronnie he come round and I said, 'I just been down on this bloke Fred's site. I've been minding him and looking after him and now I think he's shafting me. He's got to be on like two grand a week and he's paying me one and a half to mind him and I've got to bollock and clout all them mugs and after all that he's holding back on my pension, so I've decided to sack myself and take my Christmas box early.'

Anyway, Ron's up for a bit of work, so we get over there, two in the morning, broke the big padlock and reversed in; can't see a fucking foot in front of us. Ronnie's got a big torch and bolt croppers, so he's opened the warehouse and we're in. By about quarter-past five we'd loaded the lot up, we're black as arse'oles and knackered. We drove home and his lorry was practically scraping the ground, what with ten ton on board.

Back home, I said, 'Look, don't park outside my gaff because he's gonna put two and two together.'

So we stuck it outside Ronnie's, nice and sweet.

Eight o'clock in the morning, I get a bang on the door. I've opened up and there's Fred with his foreman and he's doing his nut. I was so tired when I come in I couldn't even be bothered to wash, so I'm covered in coppery shit. He's looked me up and down and said, 'You've nicked all my gear.'

I've gone, 'I dunno what you're talking about.'

He said, 'Leave it out, Len, you've got half hundredweight on your face and arms.'

I've said, 'OK, I'll put my hands up, I did nick your gear, but I'll mark your card why I done it. The reason I nicked your gear is you've been fucking using me for months to straighten up people – the brick people, the metal people and the navvies. I've been keeping your site nice and happy for a poxy one and a half a week and I ain't seen a tanner for ages. I think you're taking the piss, so I took the piss yesterday.'

He's hopping up and down, 'Len, it's got to go back, you've gotta bring it all back.'

'Well it ain't fuckin' well going back because it took me and my pal all fucking night to load it and it was the hardest work I've ever done, so you can't expect me give it back.'

He dunno what to do, he can't kick off, because he knows if I flare up he's gonna get badly hurt, mate or no mate. So he's said, 'Tell you what, I'll give you a grand as long as it's back today.'

I've gone, 'Lovely, as long as I get my back pay as well.'

He wiped his mouth, brung the cash round and it all got sorted. I still hear from Fred now and again when he's got a problem, but he only phones me now when he's got a *diabolical* problem.

How's that story, Pete? Oh yeah, going back to Ronnie, about a year after we done that little bit of business he was dying of cancer. At the back of my nut, I always wonder if it was that asbestos job I put him on to that caused it, you know all that horrible fucking dust going into his lungs. I hope it wasn't, but you know how your mind thinks...

I flew up to Barts to see him with another close friend of his, a guy named Vince; his brother was involved with Spotty's firm back in the old days.

When we got up to his room, his wife was crying and holding him and he was only about seven stone, a skeleton from what he used to be.

I looked at him and he had tears in his eyes. I said to his wife, 'Do you mind us seeing him?' And she said, 'Len, he thinks the world of you,' so I sat and held his hand and he was trying to be brave and not to cry because Lenny was there. Tears were running down his face, but there was no sound coming out.

After a while, he managed to say, 'Len, I'm done for, I'm dying.'

What could I say when I could see he was right? But I said,

'Be strong, son, you know you'll be all right,' and it choked me to say it because I knew there was no going back for him and, like I said, I've got this horrible feeling I was to blame. I gave him a cuddle and said to him, 'You know I'll always be up to see you.'

After that, when he was sent home to die, I used to go up to his house about three or four times a week, and I was taking photos up with me and he loved it because I was like a son to him, because he was a lot older than me. I told him I was fighting Roy Shaw. He said, 'You'll beat Roy, you'll beat Roy, you're the best fighter I've ever seen, you'll beat Roy.'

'Ron,' I said, 'I will do it for you,' and he held up his little stick arms like he was squaring up to me and it broke my heart, Pete, there ain't nothing worse than watching somebody you love wasting away and dying.

A week before the Shaw fight, he died. I can honestly say Ronnie was a very good friend of mine and my Val. We thought the world of him.

How was that story? That was from the heart. These stories, are they boring?

No, Len. That was quite moving.

Yeah, it was, wasn't it?

Talking of mates who've died just reminded of a guy named Freddie Davis – he's dead now, God rest his soul. He was a bank robber, Fred – good man, good stuff; he had a lovely wife, two children, good money-getter in the sixties. Anyway, he done a couple of bank jobs and he went to prison, come home and I've got involved with him as a friend and drinking partner (I used to drink in them days). One day, we was very skint, and he said, 'Len, do you fancy doing a bank?'

I said, 'Yeah, I'll have some of that, Fred.'

We had a meet with some other people – I can't mention their real names on tape; let's call them Bill, Tom and... Frank. This was, like, 1974... Can I say the location?

You can say it, yeah. We'll change it later.

It was a bank at Folkestone and it was all on a time lock – you know, no matter how you tried, them vaults wouldn't open until whatever time was put in. We met up at a pub over south London, we've got guns in the boot and we set off for the drive to Folkestone. I'm in the back with Bill and Freddie and Tom's in the front with Frank, who was driving.

We're well on our way when I said to Fred, 'There's only one road out of Folkestone, so when this goes off we got to stay in the town because there will be helicopters and everything flying about.'

He said, 'You're right, Len, good thinking.'

Bill suddenly come out with, 'I don't know if I fancy this fucking lark, what with the guns and all we're looking at 15 apiece.'

I said, 'Bill, it's too fucking late for your arse to drop out now, we're nearly there. It ain't a case of "will we", we gotta finish now.'

The plan was to go to the bank manager's house, break in and nick them by surprise. Once we done that, all we gotta do is sit with him all night until we take him to his bank to open up ready for the time lock. If the staff turn up, they can be tied up; the manager ain't gonna say nothing, he ain't gonna scream, because I'll be sitting back at the house with his wife.

We arrive at his house no problem, because it's all been sussed out beforehand, and we're sitting in the motor having a quick smoke before the off. When I look back, it makes me shudder because we've got fucking guns in the boot and, as Bill said, on their own it's worth a 15, when a panda car comes cruising down the road and almost stops right by us as the two coppers have a good look at us. I can remember Frank muttering; my arse is opening and closing like a fucking clown's hat and I wanted to laugh even though it was deadly serious. Thank God, they didn't get out, because Frank and Bill were bad enough guys to have gone in the boot, grabbed the guns and shot them dead; could've been like that nasty business with Harry Roberts up Pentonville Road. Not my game, as you know, Pete, but it might've happened too quick for me or Fred to stop them.

They drove off, thank the Lord, and we waited a few minutes, then crept round the back of the house. Fucking hell! From the front, the place was in darkness but round the back a downstairs light was on. I slid up the wall, looked in the window and could see a man, a woman and three children watching the telly. I've signalled for the others to fuck off by waving my arm, then followed them round the side. I've done my nut in a whisper: 'Some c**t has made a right fuck-up here, there's kids in the house and, for fuck's sake, no way am I gonna tie kids up.'

How does my voice come over on that thing? Rough? Gruff? You can't really hear your own voice, can you? We talk, but we don't know how it comes over. [Lenny does an impression] My name is Bob Hoskins, this is my manor and I don't want people taking liberties on my manor.

You like that, don't you? Go on, Pete, where was we?

You said you wouldn't tie kids up.

Yes, anyway, I said, 'Fred, we can't tie kids up in case something happens in the night.' They all made me right because they was good stuff and had kids of their own and we made up our minds to fuck off home.

Wasted night, then?

Well, for the big one it was, but Frank pulled a stroke that made us laugh our nuts off all the way back. We see one of them all-night shops and he said, 'I'm pulling up here to get some fags, anybody want anything?'

Yeah, we all wanted fags or bacca, so in he went. We sat talking about what a c**t he was, like blokes do, when he come flying out screaming at Frank to go, go, go, like he was in *The Sweeney*. We've picked ourselves off the back window and we're going, 'What's up? What's up'?

He laughed and flung a bundle of cash all over the motor, shouting, 'I creamed the fucking place.'

I stopped him laughing. I've put the look on and shouted at him, 'You fucking idiot, ain't you got no brain?'

He's swung round in his seat looking like his gonna shit

hisself, because, as he knows, I can turn from Mr Nice to a beast on a sixpence. 'What's the matter, Len?'

'Matter?' I've gone. 'You forgot my fucking crisps.'

We all pissed ourselves, so we ended having a good laugh even though the job was shit.

When I got in bed that night, I said to my Val, 'Fucking hell, babe, we was lucky tonight, Old Bill's only drove and clocked us while we're waiting to do a job and the boot has got guns in it. If they'd given us a tug we'd have all got a 20.'

She weren't too impressed, because she'd fell asleep again.

You hungry, Pete?

Yeah, I am a bit.

Good boy. OK, slip next door to the pub and get some bits and pieces off the fish caravan. Here's a nifty, get what you want but get plenty because I'm fucking starved.

I'll have a think while you're gone...

* * * * *

Is it on? Because I was thinking, this title for the book. What about *King of the Bouncers*?

I prefer The Guv'nor.

Yeah, it's good, very good, but what I was thinking, over in America they won't know what that means, will they?

No, but they'll soon work it out. There's a film out at the moment called Prêt à Porter or something like. Now what the fuck does that mean? I know now, but I didn't at the time, but I still went to see it.

171

I hear what you're saying, but I don't want people to think it's about the governor of prison or a Borstal.

The spelling's different, Len.

Is it?

Val! Val! We're boxing round the book title, what do you...

[Val] **You told me last night, but I think Peter's right.**

About what?

[Val] *The Guv'nor*. **You should stick with** *The Guv'nor*, **because that's what you are.**

I was king of the bouncers as well.

I know, but 'Guv'nor' sounds better.

OK, we'll just leave it up to the publisher, they know the business. Switch that on, Pete, and I'll talk about how I got called 'The Guv'nor'.

I walked into the Green Man in Hoxton with Freddie Davis, Danny Kyle and Chris and there was a poster on the wall advertising a fight between Roy 'The Mean Machine' Shaw and Donny 'The Bull' Adams. I said to Danny and Chrissie, 'I'd fucking murder that Shaw geezer in two minutes, in fact, I'd fight the two of them in one night.'

They said, 'What, you wanna fight the winner?'

I went, 'Yeah, I'll fight the winner and I'll knock the bollocks out of whichever one of them it is.'

With that, up came the landlord of the place who just kept dropping names. He'd just took over this pub from a well-known character named Lenny Gower, an entertainer, a singer and a good friend of mine. This landlord didn't like me because he knew I was a timebomb and he couldn't be in charge or a flash c**t while I was there. He's overheard me saying I want to have a go, so he's gotta chuck in his ha'porth. 'I know Roy, he's a good friend of mine and you ain't got a chance against him because he's a lunatic on the cobbles; he's the best.'

Chris has chipped in, 'Well, Lenny's a fucking raving nutcase,' and I give him the old cross eye, even though it's true.

I said, 'Well, when you see Roy, tell him I'll fight him for three grand, winner takes all, or for any amount of money he wants to fight for.'

I'm indoors about two nights later when Ronnie Norris phoned me up and said, 'Len, Roy Shaw's been in the pub looking for you, he's coming back tonight.'

I said, 'Oh yeah.'

I put the phone down, put my shoes on, got dressed and got a cab over to the Green Man. It was eleven o'clock Sunday night and there was only a few people in there, having afters. I said to the landlord, 'Roy Shaw been looking for me?'

He said, 'Yes, he was in here dinnertime and he wasn't too pleased that you're gobbing off that you can smash him, so it might be better if you fucked off, because he's coming back any time now.'

I didn't wanna make a fuss in front of straight-goers having a nice drink, so I was quiet when I told him if he spoke to me in that sneering manner again I'd tear his fucking face off; he didn't say no more. I got myself an orange juice and sat down to wait. This poster's still on the wall and that landlord must've said something to a bunch of wankers leaning on the bar because these eight- or nine-handed drunken little rats kept looking over at me and sniggering amongst themselves.

I jumped up and said, 'Oi, are you taking the piss out of me, you mugs? Because, if Roy Shaw was looking for you fucking people, you'd be hiding, you would be fucking hiding under the bed or running home to your mum. He's looking for me and I'm here on my own waiting cool as you like. So piss off out of here or I'll belt all of you.'

They drunk their drink and went, like the cowards they were.

Roy never showed, so I went home. I made a few enquiries and don't think that the geezer in the pub knew Shawie and he ain't ever been in his pub – all he was doing was trying to keep me out the place. That arse'ole should know nothing in this world keeps me away from anywhere I wanna go. A bit later I went to the Lion and Lamb and caught up with Roy Nash, who was in there playing shove halfpenny and I asked him if he can get me a fight with Shaw. He was well connected with the fight people, so I thought if anybody could sort it he could.

I see Roy about a week after and he said, 'I spoke to Joey Pyle and he told me that Roy's got two fights lined up but when he's finished them two he'll come and see you.'

I've gone, 'Lovely, that'll do me, Roy.'

While I was hanging about waiting for these people to get back to me, Danny Kyle suggested it wouldn't be a bad idea to check out the opposition; you know, go and see this guy Roy Shaw in action. So we found out when he was fighting again and took ourselves down there. I could see this guy weren't no pushover, but then I wasn't myself either. 'Course, he smashed the other fighter to bits, and as I'm watching I wanna have him, so I got right frustrated that these fuckers were sort of ignoring me.

As the bout come to an end, I said to Danny, 'Fuck this I'm gonna put it to him face to face.' He's tried to stop me, but no chance, and I'm running down the stairs shouting, 'I'll take you any day, fight me, fight me.'

I've gone over the ropes and I'm screaming at him and he's screaming at me. Half a minute and we'd have been kicking shit out of each other with no money on the table; that ain't how it works. Next thing, the ring's full of people getting between the two of us. Ritchie was there and Alex Steen and some bloke called Carrington.

Alex said, 'Quick, get out the ring, you got the challenge,' and that's all I wanted, so we fucked off down the pub to celebrate. That's when my uncle Bobby Warren got involved; he called a meet with Joey and Roy.

What was Joe Pyle's involvement with Roy? Were they mates or what?

I didn't know Joey at that time, though I knew he was a well-respected man over south London.

I've already mentioned Joe, haven't I?

Yeah, you did, a while ago.

Doesn't matter, does it? I think it was the fifties or sixties –

you can check with John – that Roy was arrested for murder, when hanging was in, and he was found not guilty. When Roy came out of prison, him and Joe got together and put on these fight shows, you know, promoting them. As I say, I didn't know Joe then, it was only years later I become friends with him when I done a lot of work for him.

What sort of work was that?

Debt collecting mainly, because if he had money owing to him I would do it for him or if there was anything he needed sorting out he just needed to phone me; so, over the years, me and Joey became friends.

Did you have a lot of trouble debt collecting, or was it enough that you showed your face?

No, I didn't have that much trouble, because what with doing it for 20 years I knew the game inside out. Let's say it was enough that I can be pretty menacing.

Cut a long story short, Pete, after waiting and waiting, Bobby eventually fixed up a meet.

I got myself in the pub and waited like before. I must've been there two fucking hours when in walked Joey and Roy Shaw. Joe Pyle introduced himself, very nice, very relaxed and very calm. Roy Shaw just stood there with glassy eyes, them fucking nutty eyes like a timebomb.

Joe said to me, 'You've been putting it about that you want to fight Roy, so how much money have you got?'

I said, 'Some people will put up three grand' – that was gonna be Ritchie and Kenny.

'OK,' he said, 'you'll get your match.'

176

I looked at Roy, standing there like he was somewhere else, and said to him, 'I ain't gonna shake hands with you, Roy, I'll see you at the fight.'

His face never changed one bit. He gave me a look and all he said was, 'Make sure you're there.'

I've gone, 'Don't you worry, I'll be there all right.'

Anyway, when we had a night for it, Danny said to me, 'Len, are you gonna train for going up against Roy?'

I said, 'What the fuck do I need to train for, the man's got to give me eight years in age, eight to ten years, I don't need to train for that old bastard.'

Well, that was the biggest mistake in my life, that was. I should have trained. I never trained, just carried on smoking and going out drinking. Come the night, I got myself down to Sinatra's Club. It was turned into a boxing arena and the place was full up with gangsters and villains. I found the dressing room, got myself in there and got my kit on. Somebody did my hands with the crepe bandage, stuck gloves on me, and I was ready for the off.

Because I'm the challenger, I don't get none of the old razzmatazz. No, I wander down to the ring, climb over the ropes and wait for Shawie.

All of a sudden, the lights went dim and all you can hear is that song, 'C'mon, C'mon'.

Gary Glitter's 'I'm The Leader Of The Gang'.

Is it? Whatever, this fucking song is loud enough to deafen you. Then the crowd's cheering and out comes Shaw and stands there with his hands up before he comes down the stairs. I said to Johnny, the old pro that was in my corner, 'Fucking hell, look at him, he's like a raging bull or a complete nutcase.'

He growled and stamped his way down the stairs, shoving people out the way and chucking chairs all over the place. Tell you the truth, Pete, it was all showmanship. The punters wanted to see a guy who'd been in Broadmoor and that's what he was giving them.

Johnny said to me, 'Don't worry, Len. You all right?'

I said, 'I ain't never felt fucking better, but these gloves they give me, every time I close them they spring back open.'

He's gone, 'That's probably because they're new.'

Roy swung over the ropes and bounced and jumped all over the ring.

I'm thinking, 'Go on, tire yourself out, you old c**t.'

The MC was the ex-stunt man Nosher Powell and he introduced Roy as the hardest man in England, 'Blue Boy' Shaw, and the challenger, Lenny McLean – dunno how many names this guy needed but it said 'Mean Machine' on his poster.

The bell went and I steamed in trying to get a decent punch in that would hurt him early on, but them gloves weren't doing me no favours because they kept opening. I wasn't punching him, I was poking him. He got back against the ropes and for three minutes solid he smashed me on the jaw. Round two the same and round three smashed me on the jaw for another three minutes. I just laughed at him, called him a wanker, called him a fucking fairy, anything to wind him up and make him lose concentration. Come the fourth round I was puffing and blowing like an old man and I was so knackered I felt like one. That's when Nosher stopped the fight. Got to hand it to him, Shawie might have been ten years older, but he was definitely fitter than I was.

It was a kick in the bollocks for me, but I only had myself to blame. I spoke to Bobby Warren about a week after and he told me I had to get fit if I had any chance of beating Roy. He said, 'Len, don't underestimate that man, there ain't no one tougher than he is.'

I've said, 'Well, I reckon I am.'

'Well,' he said, 'that might be the case, but you haven't proved it so far and if you don't shape up then you might as well forget taking his title away from him.'

I knew what he was trying to do, he was getting me wound up so that I'd go all the way to prove myself. It was working, because straight off I've said, 'Bob, get me a return and I will definitely beat him.'

I took him for granted last time and I told myself it wouldn't happen again.

Bobby said to me, 'What I'll do, Len, I'll bring my young nephew in to do all the running about, like putting posters up and any bits and pieces that need doing. He can help you train and that, then all you've got to do is concentrate on getting fit.'

I said, 'Fuck me, what does he know about this game?'

And Bob said, 'Nothing at all, but he's a quick learner.'

Anyway, Bob brought along this skinny kid with blond hair, so I said, 'Right, son, you know what you got to do?'

'Yeah,' he said, 'I got to have all the posters printed and do what you tell me to do.'

'First off,' I said, 'you can come running with me in the morning – you can time me and pace me if you want.'

I'm up early, stuck on a pair of shorts and training shoes and got myself round Victoria Park. The kid is already waiting, so I said to him, 'How far is it right round the three parks?'

He said, 'Four miles.'

'Four fucking miles, I ain't ready for that, 'specially on top of a big fry-up. So how far is it just round this one park?'

He said, 'One mile,' and I've gone, 'OK, that'll do for starters.'

We started running and after about half a mile the kid said, 'I'm bolloxed, go on, you carry on, because I'm just getting the posters done, you're the one that needs to get fit.'

I said, 'Both of us or nothing,' so what we done, we ran and walked, ran and walked the mile; after a few days, we could run the whole mile without stopping.

Bob come down the park one morning and said, 'I've had a word with Freddie Hills over Battersea and he's willing to train you with his professional fighters.'

I said, 'Bob, don't forget I'm a street fighter, I don't need fancy techniques and all that shit, I just do what I have to do from the heart.'

'Lenny, you're the best,' he said, 'but if you want to win

this fight you are going to have to work at it, improve on your moves and stamina.'

I've got tons of respect for Bob. After all, he'd always looked out for me, so I had to make him right.

I went up to Freddie Hills and he trained me for about seven or eight weeks, taught me all the moves and learned me everything he thought I needed to know. After a while, Freddie told me, if he had've got hold of me when I was a young man, I could've been world champion.

He brought a guy over who went 11 rounds with Larry Holmes and Fred was training him up. I was in the gym at the time and I was asked to have a spar with this guy, Tom.

I said, 'Yeah, I'm up for that, but does he know I'm a street fighter, not a boxer?'

They said, 'That's OK, it don't matter.'

After a couple of rounds, Chris Dundee, who was there, shouts, 'Fuck's sake, Lenny, hey – hey, take it fucking easy, you're supposed to be sparring, not trying to kill the guy.' He's gone to Freddie, 'Pull him out, he is like a wild animal.'

Afterwards, Chris said, 'Len, I can get you in a position to go for titles and earn you a lot of money... and myself.'

I said, 'No, forget it, I'm in my thirties, it's ten years too late.'

The night of the fight came and we went to the place at Croydon and all of a sudden – crash! The fight's on. I've got Bobby Warren in my corner. I come out in the first round and I smashed into Roy; I jumped on him, I punched him,

I've kicked him, because I wanted to get this over. Ding! They've pulled me into the middle of the ring and I got told this weren't on the cobbles, so keep it reasonable.

'Fuck this,' I've thought, as the second round started, and I've gone for him like a fucking lunatic and hit him four or five times in a row. Bang! He's gone right through the ropes and ended up in the second row; so I was the winner. That meant he's won one and I've won one.

But it was very unsatisfactory, Pete – know why? Because I wanted to see him on the floor proper, completely spark out, finished and dead at my feet. Well, not dead exactly, but you know what I'm saying. I wanted to finish him so there was no comeback.

It took a bit of time to organise another match, because it don't just happen overnight, but eventually we hired the Rainbow Rooms and got ourselves a date for another fight. There was a lot of money going to be riding on this and I ain't talking about the door money, even though that was gonna be about 70 grand. No, we're talking heavy money on the betting from very heavy people. Because of this, we heard a rumour there was going to be trouble at the venue, so what we did, we spoke to Ritchie, who was a very good friend and a well-respected man as well as knowing people in London and Scotland. He got in touch with his contact, Arthur, up in Scotland and, before he knows it, Arthur's come down to London with some of his men.

I'm in the dressing room before the off, an' all this kid that was selling programmes for us kept doing was going for a wee, up and down, up and down. I said, 'You're making me fucking dizzy, what's up with you?'

He says, 'Len, I'm very nervous.'

'Nervous, I said, you ain't even fighting; anybody should be nervous it should be me and look at me I'm as cool as a whatsname.'

In the end I told him to fuck off out of it so I could psyche myself up ready to give Roy some damage. I've done a few exercises, not too many, then I laid on the bench for a few minutes and shut my eyes.

I've heard the door open and I said, 'If you've come back to wind me up going for a piss every two minutes, don't think about it, fuck off now.'

I've still got my eyes closed and this voice said, 'It's me, Lenny, it's your dad.'

That woke me up, because I won't ever forget that voice. It was Irwin's, that slag Irwin's. I jumped off the table and this little old man jumped back four paces and put his hands up like he expected a punch.

When he was knocking us all about all them years ago, it was like he was a giant; now he must've shrunk or something, because he weren't the man he was. I hadn't set eyes on him since the day my mum died. Did I tell you about that, Pete?

I knew she'd died, but you haven't spoken about it yet.

Painful time, son, very painful. Thing is, we didn't even know that she was ill; didn't wanna make a fuss, I suppose. I got a call at the club one night telling me she was in hospital and it wasn't looking good, so I flew up there as quick as I could. The family was there and my Val had gone up with Boo.

I've said to them, 'Just let me have a few minutes on my own with her,' and they said OK. I've gone in and she was laying there asleep. I whispered, 'Mum, it's Lenny, your Lenny.'

She put her hand out and I held it tight, then she opened her eyes, looked strange at me and then give this little smile and said, 'It's you, son. I thought it was my big Lenny, your dad.'

That broke me up, Pete, I can tell you. You still got your mum?

Yes, I have and my dad.

You're very lucky, son. Make sure you look after them, because once they're gone you don't get another chance.

Well, I looked at her and she looked at me then she said, 'Lenny, I'm so sorry.'

I said, 'Mum, you don't never have to say sorry to me.'

She said, 'I'm sorry about Jim and how he behaved when you was kids. He isn't a bad man, it was the drink that made him do things.'

I remembered the times he beat me black and blue while he was sober as a nun, but I didn't say nothing to Mum; if she wanted to believe that, I was man enough to go along with it. Her bringing his name up at a time like this brought back some horrible memories and I couldn't stop myself saying, 'Mum, one day I'm gonna kill him stone dead for what he did to us all.'

She got hold of both my hands and sort of lifted herself

up saying, 'Promise me, Lenny, promise me you won't ever hurt him.'

I couldn't believe it – he made her life as bad as ours and she was standing up for him. I've said, 'Please, Mum, don't lay that on me,' but she put her hand on my mouth and just said, 'Promise.'

What could I say? I promised her, and, as much as it went against everything I knew, I meant it.

She gave a little smile, said, 'I'm really tired,' laid down and she was gone.

My heart was torn right out of my chest. I gave her a kiss and a cuddle and I cried. Yeah big Lenny, toughest man in the country, sat holding his mum and cried. I wiped my face at the sink and went out to tell the others, though all I could choke out was, 'She's gone, Mum's at rest.'

They've all gone in the room and as I've looked round there was Irwin, standing to one side with tears rolling down his face. It was like he was the cause of all this pain inside and, though I was out of order with Mum laying there, I flew at him in a rage and told him his fortune.

I said to him, 'You can straighten your mug, you c**t, because you was no fucking good to her when she was alive and now she's well away from you. If you'd appreciated what you had and done the right thing by my mum, I would give you a cuddle and sympathise with you, but you didn't and right now I wanna punch your fucking lights out.'

'Please Len,' he said, 'we've got to stick together as a family now Rose has gone.'

I nearly hit him, but I could still hear Mum's voice. 'Family, family? You've got some neck, you horrible bastard. Just get outta my sight, you make me sick.'

That was that, I got my Val and we went home to shed a few more tears and try and forget that man existed.

Sorry, son, I've gone right off the track again. Shall we have a drink and a smoke while I collect my thoughts?

You got upset just then.

Yeah, I did. When you lose your mum or anybody you love, it never goes away; don't matter how many years pass. Shall we leave that bit out the book?

You can make your mind up what goes in and what we leave out when we put it all together.

That's lovely, Pete, lovely. I'm still all over the place, beginning at the middle and the end at the front; can we square that all up?

No problem at all, you'll see when we get there.

Who was that at the door, Val?

[Val] **Dave. I told him you were busy, he said he'd phone you later.**

Good gel, babe, we ain't got time to waste chatting.

OK, Pete. Where was I?

Jim Irwin in your dressing room.

Yeah, he just turned up. Told the fella on the door he was my dad and they let him walk in; fucking mugs. So I've jumped off the table and shouted at him. 'What the fuck are you doing here?'

He's gone, 'Been a long time, son, thought it was time we tried to make up, you know for your mum's sake.'

I'm almost lost for words, I've got an important fight in a couple of minutes and this thing from the past is in my face. I said, 'One, I ain't your son and never was and never will be. And this ain't for my mum's sake it's for your own, because you're old, feeble, lonely and because of the way you lived your life, no fucker wants to know you.'

Pete, I ain't a bully and for a brief second I felt sorry for him, but that disappeared when he tried to give me a hug. I pushed him away and told him if it wasn't for the woman he abused dreadful in the past I'd be belting him before I done Shawie. I told him to get out and he slunk away like the coward he was; I ain't laid eyes on him since. You know, when he was giving it with the tears he wasn't even with Mum, because he'd fucked off with some bird he was in the mattress business with up north. Dirty slag, him and her.

I'm steaming, I'm angry as fuck and somebody's gonna get it. When I heard the music blaring out of the tannoys, I'm ready to kill Roy Shaw. I honestly think the crowd thought I was gonna get a hammering, and you can bet your life all the good money was on Roy. My people was right behind me, though, and I was gonna do them and myself proud.

Have you seen the fight, Peter? I'll show you in a minute, I've got it on video somewhere. Don't forget, mainly my fights have been bare-knuckle fights. The reason why we done these fights with the gloves on is once you start promoting you have to keep the worst down, wear gloves and stick to some rules; didn't always hold up, but as far as the police was concerned it was legal.

When I had a fight in that pub near your sister's, things got a bit rough and the police wanted to nick me. I was taking on Gypsy Bradshaw and what with it being televised and all that it was just gonna be a straightener, but that c**t decided to give me the nut while we was touching gloves. Forget straightener, I knocked him down, picked him up, bashed him on the head a few times, then stamped on his head. The crowd's going mad and half a dozen geezers jumped in the ring and pulled me off, but they couldn't hold me and I broke away and stamped and kicked him until he was unconscious – though he might've been unconscious already. That caused a bit of a fuss, I can tell you, Pete, because they showed it on telly and it was all in the papers and that's when the law thought they'd get a case against me. But it didn't come to nothing.

Anyway, I'm over the ropes and ready for anything. Roy's glaring at me and I'm giving him the look. Then – bang! The fight got started and we both steamed in. You'll see it in a minute, son, so I don't have to explain, but let's just say I give him a terrible beating at the end. I gotta say up until I got him in the corner he was handing it out a bit strong, but I could take it. That man's got a punch that could knock a hole in a door, and I think you could belt him all day on the body and he wouldn't even feel it. But I caught him a beauty on the forehead, drove him into the corner and it was all over bar the shouting. I wasn't counting, but afterwards Ritchie said I give him about 40 head shots. I just remember banging away and him slowly dropping to the canvas. He was out the game and I was the guv'nor. The crowd was going fucking mad, so I jumped up on the ropes held my hands above my head and screamed at them all, 'Who's the Guv'nor? Who's the Guv'nor?' And the crowd are shouting and screaming, 'Lenny, Lenny.' Above all the racket I could just hear Carrington shouting, 'It's all over, Roy,' and Roy going, 'Who done me? Who done me?' Everybody's laughing and hugging each other and the only two people that hated each other was me and Roy Shaw in the ring.

Today, even though we talk if we see each other, I don't suppose we could ever get close. I've got respect for the man, because he gave me ten years and he wasn't no pushover, but in the end I took his title off him and he ain't never gonna be happy about that. Me and him have got the same temperament, we're both very violent and that's why we could never be friends, because it would be like an atomic bomb going off. Yeah, he was in Broadmoor, he come out angry and that's when I fought him.

Pete, I bet it's surprising how much is on a tape when you start to put it on paper. Will you be able to box things about, and put it down so it flows?

Yeah, once it's on the screen we can take pieces out and generally move it around, but until then say whatever comes into your head.

So it's not boring?

No, not at all.

That's good. We can talk about the gypsies if you want. Yeah the gypsies, I don't mind them at all because they look after their own and they're good money-getters. The public don't like them, because you seem them parked up and they make a lot of mess when they park up, but where they gonna put their rubbish? You know, the council don't want to give them nowhere, or they don't want to go nowhere else where they've decided they wanna be. I've fought a lot of them and they show me a lot of respect, and I have respect for them when it's earned.

One guy, a very good friend of mine, he's a well-known gypsy. He phoned me one Sunday because his nephew and his pals were getting a lot of heavy grief from local tearaways. He's asked me to step in and I said, 'With pleasure, mate,' because I hate bullies. So me and Big Graham, who never says nothing but 'safe' and 'sweet', and another fella named Mick, went down to this pub where these guys hung out. As we've walked in I saw my mate and said very loudly, 'You got a problem, pal?'

Everybody looked at me, because everybody knew who I was, what with being the Guv'nor. He told me this wasn't kids playing games when these people were digging out his nephew, it was tough guys who didn't think twice about carrying guns and knives and using them.

'OK,' I said, 'how do you want to play it?'

He said, 'Well, I'm tooled,' and he showed me a fucking long bayonet he's got tucked in his waistband.

I had to give him ten out of ten, because he was 64 years old and game as a bagel. I said, 'You won't need that, you don't have to get involved, that's what you called me in for. What'll happen is this: when they come in, I shall give them a terrible call and if they don't listen to reason or they don't want to behave themselves I shall belt the fucking life out of them; so will Mick and so will Graham. We'll go to work on them, you ain't got to do nothing, you've done your bit at the age where you got to put your feet up.'

He went, 'Lovely, Len, I respect that, but I want to be in it with you.'

I said, 'OK, but don't get under my feet,' and he laughed.

We sat there all afternoon and it wasn't until early evening this mob came crashing in all noisy and full of themselves. They quietened down when they saw us three sitting glaring at them and it turned into a bit of a stand-off. They broke first. We got a tray full of drinks delivered to our table and the bar girl nodded towards these fellas. When we looked over, they're giving us the thumbs-up like we was old mates; bunch of c**ts. What we should've done was belt the shit out of them for giving my pal a lot of worry about his nephew, and Graham even suggested it, but he said to leave it for now. When we left, we got a tidy bit of folding, even though we said it was on the house and he'd bought drinks all day. He got in touch a couple of days later and told me those plastic gangsters had shaken hands with the nephew; so, like Graham would say, it was safe and sweet.

The same guy got in touch another time when he was

owed some serious money off some people out in the country. I didn't ask what it was all about, but I had a good idea – but I'll tell you that when the tape ain't on. Anyway, he's asked me to get his money back, so we went round to see the people who lived in a big house in the country; sort of farm, really, but more show than working.

Before we went on the farm, I said to him, 'How far do you want us to go?'

He said, 'I want you to frighten the shit out of them, because they're taking the piss outta me and some other people.'

So, I said, 'Who are we working for – you, or a bunch of people I don't know?'

He said, 'This is for me, Len, and I'll square up with you, but you'll be owed big, big favours from the other lot involved.'

I've gone, 'That's good enough for me, I'll go to work.'

There was a big luxury caravan that was used as an office – the fucking thing was probably worth more than my house – so we've headed for that. The main guy was inside fiddling with some papers when I burst in on him.

Cocky twat says, 'Can't you knock?'

I went, 'Knock, you c**t? I'll fuckin' well knock you out if we don't get some business sorted in the next few minutes.'

I got the impression this guy is used to giving orders and ain't so keen on taking them, because even though he's gone a bit pale he's still got that cocky look on his mug.

I've said, 'It's very simple. You owe money to my friend. He invested it through you with a good heart and no doubt you've had a good earner, but it strikes me that you're a greedy fuck and wanna rump him, don't you? So to save me breaking into a sweat pay what's owing to him right now or there's gonna be bad trouble for you.'

Fuck me, he still ain't folding up, because he said, 'You can't come in here threatening me. I think you're bluffing, because you're committing a serious offence by this intimidation.'

I nearly laughed out loud at the cheek of this man. I said, 'Look, I'm only gonna ask once more: are you getting the money or not?'

He said, 'I can't pay him yet because of this and that and I have a cash-flow deficiency at the moment.'

I said, 'OK, see if this helps,' and I dragged him outside and said to Graham, 'Cop hold of this weasel and don't let him go.' I walked over to a barn and luckily there were some cans of oil, or paraffin, in there. I've gone back opened the caravan door and started splashing inside.

He ain't so cool now, he's screaming, 'I'll get the money, I'll get the money.'

I've said, 'You sure?' And he's nodding his head like crazy. I said, 'Well, you should've said that 20 minutes ago,' flung a match inside and it's gone up like a bomb. I nearly lost my fucking eyebrows and a bit more.

Two minutes later, we're driving him to his bank to pick up a money order and all the way he sat in the back sobbing. My mate was more than happy and so was me and Graham, because the pay day was a percentage of the take and it was very serious dough.

Was that story all right, Pete?

Top class, Len, very good.

Shooting, Pete, you know I've been shot more than once? Hold on I got to have a pee...

Did you wash your hands?

Oi, that's my one, cheeky c**t.

I was going home and I got shot in the back. Three times they tried to shoot me – no, four, but that time they picked the wrong guy. I'll start with the one at the club, because I don't think that was connected to the others.

Ready, son, got it switched on? Good boy. I was stood on the door at the Barbican and I've got another fella with me. I did the door Monday to Thursday on my own, and Friday and Saturday I had another kid help me out called Bill Sutherland. Bill was standing there with me, we was just talking and looking at some girls by the stairs. Next thing we know, there was a terrific blast like a bomb going off and the glass in the front of the club smashed out and I got thrown up in the air. I got myself off the floor and see Bill laying at the bottom of the stairs and he's got people all round him saying, 'You all right, Bill? Bill, you OK?'

Now, 'cos I had my back to the glass and he was stood in front of me, he was protected, so I knew he wasn't properly hurt. I've shouted down, 'Never mind Bill this, Bill that, don't worry about fucking Bill, he's just fell down the stairs from the shock. I've been shot and none of you give a fuck.'

Anyway, I've run out the door just in time to see two geezers on a motorbike coming back to finish me off. Both got helmets on, but the pillion passenger was holding a sawn-off shotgun cradled across his arm. What with my adrenalin pumping faster than the blood out of my leg, I never even thought, just run at this bike. He's done a bit of a swerve and as he's come past me, I've managed to kick his back wheel. Somehow he's kept it upright, revved the fuck out of it and tore off down the road.

By now I'm standing in a pool of claret, so I've gone back to the club and I got a big hole in me, right, and blood's coming out. So I see this fucking Dennis and another guy, so they took me in the office and they took my trousers and pants down. Now they both give a big gasp, like 'fuck me', so I know it must look a mess. They got towels and stuff and first off Dennis starts putting them on the floor.

I've gone, 'What the fuck are you doing, Dennis?'

He said, 'You're ruining my carpet, Len.'

Anyway, the other guy stuffed these towels round my arris and the bleeding either slowed down or I was running out of the stuff. Somebody said they'd called an ambulance, so I leaned over this desk feeling a complete pratt and waited and waited.

I tell you, Pete, I wasn't too happy with my bare bum in the air for every nosey bleeder to check it out when they stuck their heads round the door.

After 15 minutes, I said to Den, 'Fuck this, I'll be drained out in a minute, I'm off.'

He tried to stop me, but I think he was happy to get me off the carpet.

I went outside and waved a cab down and I've gone to get

in the cab and the cabbie said 'Len' – they all know me, Pete – 'you can't get in here, you're smothered in blood.'

I said, 'Don't worry about the fucking blood, I'll get in the back and kneel up,' so he dropped me round Barts. As I got out I said, 'What do I owe you, son?' and he said, 'Fuck 'em, have it on the firm.' Decent sort of guy.

I walked in the hospital about one o'clock and the porter's sitting reading the paper. I said, 'I wonder if you can help me. I've just been shot.'

He said, 'Where?'

And I said, 'Just outside a club I was minding.'

He went, 'No, I mean where on your body?'

[Lenny laughs]... That ain't true, Pete, I just chucked it in to make you laugh.

Fuckin' hell, made myself lose the thread, where was I? Oh yeah, so this porter guy has said, 'Where you been shot?'

Well, all I had to do was turn round and it was very obvious because my trousers were hanging in shreds and the blood was still running out. All hell broke lose then. People come running, put me on a stretcher and rushed me down to casualty, put me on a drip; I tell you, I got the whole nine yards. They rushed me to theatre, I had an operation, then they put me in a ward – and who's waiting for me? Old Bill. Fucking hospitals grass you up every time a bit of lead is flying about.

Anyway, these CID geezers said, 'You have been shot, any idea who is responsible?'

I said, 'Look, I don't want to talk to you. In my life I've hurt lots of people but always with my hands and only people who ask for it, so you could say somebody, some fucking coward, has made up his mind to shoot me in the back. I don't want to talk about it, I don't even want to know who done it, and if you pick any one up for it I won't pick them out; I'll say they're my friend. So you're just wasting your time.'

To be honest, they looked bored and all they said was, 'Fair enough, now we know where we stand.' They came back a couple of days with a letter from Scotland Yard, saying, 'Mr McLean does not wish us to make any further enquiries regarding the firearms incident at the Barbican', and I had to sign it.

Dennis McCarthy and his ex-copper partner come up to Barts to see me and they brought two big bags of fruit and sweets. I said, 'Very kind of you, fellas, now what I'm gonna do is discharge myself tomorrow and I'll be back on the door for you.'

They both looked like they'd been caught with their hands in the till and Dennis said, 'No, Len, we've had the police round and they've said, when we go to renew our licence, they're going to oppose it if we've still got you minding the club. They also said nobody will take you on unless they're carrying guns because the only way they're going to take you out of the picture is by shooting you. So, Lenny, we're going to let you go.'

I've gone, 'Fuckin' well hold up, you're gonna knock my pension on the head after all I've done for you? Well, I ain't fucking going. You come to me when you was in trouble, you come to me when you was in the shit and nobody else could clean the place up. I've had more battles over your place than anywhere else. Now, with me laying here with an extra arse'ole – bang! I'm out. Thanks, Len, now fuck off out of it.'

'It's not like that, Lenny,' Dennis come out with, 'we haven't got any choice in the matter.'

'Say what you like, Den, I'll be back on that door, you see if I ain't.'

That's when his partner slung an envelope on the bed saying, 'Three grand there, severance pay.'

I've gone, 'Lovely, I'll have that, so off you go then and take it easy.'

They couldn't get out quick enough.

Friends? Fuck 'em, it just shows when people are in trouble they need you, but when there's no more trouble they want to get rid of you. I ain't got a lot of time for them people.

Have a look what that shotgun did to my arris, Pete.

Fucking hell, Len, that is a mess.

Took a big lump out and it never grew back; couldn't sit down for weeks. Why is it people think it's funny being shot in the arse? If I'd taken it in the chest, they'd have been horrified. But no, because it was my bum, it's a joke. I got the piss taken for ages.

Another time, there was this fella named Billy who used to fight on the under card. I was always top of the bill and he was the under card. This kid done a bit of minding, he done a bit of debt collecting and he was a bit useful with his fists. He got in touch with me and said, 'Len, I'm fighting at Romford on one of Carrington's shows.'

I've gone, 'Oh lovely.'

He said, 'I need to bring myself up to scratch, but the only trouble is I've got no one to spar with. Would you come up and do a few rounds with me?'

I said, 'Yeah, no problem.'

Val! Peter said any more tea? *Val*!

So we arranged to meet up at Freddie's place in Battersea. We got set up and before we started I said, 'Look, Billy, I won't do me nut, I'll just fiddle about with you. I'll let you have a couple of shots and I won't go too strong because I'm a lot bigger then you.' I got in the ring and I've put on these great big 18oz gloves. I said to him, 'I've got these big gloves on, so you won't be hurt. If I give you a belt, it'll be like hitting you with a cushion, you won't feel nothing.'

He went, 'Nice one, Len, that'll do.'

So I'm fiddling about with him and he was as slow as fuck and we weren't getting nowhere, so after a bit I said, 'I'm gonna let a couple go so you know I'm here, otherwise you might as well go on the bag.'

He's come at me and I've gone straight through his guard, hit him up the Darby and he's gone over like a sack of shit.

He's jumped back up, all red in the face, and said, 'Fuck you, you liberty-taking c**t.'

I said, 'No, I'm here to help you, all I done is tap you up the Darby. What do you think the other fighter's gonna do on the show, pull his punches in case he hurts you? Face it, you ain't ready and you ain't fit.'

He just went, 'Fuck you,' pulled his gloves off, flung them at me and fucked off out the ring.

I've followed him into the changing rooms, caught up with him, got him by the throat and pinned him up against the shower. I didn't bash him, just lifted him off his feet and told him, 'Don't you ever swear at me in front of people or I'll kill you stone dead, do you understand, you fucking mug?'

He's nodding his head, so I let him down. I got dressed and he got dressed; he went home and I went home; no more was said.

A fortnight later, I'm upstairs at home, it's a Saturday so Val's shopping and the kids are out with their mates. I'm in the bedroom and the doorbell goes. I went on to the landing and shouted down, door's open – save me keep going up and down I used to keep the door on the latch. The door's flung open and some c**t with a scarf round his face is only standing there with a gun. He went, 'Fuck you, fuck you,' and started firing up the stairs. One went in the fucking wall, the others dug into the stairs, and then he dived out the door. I'm just in my pants, but I tore down the stairs, picked up a cosh I kept behind the door and chased after him, but he's fucked off and gone.

I made a few enquiries...

[To Val] All right, babe? Yeah, put it on the table. I was just telling Pete about the time somebody came in the door and what he put in the stairs.

So I made a few enquiries, you know, put my feelers out looking for whoever it was, but nobody seemed to know nothing. What it was, Pete, it all happened so quick and with bullets flying about and that, I never got a proper look at the geezer, so I'd really nothing to go on. After a while I forgot about him. No, that's not true. I put him to the back of my mind, but didn't forget.

Weeks later, I got home one night, parked the car down the road and some geezer must've been lurking about waiting because I usually come home about the same time every night; well, morning really, I suppose, because it was usually about two o'clock. I got out my motor, locked the door and, bang-bang, I've been fuckin' well shot again. It was like being smashed in the back with a hammer, so I never even had a chance to go after who done it. I got indoors, got my Val out of bed and she rung a friend of ours who was one of them guys that do first-aid at football matches.

St John's ambulance man?

That's the one. Well, he came up and said I should go to hospital, but I wasn't going through all that old bollocks with the law again, so I told him to do the best he could. Luckily, the bullet had gone right through, so he didn't have to dig about. Val's crying and going on about I'm gonna get myself killed next time, but what could I do? I mean, it wasn't like I was asking people to keep fucking shooting me.

I was going somewhere about six or seven weeks later, and as I'm going round by Mare Street there's this fat Scotchman who I'll just call Stevie standing on the corner. He see me and waved me down. He said, 'All right, Len, all healed up?'

I said, 'Not bad, son, not bad,' and he come out with, 'I know who shot you.'

Have I told you this story, where it turns out it weren't true?

No, not yet.

Seems this Stevie had a score to settle with some guy that had rumped him over a bundle of traveller's cheques and he thought by telling me this guy was the one that shot me I'd find him and kill him stone dead; what a fucking liberty-taker. I've gone after the name he put up and before I could do this fella some damage he convinced me he had nothing to do with it, so I've gone back to the Scotchman and give him a good belting instead. He won't try that one again.

I got a whisper that these couple of shootings was down to the guy I'd bollocked, Billy Quinn. Now, why the fuck he'd wanna kill me over something so stupid as that is really beyond belief, but you never know what goes on in people's heads, do you? With a name, I had something to go on, but no matter how hard I looked for him I never found him. He's completely disappeared.

Anyway, I got on with other things. There was a fight fixed up between me and this fucking big geezer. 'Man Mountain' York was his name. Big, but you bet he was as slow as fuck. So come the night I got myself down to Woodford, where the fight was taking place, and settled into the dressing room. Somebody I knew come in and said, 'Len, you ain't never gonna believe who's in the next dressing room.'

I've gone, 'Well, this could take all night but I'll have a good stab at it. Is it Prince Charles? What about the President of America? Could it be...'

'Hold up, Len,' he said, 'I'm being serious here.'

I've gone, 'Well, don't fuckin' well ask me to guess, just tell me 'cos I ain't gonna know unless you tell me, who the fuck is it?'

'Your mate Quinn, you know, the guy you reckoned took a pop at you.'

I said, 'It weren't one pop it was fucking two, and if it's him next door I'll rip his head off.'

'Believe me, Len, he's on the under card and he's sitting next door with Yorkie, cool as you fucking like. There's a door straight through from here but it's locked.'

I've said, 'The c**t, I'll give him cool, what I'm gonna do is smash through this door and have the gutless bastard. And if the Yorkie Bar Kid wants to get involved, I'll smash him as well.'

I kicked the door off its hinges and burst through. Quinn's sitting there and he's shit himself, gone all white and lost about fucking three stone. The geezer I'm fighting sat there like a statue and wouldn't look at me, so I've said, 'Listen, Mr Man Mountain, one word and I'll hurt you, OK?'

He didn't say a word and I don't think he knew what Quinn had done.

Billy is trembling all over; he knows what this is all about.

I said, 'See you, you c**t, I think it was you who shot me in the back.'

He's gone, 'Weren't me, Len, honest it weren't me.'

I said, 'It was fucking you and now you're gonna get hurt.'

You wouldn't believe it unless you was there, Pete, but this spineless coward dropped on his knees, he actually dropped on his knees in front of me, and begged. He went, 'Len, do me a favour, let me explain, let me apologise please. I was on the gear, I was pushing it up my nose but I ain't on the shit no more, I'm as good as gold.'

I looked at him and I'm thinking what can I do with a c**t like this, sobbing at my feet? Belt him, smash him? I know he could've killed me when he took those shots, I know he could've made my Val a widow and left my kids without a dad, but end of the day these things happen and I wasn't gonna get no satisfaction hurting this prick. I've said, 'OK, get off your knees and act like a man while I give you a warning. Don't ever cross my path again or else you'll end up stone dead.'

He's shaking like a leaf and said to me, 'Shake my hand, Lenny, shake my hand and let me know it's all over.' So we shook hands.

That's for the book, Pete – because I lied. We didn't shake hands, because I didn't wanna touch that druggy scum, all I done was tell him to forget his fight and fuck off quick and he did. Why I say we shook hands is that about a year after he wound up dead with a bullet in the head. See, I couldn't go too strong there because the man's dead and they haven't found the murderer. I'm treading dodgy ground telling you, I got to be very careful. I know a few people been pulled in over his murder because they had problems with him before he died. Well, I had a problem with him, so people think I straightened him up but I didn't and I don't want anybody to think it's anything to do with me. So you see, Pete, I was boxing round that. I felt sorry for his family because they lost him and it weren't their fault, but if you go the way he was going you only end up one way. When you see me telling stories and it's going on that tape I have to be a bit delicate, I have to be very careful. I know you're a professional writer and you're not a fool and you will write round things. Just remember: I didn't kill him or have him killed, you know what I'm saying.

There was a funny period a few years back when it was like open season on Lenny. I'm either being shot at, fucking shot for real or people are threatening me with guns. Like Old Bill said to Dennis, nobody's got the bottle to face me and say, 'Len, you and me one to one because I've got a grievance with you.' No, these cowards, these monkey fucking cowards, have gotta sneak around and try and do me in the back or from a distance.

There was a rumour going round that there was some people flying about with guns looking for me. I said, 'Pass the word around, I'm not hard to find, I drink in a pub called the Green Man every day.'

I was sitting in there one day when a guy come in, a guy I used to know in them days by the name of Johnny Price. He wasn't a bad fella. He said to me, 'Lenny, can I borrow your motor? I'm just going round to so-and-so and I'm running a bit late.'

I said, 'Yes, you can borrow the motor but be very careful, have your nut about you, because there's a little firm going about with guns.'

'All right, Len, I'm only going round the corner.'

I said, 'OK,' so I give him the keys and he drove round the corner to a pub in the Nile.

He parked the car and got out the car and walked about four yards and a car skidded – looked at from the back he must resemble me, because he was tall and he was big; they must have thought it was me because it was my car. Anyway, a car skidded, a man jumped out with a balaclava on, sawn-off shotgun and blew the muscles out the back of his legs, got back in the motor and drove off.

After a couple of hours in the Green Man, I wanna go home and I'm fuming because he ain't brought my car back. In my head I'm telling myself he's in trouble when he does turn up. 'Course, I don't know he's in the biggest trouble he'll ever have in his life and I don't find out until a pal comes in and tells me there's been a shooting and Johnny's been shot getting out of my car.

I made a quick enquiry and found out where he'd been taken to, got a cab down to St Lewis hospital and was directed up to a private room. Johnny was laying there white as a ghost and he was on a drip and when he clocked me standing there all he kept saying to me was, 'Len, why?'

'Why?' I said. 'I told you to keep your eyes open, I told you to keep your nut about you.'

He said, 'Len,' his exact words was: 'Len, can you just leave the hospital, I don't want to be seen with you – you're too dangerous. I'm probably crippled for life and it's down to you, so keep away from me, don't talk to me.'

He said some harsh things, but I couldn't blame him. I said, 'John, don't worry about it, I will put a stop to it and pay them bastards back for what they done to you.'

Now this was completely out of character for me, but I got hold of a shooter because I was raging inside about that poor geezer laying there and his wife and kids all crying, so really I wasn't thinking straight. Well, the guy who I borrowed the gun off, thinking he was doing me a favour blew down Ritchie Anderson's ear and he came flying round to see me.

He said, 'Look, Lenny, this is silly, you're always telling everyone that you don't need guns because your hands are all you need and here's you tooled up for a war. One man has ended up in a wheelchair and may never walk again, you're flying about with a gun and there's this other firm flying about with guns, the only people that can win is the Old Bill, because someone's either gonna get plenty of bird or stone dead. I know who these people are. Get rid of the gun and I'll set up a meet and I expect you all to shake hands.'

After Ritchie had a word with this firm, we had a meet and sorted it out. I don't need to go into all the details, just that it was nothing to do with this particular family as such but someone on their firm who had the hump with me over some bashing I couldn't even remember. With me growling and Ritchie getting involved, they thought the best thing to do was straighten out their people, pay some compensation to Johnny and move on.

Just shows you, Pete, guns are nothing but trouble because they make tough guys out of cowards. Caught with a gun you get ten years; use one whether you kill somebody or not you're looking at a 20. Yet mugs like Quinn and others are willing to suffer that over some petty argument or a bit of a slap that they probably deserved anyway. Funny old world, innit?

You said you were shot three times and shot at once; you've just spoken of three things.

Good boy, at least you ain't falling asleep. OK, let me have a think. There was the Barbican, there was inside my house, there was outside my house and the time Johnny copped it; how many's that?

That's four shootings, but only twice actually wounding you.

Now I'm getting fucking confused. One in the arse, one in the back and one in the leg, you're right, son; how the fuck could I forget that one, because I definitely nearly died. I'll tell you that story, then remind me there was another one where I got shot at, OK?

Val! Where was I that time I got shot in the leg?

[Val] **The Barbican.**

No, that was my bum; I'm talking about my leg.

[Val] **You didn't get shot that time, you got stabbed and it went bad.**

Fucking hell, I didn't get in until four last night, Pete, so you'll have to bear with me.

OK, I wasn't shot I was stabbed but that turned out worse, funnily enough.

Usual thing: bunch of wankers are in the club and full of piss. Probably nice enough lads during the day, but once they get with their mates and chuck a gallon of ale down their throats they become aggressive, nasty and objectionable and I have to take their shit. It was getting late and they weren't making no move to go home, so I've asked them politely to drink up and go home to bed. Now, they wanna be leery like the other lot I told you about. I got the usual fuck offs, and that's like water off a duck's back to me when I'm at work, but then they wanna square up to me.

Three of them have come at me, and that ain't a problem until the biggest c**t pulls out a knife – a flick knife. He's holding it low, like he's seen in the films, so I easily kicked it out of his hand just before I punched him between the eyes. Didn't knock him out, but knocked the fight out of him. I've grabbed another one of them round the neck and twisted him round and as I've done that I got a terrible pain in my thigh and my leg just folded under me. These kids have fucked off at a run and when I looked down I've got the knife stuck in my leg, right up to the handle.

One of the doormen run over just as I was trying to pull

this thing out and he's saying, 'Leave it in, Len, you ain't supposed to pull it out.'

I've gone, 'Fuck off, I ain't walking about like a fucking knife rack,' and I gave it a tug. He was right, because now the blood's flying out. He wrapped his tie round my leg and the bleeding stopped, then he shot me down to the hospital.

They sorted me out and told me to keep off it for a couple of weeks and I didn't say but I had too much work on to do that. That bastard kept me awake all night and the following day I was due in the City to do a bit of a minding job. Not heavy stuff, just standing in this boardroom to keep an eye on things. Well, this meeting went on for about six hours without a break and in the end I thought my leg was gonna burst into flames because the heat from it and the pain was driving me nuts. By the time I got into bed that night it was like twice the size – and it was big enough to start with. I didn't say nothing to my Val, because she can be a worrier.

Next morning the fucking leg has gone black and I had no choice but let Val call an ambulance. Turned out it's gone gangrenous. Now, the problem with that is, if they cut you, the poison spreads all over and you die, so the only option is to cut the leg off well above the bad bit and it should be OK. They put a morphine pack on me, that pumped the drug around my body 24 hours a day, and really I don't remember too much about it apart from little bits when my brain seemed to clear.

Now, I didn't know what the surgeon was discussing, because my brain was all fuzzy, but one of those times when it cleared I looked at my Val, who never left my bedside, and she was crying. I've took her hand and told her I loved her and we'd soon be going ballroom dancing again. That made her smile, because she knows I ain't ever danced in my life. Then she went back to crying. I said, 'What's up, babe?' And she told me they were considering amputating my leg.

I remember looking at my wife and saying, 'Whatever happens, don't let them take my leg off, I'd sooner die than hobble about on crutches for the rest of my life.'

She said, 'You haven't got any choice, Len, if they don't take it off you'll die, they've already told me that.'

Then the sister came up and I said the same to her: 'Don't let your people take my leg off. I'm Lenny McLean, I'm a street fighter and I've been fighting all my life, you can't take my leg off. You take my leg off there'll be fucking mugs out there queuing up to fight or get their own back and I couldn't live with it. I got too much pride. I'd sooner die.' She walked away and I said to Val, 'Val, before this stuff knocks me out again I want you to promise me that you will sign the papers to let me die rather than them take my leg.' She just cried and shook her head and I said, 'Val, please, if you love me and I know you do, make me that promise.'

I was already slipping off to sleep when I heard her whisper, 'I promise, God help me, Len, I promise.'

You occasionally read in the papers that a nurse has done something wrong or even killed patients. What you don't read about is the thousands of nurses who are angels, who treat people like their own and care about people even though they get shit money. I was very lucky, because the sister in Bank Cross hospital – she's called Mandy, I forget her second name – was an angel from heaven. When the top man come down to organise my operation, she stood her ground and asked him to let her keep trying the drugs for a couple more days. Val told me this. He stood there shaking his head and she was all fired up and arguing with him. In a way, she was well out of order, because these doctors are like gods, but she was like a little terrier nipping his ankles until he reluctantly gave in. Me? I was more or less unconscious all the time on this drip, on this morphine thing.

Two or three days later, I started coming out of the druggy state and could take notice of what was going on and it was then this Mandy come up to me and Val with a great big smile on her face saying, 'Brilliant news, the drugs have done their job and the gangrene has missed your bone by a fraction of an inch, so your leg will be all right.'

Pete, I can't tell you the relief I felt. While I was awake at different times I never let anybody, not even my Val, know how I really felt inside. Yeah, I was scared, yeah, I felt sick at the thought I'd never see my kids grow up, but I kept it inside.

After that, I got stronger every day and some weeks after I was released from hospital and as a thank-you I bought all the nurses chocolates and tights – well, Val got them – and I even stood on the picket line outside the hospital because they was asking for more pay. I don't think I will ever forget what they done for me.

A long time after, I said to Val, 'You know I asked you to sign them papers so I could die rather than lose my leg? Would you have kept your promise?'

She said, 'Lenny, I never had to make that decision so please don't ask me to think about it again.'

I knew by her face I'd be better off leaving that alone.

Would you honestly have wanted to die?

Well, normally I wouldn't, but you have to remember the sort of life I lead. Some people say I'm cocky or arrogant or even that I'm a bully, but I ain't none of those things; I just am what I am. Fucking hell, I sound like Popeye. Do you remember that?

[Lenny sings] 'I'm Popeye the sailor man, I'm Popeye the sailor man, I am what I am 'cos I am what I am, I'm Popeye the sailor man...' [laughs loudly]. Loved him at Saturday pictures.

Seriously though, son, I don't know any other way to live if I'm not sorting out a bit of trouble or doing what I do, and with one leg that would all have been out the window. So, yes, I honestly would've been better of out of it.

You said to remind you of another shooting.

Ah yes. That could've been another serious thing. I kept getting asked to do a bit of work for these couple of geezers but my gut instinct was there was something not right about the whole thing.

These guys were two Rastafarians. And there ain't nothing wrong with that, like I've said before, but there was something about the way they kept hopping about made me think they were on something. I fucked them off, told them, 'Thanks for the offer of work, boys, but I'm too busy.'

They don't listen and kept ringing and calling until I got fed up with them. They even turned up at the club one night and I had to bollock them and told them if they was thinking of pestering me one more time they'd better think about getting a ticket booked for Barbados or wherever it is they come from. One of them said he come from Brixton and I growled at him because I wasn't in a good humour.

They never got in touch again, but some pikey-looking geezer come to me one day and asked if I'd mind him while he did a bit of business, because he'd heard I was the best. I had to make him right there and when he chucked a couple of names up as a reference I didn't see a problem in helping him, 'specially as he was offering top dollar. All I had to do was mind his back while he traded cash for a load of nicked bonds. The business was gonna take place somewhere near where your friend, sorry, Pete, where your sister lives.

On the night, I've parked up near the place, then he's picked me up and we've driven the short distance to the meet that was on some wasteground where they was making a start on building the Dartford bridge. We sat in his motor, then, after a bit, this old Ford comes driving in, stopped and the lights flashed. OK, here we go: do the business I can be home in ten minutes. We got out and Bill – his name was Bill – is carrying a big bag of cash. Two fellas got out the Ford and one of them's carrying a bag as well. I've stood back a little bit and this guy's minder done the same. I see Bill hand over his bag then, bang, bang, he's dropped down. I've run at the guy who done the shooting, but him and his mate jumped in the motor, started it up and fuck me the windows gone down and it's my turn. Bang-bang-bang-bang. Four fucking shots go whistling past me, then they're off.

I never even had time to think how close I was to being dead. I went back to Bill who was bleeding bad from the chest and moaning. I said, 'Don't worry, pal, I'll get you to hospital.'

Then he said, 'Did you get the drugs, did you get the drugs?'

I've gone, 'Drugs, you muggy c**t, fucking drugs, this was supposed to be bonds,' but he was out of it. Though I felt like it, I wouldn't even let a dog die in the mud, so I've picked him up, slung him in the back of his motor and driven up on to the main road. I put the hazards and the headlights on and left him there for somebody to find. Oh yeah, I turned his pockets out and took his bundles for my wages. If he lived he wouldn't say nothing and if he died Old Bill would probably nick it for themselves.

The underworld, if you wanna call it that, is a very small place. You can't take a piss without somebody or other passing the word on. So a little end to that story is that it turned out those Rastas had put the pikey up as a front-man after I said I wouldn't deal with them. Well, tough shit, they lost a fucking bundle over that deal, but Lenny hadn't got his two pen'orth out of them yet. If I'd planned it, it couldn't have worked out better. I got the whisper that these guys hung out in a café over Mile End way, so I've gone over expecting to waste my time waiting.

I've walked in and the place is empty except for those two c**ts huddled in a corner planning their next drugs deal. Ever seen a black guy go white, Pete? Well, it ain't really white, it's a sort of dirty grey, and that's what these guys went. I give the bloke behind the counter a look and he disappeared out the back. Then, without breaking stride or saying a word, I crashed into both of them with a left and a right. They've both fell off their seats with busted jaws, then I really went to work. You've seen what Bradshaw got for a lot less. Well, they got a bit more.

As I'm walking out, the owner stuck his head out from the back and said, 'I didn't see nothing.'

I've gone, 'Have a nice day, pal,' and fucked off.

Druggies see, I fucking hate them because they deal in misery and bring nothing but agg to decent people. I don't believe in killing other people's kids. I got no time for people who are doing drugs – they're no different from nonces. They're selling drugs to kids and drugs kill kids. Apart from me, you know, saying that they are killing kids, I've got a lot of good friends who have dealt in drugs who are absolutely smashing people, but how they get their living I don't agree with. But as people they are nice people and I've got a lot of time for them even though their principles are a bit below the path. It's a terrible business and, do you know, if someone was selling one of my children drugs they'd be dead in the most horrible fucking way and I would go to prison with a smile and I think a load of people that have got kids would feel the same. But unfortunately, that's where the money is, it's in drugs. I wouldn't touch it for ten million pounds. I got my money the hard way and I can hold my head up.

I'll tell you about a very, very close friend of mine. I won't say his name on that tape, but you know who I'm talking about, Pete, because I know you'll treat everything I tell with respect and confidence.

OK, well, like I said, we were very close and this guy was as much a brother as Barry, Kruger or even my cousin Tony. But, as often happens when you grow up, you lose touch and eventually we went our separate ways. I heard he got involved with one or two different people and he became a conman and it weren't long before he became one of the top conmen in the country. A few times he's had a few pulls when a deal went wrong, but he's stuck my name up and got out of it. He started doing bigger and bigger things but then, like a lot of people when they've got too much money and too much time on their hands, he got involved in small drugs and then big drugs and he ended up on heroin. At one time he ended...

[Breaks off as his son enters] Hello, Tiger. OK, see you later, son. Oi! Oi! Don't let it run right out of petrol, will you, son? Don't bring it back empty.

Kids! Never think they should put petrol in the motor when they borrow it.

Where was we? Yeah, he had a big house in the country, all paid for, he had about a quarter of a million pound in the bank, he had a Porsche and he was really cracking away. Then, after he started on the heroin, after two years he lost everything: his family, his wife, his kids, his house, every tanner he had and he went down from about 12 stone to about eight stone; lost everything down to that fucking shit, that horrible white stuff.

One day his wife phoned me in tears and said, 'Lenny, he's bad on heroin and I know it's going to kill him, can't you help him?'

I said, 'Well, I can give him a talking-to but if I know people on that stuff they don't care about anybody or anything, all they think about is where can they get their next hit. All I can do is try and cut his supply off and then try and support him through the worst. Can you find out who's supplying him, who his dealer is?'

Back then, Pete, you didn't pick it up on street corners like today, you got yourself in with a dealer and he looked after you – if that ain't a fucking contradiction.

Well, one day she phoned me up and said, 'Len, I've found out who's been selling him the heroin,' and she give me the name of a guy out of Hoxton. She was sorry she didn't have an address, but, like I told her, with a name I'd find him in two minutes.

I got myself round to his address and waited in my motor until I see him coming up the road. These people are paranoid, with fucking good reason, and once he was indoors there would be no chance of him opening up unless he thought I was one of his regular punters.

He's reached the door, had a good look round and as he's put the key in the door I've jumped out the car, run up the path and pushed him through the open door. He scrambled off the floor and I hit him on the chin. I knocked him right down the passage and he crashed his face into the post at the bottom of the stairs. He tried to run up the stairs but I caught him by the leg and bounced him back down. He's screaming like a kid – he's a fully grown man, but he's screaming like a baby, smothered in blood and screaming like a pig. I've stood back and said, 'Listen, you c**t,' then he was off up the stairs again. He went up four flights and left a trail of blood all the way, but there was nowhere to go. I'm a big fella, but I was so wild I went up behind him like a greyhound and grabbed him as he went into a room. I had his shoulders and I let his own momentum carry him forward until his head smashed through the window. I hoisted him up, pushed him across the broken glass and hung him out the window – and I mean right out.

I said, 'What I want to do is let go of you and see you hit the ground because what you're doing is supplying drugs to people and you know but don't care that eventually that shit is gonna kill them, you fucking slag.'

He's crying and begging, saying, 'I'm sorry, I'm sorry, what it's all about is...'

I said, 'Shut up, you c**t, I'll tell you what it's all about. You're making bundles of money out of killing kids and a very good friend of mine. I've been asked to have a word and

I have now, in my own special way, so the selling stops here today. I'm gonna have you watched and, if I find out you so much as sell even one tiny spliff, you'll end up as a piece of bacon or a sausage because I will make sure you get fed to the pigs on a farm in Kent.'

I left him crying on the floor in a big pool of blood and that beating must've done a bit of good because I know for a fact he's never sold another drug.

Trouble was, it didn't do nothing to help my pal. I don't know where he's getting his gear from now, because he's still on the shit. Somebody said to me, 'Lenny, you'll be protecting him till the day he dies, just forget him and let him do his own thing.' But I haven't give up on him, I'll always have a soft spot in my heart for him. It cuts me up that one minute he's a livewire, next minute he's a wreck of a man with nothing to live for really except his next injection. Wherever he is in the world, please God, I pray he'll clean himself up or it's a fact he'll end up stone dead.

How's that, Pete, is that a good story? Or is it a sad story?
Very sad, particularly as he's got a wife and children.
Yeah, that is the worst part. But the embarrassing part about it is this. As much as I think the world of him and I love him like a brother and I would never see any harm come to him and if anybody hurt him then God have mercy on their soul, I can't have him round my house. He phoned me just after I got out of prison after that murder charge and I had to give him a dodgy address. I said I've moved because the thing is I don't want any drug addicts round me or my family.

Anybody that sells drugs to kids are the lowest of the low. How can a man get fat out of pumping drugs into teenagers? And I'll put it in the book that they're slags and no better than them that rape old ladies and interfere with babies. They won't like that, will they?

I might have mentioned this before, but, in all the clubs and pubs I've minded, I've always been the leader and I've always carried the other minders. I ain't got a lot to say about most of them, because I've always done the business and they've followed. I suppose the craftiest, cunningest minder I've ever worked with is a guy named John. When there was trouble he'd want to go the other way, the long way round. I used to say to him, 'What you doing? The trouble's over here.' I used to rush the short way and he used to go the long way round.

He'd say, 'Len, whether we rush or whether we go slow, we still get the same money and don't get no better thought of.'

I'd say, 'John, you don't know what you're talking about,' then he'd say, 'Well, Len, if you remember, you went the short way round and got yourself nicked for murder,' so I suppose I had to make him right.

Give him his due, he was always by my side when I was having trouble or when there was trouble in the club; he was always ready to back me up. I remember one night, we was minding that club together, I got called down to the dance floor, the main bar, and there was a little firm there, six of these brothers, all from the age of about 24 to about 38, and I said to them, 'When you're ready, boys, can you

221

drink up and mind that road as you cross over for a taxi. Goodnight, boys.'

They went, 'Fuck you.'

I said, 'Do what?'

They went, 'Fuck you.'

I said, 'No, fuck you lot.'

Anyway, one of them has pulled an axe out, the oldest one. He said, 'Do you want some of this?'

I said, 'Yeah, come on, I'll have some of that,' and, as he's gone towards me with the tool, John is just behind the guy, so he's kicked his hand and the axe dropped. I've hit this black guy on the chin and knocked him spark out, then the two of us unloaded the rest.

Once we've seen off this bit of trouble, all the other doormen suddenly appear from nowhere. Me and John were on our own until we've laid all these guys out, then we're mobbed by minders once the brothers are stretched out on the floor. I've said to them, 'Get rid of this lot, they can't hurt you now because they're all spark out. No, no,' I said, 'leave that one, the main one, the one who wanted to go to work with the axe, we'll deal with him.' I said, 'John, get this c**t's feet and drag him into the back room, I'll give him bayonet.' I told John to hold him up by his arms, because he was still unconscious, then as he's held him up I've hit him like he was a punch bag. I doubt whether he felt a thing, but he would when he woke up. Then we took him outside and slung him in a skip.

On another occasion, there was me, John and another guy

named Peter. Unusual name for a black geezer that, don't you think? Peter was a black bloke, a very nice fella, and an absolute gentleman. There was some black blokes from the Broadwater estate, they was about eight-handed and they was causing trouble, so they buzzed up for me. As I'm on my way down, the governor shouted out to me, 'Lenny, why don't you let Peter talk to them, because he's black, and he can brother them up; might save a bit of aggravation?' I went, 'Marvellous, go on then, Peter, you go in and do all the brother talk and we'll nip it in the bud.'

So he's giving them all the talk and it's all being smoothed over, then one of them looked at me and said, 'What you looking at, you honky bastard?' That was it, all hell broke loose. I smashed him up, I smashed about four of them up, and Peter and John got stuck into a couple more. We've hurt 'em and slung them out the door. The next night somebody's come into the club and said, 'Len, there's three black guys looking a bit dodgy outside. There's one by the corner of the post office, one over by the garage and one where the cars are parked.'

I went, 'Oh, yeah, it's them mugs come back from the night before.' So what we've done, we've slipped out the back way, I've got hold of one, John's got one and a kid named Graham – nice kid, good boy – he's got hold of the other one. Bang! We've sprung them, knocked them out and searched them and found they were all carrying guns; these c**ts meant business.

What I mainly used to do was leave the doormen outside minding the door with their bow ties, looking like circus ringmasters, while I got nice and comfortable in my office. I was like the reception manager, really; I was in charge of the club. One time I was in the office having my bit of dinner, the door's opened and John come in saying, 'Len, we got a bit of agg.'

I went, 'For fuck's sake,' so I've put me knife and fork down, and gone out and there was these two guys and, on my kids' lives, and this is true, I ain't seen any bigger, they must've both been about six-foot nine each and weighed in at about 23, 24 stone.

I said, 'What's the problem, gents?'

They said, 'What do you mean what's the problem?'

I said, 'I'm having me dinner in the office and they've called me out and said there was a problem with you two.'

One of them said, 'There's no problem, one of your monkeys seemed to think I was messing with one of your staff, but she's my old woman.'

When I looked, he's pointing to an 18-year-old girl, an absolute beauty queen in a little leotard, one of the waitresses. I said, 'Don't talk to me like I just come off the boat, she can't be your wife, she's a princess and wouldn't look twice at you two fucking ugly fat dinosaurs, so don't take the piss, just drink your drink and go.'

They said, 'OK, we'll go, but first we're gonna knock the bollocks outta you, 'cos you've got too much mouth.'

I've gone, 'OK, well have some of this' and tore into them. I've gone bang! – hit one with a right hand, one with a left hook – bang! They've both gone over like a sack of shit. I thought, 'No, you can be hurt now, you two,' so what I done, I spread-eagled them and punched them right up the nuts, so in the morning their nuts are gonna be like an elephant's. I said to John, 'I'm gonna finish my dinner, so you get some boys and drag them out and make sure their heads are hitting the steps, because they took a fucking liberty: they made my steak go cold.'

After a while, a couple of my doormen come into the office with their shirts and ties all over the place. I thought those big guys had come round and kicked off, but it turned out they couldn't lift them. I've said, 'For fuck's sake, use your brains: fucking roll them down the steps.' And they did, and we never heard from them again.

Another time, I'm minding this club, sitting around and having a chat and a laugh, when a guy come in with one of those big flowery dresses on, a full robe like an African robe, a big, black guy, built like a brick shithouse, a well-muscled guy. He's walked in and introduced himself as Cool Ken, supposed to be the guv'nor over in Peckham. I've asked him want he wanted and he said, 'I want a job here.'

I said, 'Well, I don't do the hiring, I do the firing if it comes to it, but I suggest what you got to do is leave your name with the receptionist and then we'll contact you in a few weeks if a job comes up.'

'No, you don't understand what I'm saying: I want a job now. What if I take over your job?'

This c**t's getting me going now. I said, 'I don't think you wanna work here at all, you've come along tonight to wind me up and make a reputation for yourself, so come on, let's go to work.' I went crash! – right-hander – and he's gone over, then I went left hook and he's out. But I ain't finished with him, because anyone comes looking for a reputation I've got to hurt them, so, while he's unconscious, I'm hitting him, about another six, seven times. I did my normal: I spread-eagled him and punched him up the bollocks so later on he remembers he's had some. I've done his ribs and I've done his jaw but I've had enough of him by then so I got the chaps to dump him round the corner.

Half-hour later I said, 'You better check on him,' but he was gone, so he must've been OK. Turned out he'd been picked up and taken to hospital and from there he sent me a message saying he'd been out of order and could we shake hands when he come out. I sent a message back telling him, if you ever see me, cross over the road because I don't want to talk to you. See, the reason I got the hump with him was he come out of his way for a challenge, he got a belting and now he wants to be my friend; I don't want or need friends like that. I don't want them people round me.

I don't wanna bore you with too many stories of hurting people but there was one drug dealer I went over the top with. **What, more than the one that was selling heroin to your pal?**
Yes, son, much more and my excuse if I need one is that I was so full of hate it's a wonder I didn't put his eyes out. I was in the club like I am most nights, and one of my guys, Tony, who'd only been on the firm a few days, come to me

while I was looking down on the floor from the balcony. He said, 'Excuse me, Mr McLean,' and I had to look twice at him in case he was taking the piss – he wasn't.

I told him to stick with Len or Lenny 'cos he was making me feel old but inside I did appreciate his politeness.

He said, 'See that fella down there?' and he pointed to one corner. 'I've come across him before and I thought you might need to know he's a serious drug dealer who's not long out of prison after some kids died from the dodgy stuff he sold them.'

I've gone, 'You're fucking joking!'

He said, 'No, I'm serious, honest.'

I've said, 'I know you are, son, that's just an expression to show I'm fuckin' well stunned that a piece of shit like that's in my club. Tell you what, Tony, I want you to keep a very close eye on him 'cos I wanna know every move he makes. If he picks his nose, you tell Lenny, OK?

From up top I kept an eye on this geezer myself and when I couldn't see him I knew Tony would be right behind him 'cos he seemed a good kid. A while later, my young doorman come over my intercom saying this bloke's gone in the toilets with a couple of blokes. Now he's either as bent as a nine-bob note or he's selling and my money was on the last choice. I've gone down them stairs in 20 seconds and on the way I've got hold of John, another doorman; Tony was outside the door We all burst into the toilets and there's these three doing a deal. I've grabbed the two punters and thrown them both towards my boys, saying, 'I want these two searched, their names and addresses and if you have to belt it out of them; leave this other c**t to me. Oh yeah, and don't let anybody in for a bit.'

Now this dealer fella don't know whether to shit or shave; he stood there stunned trying to think how to get out of it. I've swung him round so his back's towards me, got my fingers in each corner of his mouth and pulled. While I'm almost ripping his mouth, I'm telling him to spit out whatever he's got tucked in his cheeks. He's shaking his head and I've said, 'Ten seconds an' you're gonna have the biggest smile in London.' He spat and out come four little packs of white powder.

Pete, I've fucking lost it, 'cos I've said it a hundred times, child molesters, old-people bashers and drug dealers are the things I hate most and here's a convicted child killer, through supplying, and he's dealing shit in a place I'm looking after.

He knows what's coming and he's pulled away from me and tried to get in one of the cubicles; waste of time. I've said to him, 'You child-killing piece of shit, prison didn't teach you a lesson so now it's down to me.'

He started screaming that he'd been fitted up by the law but I cut that noise off with a couple of right-handers.

I beat him, Pete, I beat him for every kid that had died or had their lives fucked up. It didn't take long for him to be completely out of it and with him laying on the floor I've kicked his legs apart and put my gas lighter on his nuts. I don't need to tell you the pain he would be in when he woke up might, just might, make him think twice about the business he was in.

All dusted, I got a couple of my lads to bung him in a motor and drop him outside Barts. Never heard another word about it. The two punters got slung out after telling them their details were gonna be passed on to the police, that was bollocks but I bet it give them sleepless nights for a while.

Looking back, p'raps I went a bit strong but you have to think these people ain't no different from killers with guns and knives.

In my life, through what I've had to do for a living, through the fights and club fights, I got a reputation as being the toughest guy around and because of that, they come from all over and want to fight me. I give it to them, because I can be very obliging, but I'm hoping now as I'm getting older I'm getting a bit wiser and all I want now is for the film and the book to go and then I'll get away from all the shit. Dealing with druggies, lowlifes and scum, that's all in the past. What I want to do now is, I'm looking round for a bit of cream. Don't get me wrong, Pete, I've had a good life on the whole, what with my lovely family and a bit of dough in my pocket, you could say I've had the bowl full of cherries, but what I want to top it off is the cream. I've had no cream, all I've had is plenty of agg and now at my age I want some thick cream poured over my cherries.

How's that, son? Wanna ask me some more questions?

When you were younger, did you go after people to gain a reputation?

Yes, I suppose I did. It's what being young is all about, you know: young stag taking on the older one, that's how life keeps moving on. But I never took liberties, even though I made a fucking nuisance out of myself. Once you've got your own rep and you're known as the Guv'nor, the hardest man in the country, then there's nowhere else to go.

It brings its own responsibilities, though, because it ain't like becoming world champ at boxing then sitting back on your arris and spending all the money you've made; it's more than that. Like my uncle Jimmy, you become a figurehead for people to look up to, so you have to always do the right thing. You could say I'm retired now, but that don't mean slippers and the armchair. I'm still looking after people and doing what I've always done. Only difference is, I don't go on the fight circuit no more.

Now that you've retired, who's filled the gap?

Funny enough, I don't know anyone. At the moment there is no Lenny McLean out there, because I would've heard about it him. I ain't blowing my own bugle, but, when they made me, they broke the mould.

The reason why I give myself a gee is because I've had my back against the wall time and time again. I've had people pull guns on me in clubs and I've knocked 'em out and took the guns off them. I learned a long time ago that 99 people in 100 won't ever pull the trigger of a gun. They think they will, otherwise they wouldn't point it at you, but when they look at your eyes their arse drops right out. I remember one night a geezer pulled a gun on me because I refused him entrance. He wants to blow my head off because I said he can't come in the club. I said, 'Go on, you c**t, shoot me.' He hesitated, so then I know he's not going to pull the trigger. I hit him on the fucking chin, he's gone over and his pal's picked the gun up. And just then Old Bill's come driving round the corner; they jumped out and said, 'What's going on?'

I don't wanna say this young slag tried to shoot me, because he'd get a five or a ten. So what I said was, 'This drunk just tried to fucking nut me.'

They said, 'Len' – because they all know me – 'look, Len, we've told you before and we'll tell you again: stop knocking people out. We'll turn a blind eye this time.'

What it is, we used to look after them, used to send all their Christmas beer round to the local nick, so during the year they give us a bit of rope. The black kid comes to and they had a word with him. He didn't want to press no charges because he fuckin' well knew he had a result. Old Bill fucked off and the kid ended up saying, 'Thank you, can I have my gun back?'

I said, 'No, fuck you.'

How's that for a story?

You ready for a break?

Val! Peter said any more tea?

Have a smoke, son, but don't drop ash on the floor. She talks about you every night after you've gone and she's hoovering up. Ain't that right, Val? You say he's a messy fucker. She ain't answering, don't want to embarrass you. Did Geraldine give you a call yet?

Yes I spoke to her on Tuesday, I didn't know what to say really, what can you say when somebody's lost a child?

Bad, bad business, Pete, but that Hatch guy will suffer for the rest of his life. Do I need to put this on tape?

You can if you want. We can always take out bits later.

Good boy, you know what you're doing. Well, this was all in the papers at the time, you know, when Geraldine's young nephew got murdered by that scum Colin Hatch and dumped in a plastic bag in a lift over their way. They caught up with him and he got lifed off, but what satisfaction is that to them people that loved that little boy to bits.

She said the worst thing for her was watching him smirking in court.

Yeah, that wound me up as well. The law had warned the family that if anything happened to that evil c**t they'd be knocking on the family's door. How could they want to protect somebody like that, ain't they got kids of their own? We got to box a bit clever here, son, because we don't want to have any nickings, so what we'll say is I couldn't dream of going against the law and having that guy hurt. I'll leave that for you to work out how to put it. The truth is, there ain't nowhere to hide in the prison system. If you can't get word from other cons, there are always screws ready and willing to take a bung for giving up information. End of the day I'm sure somebody will oblige that horrible piece of shit when he ain't expecting it, but it won't have been Lenny who organised it. You know what I'm saying, son.

'A nod's as good as a wink to a blind horse,' as my granddad used to say.

Yeah, I've heard that one.

Don't let your tea get cold. Where was I?

I know, got a funny little story, Pete. A pal of mine asked me to help him move a bit of scrap for him, like load it on his truck and go with him to weigh it in. He said he'd give me a day's pay and, at that moment in time, because I was younger then, that would come in nicely. We're shooting the shit while we're loading up and he asked me how things were for me. I've gone, 'George, times is diabolical, nothing much going on and I'm fucking skint.'

He's looked at me and said, 'Family all well?'

I've gone, 'Yeah, lovely, thanks.'

So he said, 'Yourself, you get bigger every time I see you, so you must be good.'

I said, 'Couldn't be better, strong as a bull.'

'Well then, you've got all that counts, because if you've got good health, you've got happiness, so don't ever worry about money. As long as you've got enough to put a bit of steam on the table, don't ever think or worry about money, it can't buy you happiness.'

On the way over to Yellops in east London, we've come round a corner and crash!, he's run into a skip sitting at the side of the road. He weren't going fast, so it didn't even shake us up, but it broke the headlights on the truck, broke the front grille and bent up the bumper. Fuck me, he wasn't too pleased, but we carried on to the scrap yard and he ain't saying a word and he's got a face as long as a kite. He weighed in, then told me what he got and how much he'd had to pay for the scrap in the first place and he's not that much in front. I was laughing, because he was looking miserable. I went, 'What's the matter, George?'

He went, 'Nothing, I'm just fucking pissed off about me truck.'

I said, 'But when we was on the way down to the job you said that all you need in life is your health and happiness. Well, you ain't too happy now, are you, son?'

He said, 'I'm happy enough, Len, but, fuck me, I've done a day's work, by the time I've paid you, time I've paid for this damage and me petrol, I'll wind up with about 40 fucking quid.'

I went, 'Never mind, George, you'll still be able to put a bit of steam on the table, so straighten your mug up because at least you got happiness.'

He told me to fuck off, but he was laughing at himself.

A few years after, poor old George got 18 years for a blagging, and he's still away now, but he's a good man, George. You see, sometimes it's too easy to say things when everything's sweet.

It seems that every time I'm talking about someone in trouble or talking about faces and villains, I always say they're good men. Now, that ain't just something to say, because they are good people, they're streetwise and fucking loyal. I've found the criminal or the streetwise kids that have come from the streets have been brought up the old way, with values that don't exist today in the straight world. OK, they'll thieve and get up to this and that, but bottom line is they look after their own when the chips are down. I sit in my clubs and other places that I look after and I look round at some of the office workers and businessmen, drunk, laughing and giggling, not a care in the world, and they seem to sneer at people like us because we're the other side of the fence.

One day a guy comes over to talk to me. He said, 'I was reading about you in the papers, Len, you got nicked for murder.'

I went, 'Yeah, but I never fucking done it.'

He said, 'Can I bring my friend over?'

'He'd be another fucking office worker,' I thought.

The kid said, 'He's my best pal.'

I said, 'No, you're not pals, you're acquaintances, you ain't got no real genuine pals.'

He said, 'I'd do anything for him; if he was in trouble I would be there for him.'

I said, 'Listen, when you're sitting here with booze inside you, you'll say you'll do anything for him, but let me tell you about our side of the fence and your side of the fence, and how different we are to you.

'I put my hands up to murder to get a kid out of it. I didn't know that in 18 months' time I was gonna walk out after I'd been to the Bailey. When I put my hands up in Vine Street police station, I didn't know I was gonna get out of it, because as far as I was concerned I was guilty. I couldn't understand how it could've happened after one tap, but these things do happen. In my heart and in my mind I was looking at a life sentence or a rec of 25 years. You just said he was your best pal, but you people wouldn't put your hands up to a parking ticket to get someone out of it,' I said. 'That's why we're miles apart.'

Pete, son, I don't think that kid had a clue what I was talking about, because he come from a completely different world to me. But make me right, son, is Lenny stupid?

Far from it, Len.

I don't know nothing about geography or history or book reading, but I've got it up top where it counts. If I'd been born in St John's Wood or somewhere nice, I might have been a college professor or even a doctor. But I wasn't, I was born on the wrong side of town, where you had to fight and kick and bite, to get everything that you wanted. When you think about it, you know, the general public, they don't know what life's all about. They don't know, and they don't want to know, about the police fucking planting things and fitting people up and putting 'em away for years. They don't know about that side of life, and that's why I can't talk to them. I have them on me ear'ole about a minute and a half and then give them the elbow because I can't have 'em near me.

Let me tell you about something that happened to me – well, not to me, to my friend, this guy Albert. Albert, he's about six foot eight, 24 stone and he's a big black guy. To look at him, he looks very menacing and very powerful, but when he opens his mouth you can tell he's a placid teddy bear. He's at college now, studying for a master's degree in computers; very intelligent man and a very nice man. Anyway, he was in a club one night, minding his own business having a drink, and he's talking to a young lady behind the counter, trying to be pleasant. Some doormen have come up and – no doubt because he's black – what they've done is, they've dug him out and, because he don't look for trouble, as he's come to walk away they've attacked him. He's belted the four of 'em, and hit one of them across the head with a big champagne bottle. The next thing, he's nicked – they've nicked him, the slags, they wanted to give him a seeing-to and because he stood up for himself against four of them they've nicked him. He went to court and he's got a seven, Section 18. I met him in Wandsworth and he told me he was up for an appeal. I've come home after serving 18 months, and not too long after Albert won his appeal and come out as well. He went back to his studying at college and tried to put his bad experience behind him.

One Friday night he called into the club to see me. Now on a Friday I sit right out of the way. I mind the club but I don't stand on the door, I leave that to the new fucking generation who wear bow ties and look like they come out of Billy Smart's Circus. Anyway, I was sitting in the club at the back, drinking my coffee or lemonade, and I said to

Albert, 'Go on, son, slip over to the bar, get yourself a drink and get me a nice lemonade and make sure they put the lot on my tab.'

So off he goes and as he's waiting to be served there are about five muggy drunks, office blokes, been in since five o'clock, drunk as sacks because they been drinking fucking pints all night. One of these mugs has pinched Albert on the chest and said to him, 'You're a big lump, show us your muscles.'

Albert's stepped back and said, 'Excuse me?'

So he said, 'Get your shirt off and let's see your muscles.' Remember, Albert's just got out of the nick and he's still on a ticket, so he has to avoid any trouble at all costs, so he's picked the drinks up and walked away.

When he got back to my table, he's fuming. I went, 'What's the matter?'

And he said, 'It's all right, Len.'

I said, 'No, tell me, what's the matter?'

He said, 'I was queuing for the drinks and this geezer has pinched me on the tit. I wanted to knock him down, but you know how it is, Len.'

I've gone, 'What is he, a poof? Well, I can under-stand you can't say nothing because you just got out of nick but there ain't nothing stopping me giving these c**ts a pull, so sit there I'll go give 'em a tug.'

I went up to the bar and these five mugs are all sitting there. I said, 'Oi! You bunch of wankers, who pinched the big fella's tit?'

This geezer's looked at me through all the piss that was giving him courage and said, 'I did, so what?'

'So what, you c**t?' I said. 'I'll tell you what I'll do. I'll smash into the five of you and put you all in hospital because you have took a fucking liberty. Now, when I belt the five of you and Old Bill come down to the hospital tomorrow, will you say, "We took a diabolical liberty and Lenny smashed us to pieces because we asked for it. We're the liberty-takers and it wasn't Lenny's fault." But you wouldn't, no you wouldn't, you fucking muggy c**ts. What you would say is, "No, we wasn't doing nothing, we were having a nice quiet drink and Lenny come up and belted us for nothing." Once they'd lifted me and got me in front of the judge, he'd say, "Mr McLean, you are a very dangerous man; I got to give you five years in prison," and that would be down to you fucking drunken mugs pinching my pal's tit. We hate you people. And why do we hate you? Because we have to live our lives round mugs like you, because mugs like you say and do the wrong things, and we smash you and belt you and we get fives and sevens and tens, that's why we fucking hate mugs like you. Now, drink your booze and fuck off, you're barred. On the other hand, if you want to come back in this club you can on one condition: and that is, if the fucking lot of us goes in that office now, I shut the door and we have a fight. I'll fight the five of you. If you're willing to do that, you can come back tomorrow.'

One geezer said, 'No, we don't need this,' and I said, 'No,

I don't need it either, but you started it.' With that, they drunk up and walked out.

Albert said, 'What did you say to them?'

And I said, 'I just asked them to leave.'

He said, 'Len, what did you really say?'

'I told them don't go around fuckin' well pinching people's tits, or I'll paralyse the fucking lot of you.'

That made him laugh, so, wherever you are, Albert, I'd just like to say crack away, son, because once you got that degree you'll never look back.

Right, what shall I talk about now? Yes, I started knocking about with Ritchie Anderson after I met him on the Downs, where Kenny had organised a fight for me with some pikeys. I done the fucking lot and we walked away with about 1500 quid, it was a nice day and a very nice earner for bruised knuckles and perhaps a cut lip.

You said the stake money wasn't always easy to get once you'd beaten whoever you were fighting.

Yeah, I did say that, and one time sticks in my mind more than the others. Kenny had sorted out a bareknuckle fight with these Irish guys. Their man was supposed to be the toughest guy around, and he hated the English. I've turned up and the yard is rammed with these guys, all ready to see me get the shit belted out of me; some fucking hope. I see their guy – well, I guessed it was him because he was the biggest fucker there and he was surrounded by his cronies, and they're all giving me the old cross eye. As I walked towards Kenny's made-up ring, this Irish twat muttered something, looked at me and the others all laughed. He might've been telling his mates a joke for all I knew, but I doubted it, and I take exception to people muttering and giving me the old cross eye at the same time. I've gone, 'Oi! You c**t, you got something to say about me, say it so I can hear.' So he sneered and said something in his Irish language. That was all I needed, I flew at him and belted him full in the face.

Kenny's screaming, 'Hold up, Len, the money ain't in,' but I was gone; I'd lost my fucking head.

Before he could recover from the belt in the face, I swung a left into his Darby and caught him with a right to the head and he flew backwards and tripped over a caravan tow bar. I stamped on his chest and kicked him in the mouth and the fucker still got up, so I made an axe out of my two hands clasped together and hit him full on the temple; his head flew back and smashed the caravan window. He was down and completely out.

Kenny's doing his nut about the money, so I've shouted to the other gippos, 'I done him fair and square so settle up with Kenny and fuck off.'

A biggish guy said, 'Fuck your money, you caught him when he weren't ready, you went dirty.'

I said, 'Don't talk to me about dirty, you c**t,' and knocked him spark out.

Then the rest of his clan wanna mix it. I was between a caravan and a fence, so they couldn't surround me, so all I had to do was keep punching and kicking as they came at me in twos. I even had time to laugh inside when some fella's false teeth went sailing across the yard after I hit him in the jaw. The big guy, the one I was supposed to fight in the ring, came to and he was laying there with his hands over his face, and to make sure he didn't wanna carry on I punched his face through his hands. He laid back down and I give two or three more until the blood was running out his fingers. That's when somebody was shouting, 'You'll get your money, you'll get your money!'

I've looked around and there's all these guys laying on the deck either spark out or moaning and groaning and I said, 'Too fucking right we'll get our money, and it better be tonight or else.'

To be fair to Kenny and me, I done what I turned up to do. I beat the guy, I broke his ribs – I always hurt 'em up the ribs – I broke his jaw and I done his eye; I belted him a terrible. So, when you weigh it up, we were entitled to our wages.

As I might've known, they didn't bring the money that night, instead of that they came with shotguns and fucked a load of Kenny's motors. Shot the windscreens out, blew holes in the sides – and we're talking tasty motors, not like the shit he sold me – then fucked off. I suppose they thought they were putting the frighteners on, but they must've been strangers around there because they didn't know what an evil bastard I can be. It's cost my mate a fortune in wrecked cars, so now we're talking stake money and big compensation and I was gonna get it.

I found out where the main man lived and it was on an illegal site not too far away. I also found out he lived on his own, otherwise I would've had to handle it different because I never involve family and definitely never go strong if there's gonna be kids around. I've driven round to this site about three in the morning, it's windy and it's raining, so any noise is covered and the dogs are tucked up somewhere; couldn't be better. I found the geezer's gaff, and that wasn't too difficult because it was the fanciest on the place. I crept up, stuck my fingers down the crack in the door, ripped the fucking thing clean off and dived inside. I dunno if he was expecting trouble or always slept with a shotgun by his bed, but before he really knew what was going on I had two barrels pressed right on his forehead, hard. He can't speak, but his eyes have opened up like two big saucers. I said, 'I outta pull both triggers right now, you fucking gutless coward, but I don't need guns,' and I turned round and used it to wipe all this expensive china and crystal off his shelves. You know what gypsies are like, they give the impression they've got fuck all then fill their places up with thousands of pounds' worth of gear.

I said to him, 'You've got a couple of minutes to weigh me out ten large or I'll burn this place with you in it.'

He looked a comical c**t, because he's got these two red circles on his forehead, but I wasn't in a laughing mood. He's climbed off the bed, stark bollock naked and I could see he'd pissed himself and could hardly stand. He was trying to say he ain't got no money, but I stopped him right there and he knew it was a waste of time. He dug a roll out of a cabinet and when I counted it there was only six or seven grand, so I give him a few growls and he pulled out a panel by the fireplace and handed it over. That bundle brought it up to about 12 long ones, so I peeled off the two, flung it at him and told him I was no thief, I was only taking what was owed. I squared up with Ken and we never had no more trouble.

I'll tell you though, Pete, he was a very lucky man. He's done my pal over with shotguns and he never got belting; not even a dry slap.

After that, though, Kenny said, 'I don't want no more fights round here. All me fucking cars are done, I don't want the aggro.'

I said, 'You got paid for them cars and what with them being ex-hire they was probably worth fuck all anyway, but, if you wanna do the business somewhere else, that's OK with me. Tell you what,' I said to him, 'there's a kid from Tottenham wants to fight me bare knuckles, but, if you set it up with gloves on at Woodford football ground, you can promote it and we'll both make a bundle.'

That put a smile on his face, because he did like his pound notes. I think he made about £14,000 out of that when I hammered the guy. I've done a lot for Kenny because he's a nice guy and if ever he's got a problem I will always be there at a hundred miles an hour. His car lot's gone now, been turned into a park, but he might have some posters somewhere.

You said you'd come back to the business about the murder.
Yeah, I did, didn't I? How far had I got?

Errrr, you were in the police station. No, you were on your way to Wandsworth after being charged.

Fucking hell, you've got a better memory than I have, Pete. OK, let me think about that for a minute.

I'll go back to when I was in the station, if that's OK? I was being interviewed in Vine Street police station and one of the detectives said, 'I remember you from years ago.' It wasn't Cater; it was another DI that happened to be in the room. He said, 'I was based in the area and you were a crazy man, always fighting.'

I went, 'Yeah, that's about right, but I don't remember you.'

He said, 'I remember when you had a fight with a man named Briggs, you hurt him so badly he nearly died. Am I correct?'

I said, 'Yes that's correct, but it was a very long time ago and me and Jimmy are friends now.' What I'd forgotten was they had the tape running. I heard a funny noise and I went, 'Hold up, this ain't on tape, is it?'

He said, 'Don't worry about what's on tape.'

I've jumped and shouted at them, 'You monkey c**ts, I got nothing else to say,' and that's when I started saying I'm John Wayne and Michael Caine for three hours and that's all they ever got out of me.

So, to cover my back, I got Val to ask John to go and see Jimmy, because I reckoned they was gonna use the tear-up I had with Jim at the Bailey. I said to her, 'Tell John to make sure that Jim denies that I had a fight with him.'

John, being good stuff, had a quiet word with Jim and he

agreed to go along with it. He said, 'Tell Len I ain't no grievance with him, 'cos it all happened 20 years ago and we was both fucking out of order then. I don't talk to the police, I don't help the police and if it comes to it I will come to the Bailey and say, "No, Lenny didn't do nothing to me. Lenny and me are old friends, we go back a lot of years."'

I've got to give Jim ten out of ten and wherever he is I wish him all the luck in the world. Shall we put that in the book, Pete?

Yes, I think you should, because from what you've said he really doesn't owe you any favours, does he?

You're right, son, he doesn't, that's why he deserves a gee. As I've already said, that was the only fight I really regret in my whole life. He didn't deserve it and it was over a bird that meant fuck all to him.

We don't talk to police; we sort our own problems out. As far as me and everybody else in our world are concerned, the police are here to see our children across the road. We don't want nothing to do with them, because, when it comes to real work like catching child killers and them that batter old ladies, they are a waste of time. Shit hot when it comes to speeding tickets, but usually for what good they are you might as well do it your fucking self. We don't talk to them, we don't say good evening. I'm not interested in them; we are our own police force.

We don't have to go on about them, do we? I don't really like them.

So, how's it looking, Pete, how's it coming? Can you doctor it and polish it?

It's looking all right and coming along well, mate.

[Val] **Anyone like a drink before I go out, or don't I have to ask?**

Yeah, go on, babe, I think I'll have a coffee this time.

[Val] **What about you, Peter, tea or coffee?**

Tea as usual, Val, ta.

I was telling Pete, about Jimmy and how we hate the police.

[Val] **I heard you, but you didn't tell him about when you helped that policewoman. So you're contradicting yourself.**

Oh yeah, forgot about that, but that was completely different, that young girl shouldn't have been on the streets.

[Val] **Tell Peter, then.**

Bloody hell, Val, whose book is it? OK, I'll tell him.

What happened was, I was outside the Hippodrome – this was about half-ten at night and it wasn't too busy, so I was just looking round, saying hello to people and having a smoke; normal Wednesday, really. I see a couple of drunken arse'oles coming down the road right opposite and they're kicking a bottle up the road until it smashed, then they start kicking shop windows. I'm just thinking, 'When they get a bit closer I'm going to bollock the fuck out of them,' when a policewoman came out of a side turning in front of these pratts. OK, they're as drunk as sacks and in the morning they might turn back into nice guys, but at that time they thought it would be funny to fuck around with this officer. They knocked her hat off and when she got a notebook out they knocked that out of her hand as well. They was laughing like drains right up until I crossed over the road and knocked them down. One of them managed to get up, because I'd pulled my punches, and he run off. The other one wasn't quick enough and he got the toe of my shoe right up his arris before he could get away.

That's a good story on its own, but it didn't end there. The next evening this tiny little girl come in the club, spotted me and come over. She said, 'I've come in especially to thank you.'

I said, 'Excuse me, short stuff, but you can't come in here unless you're 18 – and what do you mean "thank me"?'

She said, and she was laughing, 'I've got ID,' and she showed me a Metropolitan Police card.

I've gone, 'Fucking hell, excuse my French, you ain't...' and she said, 'Yes, I'm the policewoman you helped last night.'

I've gone, 'Think nothing of it, sweetheart,' because I was a little bit embarrassed. Anyway, she's gone and I didn't think no more of it.

A week or two later, I was outside in the same situation. I spend a lot of time standing and looking and thinking about the meaning of life – leave that bit out, I'm only kidding. So I'm standing there and this proper old couple are walking up the road. I mean, I could've smoked two fags in the time they come up the road. As they've got almost up to me, this big ugly fucking Rasta came barging along. He shoved this old dear out of the way and, as her old man's said something, this c**t has stopped, come back and punched the old fella in the mouth.

That could've been your mum and dad, Pete, or it could've been my mum and dad if they'd lived long enough.

I only had to go two yards to belt this animal to the ground. Then I thought, 'No, you disrespectful c**t,' and I picked his head off the ground by his hair and give him four or five solid belts.

Now, it was just my luck or bad luck that a police van come along as I'm belting this guy, so as I've stepped back I'm surrounded. They know me, or some of them do, so, as far as they're concerned, Lenny McLean has been up to his old tricks: belting the shit out of innocent people. The old couple have disappeared, so I'm on my own. Then I see the little girl all done up in uniform and she was talking to what looked liked a CI and next minute he's come over saying, 'If this man,' who was being loaded into an ambulance, 'if this man insists on pressing charges against you we'll be back to see you, but for now I have no interest in what happened here.' Then he said, 'By the way, thank you for the assistance you gave one of my officers when she needed help.'

How's that, Pete, did you like it?

Like Val said, a contradiction of what you said earlier, but, yes, a good story.

Come on, son, when I said I won't have nothing to do with

the law, I meant I would never help them to put somebody away. Do you think I'd look the other way if a copper was being stabbed? 'Course I wouldn't.

OK, now I'll pick up when I was taken up to Wandsworth.

When I first went to Wandsworth, we were all sitting in the reception area. As you go through the gate, you got three screws up on the desk, like on a bench, as you walk through, and you give them your number and they tell you how long you got. Anyway, I went through the reception and then over to the wing; the screws tell us all where to go. When you're walking up on all the landings, everyone's looking 'cos everyone knows who I am. They were all shouting out, 'Lenny! Hello, Lenny; all right, Lenny, result! Good luck!'

Anyway, this guy come over and gives me some tobacco. He said, 'It's all right 'ere, Len, it's not as bad as people say.'

Anyway, another guy I knew from the clubs come up and said, 'Hello, Len, what the fuck you doing here?'

I said, 'Been done for murder, but the truth is I'm fucking innocent.'

He laughed and said, 'Join the club; we're all innocent in here.'

I've gone, 'Hold up, I'm serious, you twat.'

But he carried on laughing and said he was winding me up. Nice fella and one of your own. He said, 'I'm going to try and get you to team up with me,' but a while later he come back saying, 'Sorry, Len, they won't have it 'cos of the charge you're on, you going straight to A wing.'

Anyway, they shipped me off to A wing.

As I'm walking along the landing carrying all my bits and pieces, I bumped into a geezer who introduced himself as Frank. He said, 'We've all been reading about you in the papers, you're a bit of a celebrity because, along with all that shit about murdering that guy, the papers have been digging up all your fights – well, the legal ones, anyway – so I'm pleased to meet you.'

We shook hands and he's took me to his cell and showed me a big cardboard box and in it there's biscuits, tobacco, coffee, tea, everything you could think of. He said, 'Me and the boys, we heard you was on your way, so what we done, we had a whip-round, got you this.'

I went, 'You're a star, Frank, I owe you for this.'

He said, 'Have you done A cat before?'

I said, 'No, come pretty close but this is my first time.'

He went, 'Len, what it is in A cat, you're banged up 24 hours a day, you get half-hour exercise and if you get any visitors they all have to be checked out by the police.'

'I know,' I said, 'a pal of mine, Joey, is banged up in Whitemoor and I didn't pass the test to be able to visit him.'

He said, 'Listen, I heard the screws talking and they're very worried about you.'

I said, 'Well, if they think I'm gonna top myself, they can fuckin' well think again.'

'No, no, no,' Frank said, 'they've heard about your reputation and they're shitting themselves because they've gotta look after you.'

I said, 'You wait, Frank, you wait until they let us out and I'll have a laugh.'

So what happened was, dinnertime come and Frank went to this screw, 'This is Lenny McLean and I've been telling him you give us hard time and you're a right bastard.'

Actually, he was one of the few decent screws in that nick, but Frank was having a laugh.

I've put my bad face on, give a bit of a growl and said to the screw, 'Oh, like that is it? Well, step over here, because you and me need to have a talk.'

This poor c**t didn't know whether to have a shit, shave or a haircut and he wasn't too sure whether he should blow his whistle. I stepped up to him, put my hands under his armpits and lifted him clean off the floor. He's going, 'Put me down, put me down,' so I've given him a kiss on the top of the head and put him down and said, 'Be nice, or you'll get some more.'

All you could hear was the other cons laughing and pissing themselves. An hour later there was a very well-drawn cartoon going round the prison showing me giving him a kiss – one even ended up in the governor's office. After that he was all flustered, but he had to hang around because he was on landing duty. I said to him, 'Do me a favour, after dinner, unlock me. It don't matter, I ain't gonna escape out of this place, am I?'

He said, 'No, I can't do it; it's more than my job's worth.'

'OK then, to stop you worrying about me going over the

fucking wall, even though it's 20 foot high, lock me up with Frank.'

So after dinner he's unlocked me and said, 'Go on then, get yourself in with Frank.'

I remember I was in the cell one day, it was summer and it was red hot. I'm sitting in my cell, and in A-cat cells you got a toilet, a basin, a cupboard and your bed – you are never out of there and you're on camera everywhere. I was feeling a bit depressed that day, because I was missing my Val and the kids and weighing up the possibilities that this might be my life for the next 25 years. I mean, I was pretty strong, but I can understand why a lot of guys – especially young guys – kill themselves, because it drains the life out of you.

I'm thinking to myself, 'Fucking hole, I'm on a murder charge, I'm looking at life for giving a slag a right-hander' – no, scrub that, Pete, not 'slag' – 'for giving a man a right-hander who's pissing and wanking over young girls.' I was fucking fed up sitting waiting for a life sentence. Also, I've got my wireless in there, you was allowed to have your wireless, and also I've put a tape on and it's my wife's favourite song: 'Will You Still Love Me Tomorrow', so I'm listening and it's depressing the fuck out of me and I'm thinking, 'What a state to be in.'

All of a sudden the flap of the door opens. I looked up and said, 'Who the fuck's that?'

This voice said, 'It's me, Frank,' and he stuck his head in the door and said, 'Len I'm making a stew.'

I said, 'Do what?'

He said, 'I'm making a stew because yesterday's dinner wasn't eaten and I always make a stew out of the leftovers. How many dumplings you want, one or two?'

Now, I'm thinking: 'He's asking me how many dumplings do I want. I'm on a murder charge looking at life in prison. I'm banged up an A cat and probably the next time I see the East End I'll be so fucking old either Jamie or Kelly will be shoving me along in a wheelchair and Frank's asking me how many dumplings I want.'

I went, 'No, I'm not interested I feel like shit and I ain't got no appetite.'

He said, 'You gotta eat, Len.'

So I said, 'OK, Frank, gimme half a dozen.'

About an hour later, the doors open and he's brought in a paint tin all cleaned out and full of stew, saying, 'Go on, get that down you.' I cleaned the tin out, but I wasn't really hungry.

I used to spend a lot of time in his cell listening to Jim Reeves or Patsy Cline. I know I spent most of my time in the clubs, but all that loud shit music never did it for me. You can't beat a bit of country.

Frank had been in A cat three months and he knew everybody. He introduced me to a few people on the landing. There was one IRA geezer with a beard and I said, 'What you in for?'

He said, 'Well, I've blown this up, I've blown this building up...'

I know he was IRA, but talking to him he seemed a very normal guy and if you didn't know what he'd done you'd take him for a postman or a baker. I can't ever say I agree with what them people got up to – absolutely diabolical to blow up women and kids and innocent people – but what you have to accept when you're behind the door is that you cannot judge. That's for them outside to do; all us cons can do is make the best of things and try and rub along. There are exceptions, and I don't think I have to spell out who they are, and a few geezers found themselves on the wrong end of a pail of scalding water or else they tripped over and fell down a couple of flights of concrete stairs; you know what I'm saying, Pete. Other than that, you live and let live.

One day a screw come in my cell and said, 'Len you've been checked out, you can go on the landings.'

I thought, 'Lovely.' I've shouted to Frank, 'I'm going on the landings, I'm gonna keep in touch with you, though. You can keep me Patsy Cline.'

He was well pleased, because he liked her as much as I did.

As we're walking towards the landing, I said to the screw, 'Where we going?'

He said, 'You're going to C wing.'

I went, 'OK, but first I wanna see the governor.'

He said, 'No, you don't see the governor these days, 'cos it's all changed – you see the PO. Why do you want to see him, anyway?'

I said, 'I'll tell you why. You know I'm a well-known street fighter?'

He's gone, 'Yeah, we know everything about you, it's all in your records.'

'Well, if you put me on the wing and any of them Jack the lads, them up-and-coming young kids, want to make a name for themselves, look out for a bit of trouble. I'll mark your cards now so you know where you stand.'

He said, 'What do mean by "trouble"?'

I said, 'I'll throw them right over the tops, I'll belt the life out of 'em and I ain't gonna stand for no nonsense.'

He said, 'I'll speak to the PO, you're on 336.'

I went up there, I unpacked me gear and he come up again and said, 'You're going straight on the ones, that's the cleaners.'

I said, 'Why's that?'

He said, 'Well, we don't like the idea of you threatening to throw people over the tops.' He told me to report to the number one and he'd give me a job – number ones are cons same as everybody else but they've earned the privilege of being trustees.

I went over and walked into his cell.

He went, 'Hello, your name's Lenny McLean and I'm pleased to meet you.'

I said, 'Forget the polite shit for now. I'm gonna mark your card: I don't want no fucking hard work, I don't want no fucking heavy jobs, I want it nice and easy, right? I got a murder charge hanging over my nut, this cleaning bollocks ain't my game, all this fucking about, so give it some hard thought before you offer me anything I don't like.'

'Len,' he said, 'what we gotta do is this, the easiest job out the lot, and that's just washing the showers down. All you do is wash the showers down, mop the floor and you can be all done and laying on your bed inside half-hour.'

I've gone, 'Lovely, that's right up my street.'

I went to the showers that night to do the mopping and fuckin' well washing down the showers and there's a mugging pile of what must've been 300 pairs of dirty pants.

The one said, 'Oh, I forgot to tell you, you got to pick the pants up and put them in the big bin.'

I've said, 'On your fucking bike, I don't pick up nobody's shitty pants, that ain't my game.' I see a young kid stood there – God knows what he was in for, because he looked about 12 years old, so I said, 'Oi, short stuff, come here, this is a little job for you. I'll sort you out half-ounce every week and all you gotta do is come in here and pick up all them dirty pants and put them in that bin.'

He went, 'All right, Mr McLean.'

So that was me sorted; I got the kid to do them and we was both happy.

I met this guy named Tommy – or, to put it more truthfully, I went out of my way to meet this Tommy, because he was in charge of the stores and in the stores they had the best shirts, the best of everything, all the best underwear, not second-hand rubbish. We could wear our own gear, like tracksuits, but the best towels and sheets you had to be in the know to get hold of. I've said to this geezer, 'Listen, you ain't too clever and you ain't too bright, because if you was a bit sharper you'd be making bundles for yourself.' I said, 'Right, I'll tell you what to do. When you're in the officer's mess, because they trust you and all that, I want you to phone up my wife and ask her how she got on with my brief and at the same time find out in general what's happening with my case; do that and I'll see you don't go short.'

So he's crept into the mess and he's mopping around and when no one's around he got himself under the table and phoned my Val.

A bit later he's come in my cell and told me he'd spoken to my wife. I've made some coffee and he told me what she'd said. He said, 'Your brief has spoken to some expert and he's looked at all your papers and it seems no way could that guy have died three hours after you gave him a belt, even if you did break his jaw.'

I said, 'Hold up, I never broke the guy's jaw, I've broken too many to count and I'm telling you, Tom, this guy walked away still talking.'

'Well,' Tom said, 'your guy did say he thinks it all points to him dying while the police were trying to control him.'

I got very close to Tommy and another bloke because, when you're all facing a murder charge, the thieves and the petty robbers steer clear, so you sort of band together in a little group.

One day I see this other bloke sitting there and he's got a wet towel on his head. So I've asked him what's up and he told me there wasn't too much money flying about outside and his wife can't afford to visit and she was having trouble keeping up with the bills. I said, 'Don't worry about it, when Tom phones Val tonight I'll get him to tell her to phone your wife and to meet up somewhere and Val will give her £200.'

He was made up and the next thing what happened was he said to me, 'You know, Len, my missus is gonna go after bail for me, and then I can help her out. Only trouble is, it costs a few quid to get it all rolling.'

I knew him or his missus was taking me for a complete and utter c**t, because you never, ever get bail on a murder charge. But what the fuck, if he was so desperate for cash that he'd spraunce a friend, a friend who's in the same boat as him, well, that's on his conscience. End of the day, it's only money. Val met his wife again and that time she gave her £600, and just as I expected she fucked off with the money. He was a fucking good actor if he didn't have nothing to do with that scam, because he cried that now he wasn't going to get bail and he cried because she'd taken off. I give him the benefit of the doubt and never let on what I suspected. Whatever, I didn't blame him – and I didn't blame her, because they was both under terrible stress.

Talking of being knocked, I lent money to a geezer and if I ever lay my hands on him, that slag out there, if I find him I'll strangle him. What happened was, a good while before I got stuck behind the door, this guy come to me because he was in trouble for ten grand, so out of the goodness of my heart I lent him the ten. He got out of trouble, but he didn't manage to pull the money together, so he begged me to let him give me a hundred a week. OK, it ain't fortunes, but better than a kick in the nuts. He managed to pay every week for a little while, then he got himself banged up on a fraud charge. His wife come to me in a terrible state because she was slipping behind with the mortgage and everything, so I said, 'Don't worry, while he's away I'll pay your mortgage.' I paid the mortgage and if she had a problem I lent her money. He's waiting to go to Ford Open nick, but the paperwork was dragging on and on, so I thought the quicker I help him get a move, the quicker I get my dough back.

That might sound a bit mercenary, Pete, but you have to remember I had to earn my money the hard way – nobody gave me a handout on the way, so why shouldn't people who borrow money pay it back with a bit of interest? You read it in the papers and they're talking about moneylenders being the scum of the earth and the poor victim is having a breakdown because they can't pay back the loan. But that fucking victim had a nice holiday or bought a new car out of somebody else's pocket, then once the money's gone they start crying.

I had a screw in the prison system in my pocket because I'd done him a few favours, so I met him and arranged for him to move along the paperwork so my pal could get moved. He was in Ford within the week and well happy, because it meant if he kept his nose clean he could be looking at home leave, then release. I visited him and, when he brought up the subject of the money, I said, 'We'll sort that out when you come home.'

He come home and I gave him a few quid to get him on

his feet and after a while he started to pay back a bit. I suppose he give me three or four grand over a time then I got nicked for the murder and I ain't seen nothing of him since. I hope you read this, you slag, because one day Lenny will catch up with you.

How am I doing, Pete, you finding this boring?

No, Len, the complete opposite.

Val! Peter said should he have bought a flask with him? Know what? I get down the club after doing this all day and I ain't got no voice to bawl at people with. I'll do a bit more then we'll call it a day, because I am bolloxed.

It's funny, people say to me, 'You've got a cushy number sitting down all day writing or talking to people. It's not really work, is it?' It might not be digging holes, but as you're finding, Len, it can be very tiring.

You're right, son; all this has opened my eyes. I thought it was gonna be a piece of piss and all done in a couple of days.

Anyway, I'm on the cleaning one day, doing the showers, and two screws come in and say, 'Lenny, doctor wants to see you.'

I said, 'Doctor? What the fuck do I need a doctor for, I'm feeling top of the world?'

'No,' they said, 'psychiatric kind of doctor.'

I said, 'That's the game, is it? They wanna ghost me off to Broadmoor, well, fuck 'em, my brief will have something to say about that.'

These two screws are getting a bit nervous, because they

think I'm going in to one, but they was safe.

'You'll have to go up in front of the PO, then,' they said.

So an hour later, I'm in his office. Straight off, I said, 'What's all this about me having to see the nut doctor? I reckon you're taking a liberty and taking the piss.'

He said, 'There's an example of the problem: your aggressive attitude. You are a very threatening man and my officers are finding themselves intimidated every day.'

I've said, 'Well, that's news to me; I thought I was handling being stuck in this stinking fucking piss'ole very well.'

'That is your opinion,' he said. 'From where we're standing, you are very difficult to deal with. You keep growling and flaring up at the other prisoners; you threatened to throw a prisoner off the balcony the other day and I'm sure you cannot remember what you said to my officer the other day when he simply bade you good morning.'

'Well,' I said, 'there ain't nothing wrong with my memory and, as it happens, yes I remember exactly what I said to him. I said, "What's fucking good about a morning slopping out shit and piss?" I've been stuck in that pisshole of a cell all night long and you want me to be polite. I got a murder charge over my head day and night, so I don't give a fuck if it's good morning or goodnight or goodbye. So get off my back, keep out of my sight, otherwise I'll knock you spark out you fucking northern c**t. How's that... Sir?'

Sarcastic bastard said, 'Are you expecting applause for that amazing display of memory? Every time you open your mouth, McLean, you make our decision to put you under observation the right one. Report to the doctor as and when you're told.'

I wanted to unload the pratt on the spot, but it wouldn't do me or my family no good and when it was read out in court I could forget any fair trial. So I wiped my mouth.

I saw the doc and he told me he wanted to keep me in the hospital for a week, just for observation, you understand, because they are a bit worried about me because I keep frightening the officers. So the doc give me an injection, he give me 250 milligrams of Valium and some other drug with a fancy name and they doped me up to the fucking eyeballs. They fucking doped me up so much I didn't even know what day it was. That's a week out of my life I'll never see again.

After about a week, they must've cut the drugs down, because I felt more awake, until they come round with a little plastic cup with pills in, then I'd sort of go downhill. I caught on quick and started holding these things under my tongue until I could spit them out and my head come back to normal. The doctor turned up one day and he sat down by me and said, 'I know you're not taking the pills. I should report this and then you will be forcibly injected until you are under control.' He spoke quick enough to stop me getting up and strangling him; how dare they treat me like some fucking dangerous psychopath? Like I said, he was quick as he said it, but he said that could be avoided if we come to a little arrangement. This geezer didn't look like a poof – not that you can always spot it – so he must have something else on his mind. He said, 'We can't talk here, so I will send for you to come to my office shortly.'

Two screws eventually turned up and escorted me to the doctor's office. I acted very placid, so they must've thought I was well drugged up. I went in and the screws stayed outside the office. I sat down and the doctor handed me a sealed letter. When I opened it up, all it said was, 'Len, look after this doctor, he's OK, he done me a lot of favours.' The letter was signed 'Connie'.

Now, Connie was a right old lag and I'd known him for a long time. Never met up with him too often, because I think they had a special revolving door for him on the prison: in for a few years, out for a few months then back in again. He was as sound as a pound, though, so if he's writ this letter it's kosher. I said, 'What's the matter, doc?'

And he said, 'A friend of mine, a much-respected man, has a son of 14 years old and he's being sexually abused by – and he showed me a photo – by a very well-known television star.'

I said, 'Yeah, I know him; he was in this and that and in so-and-so.' I said, 'What do you want? Give me that phone over. Dirty animal; I'll slip some people round to give him a proper seeing-to.'

He said, 'No, Lenny, we don't want that, what we want is heroin to be put in his house. We check when he is at the theatre, we want someone to put heroin in his house so the police can arrest him and he will end up in here and I'll get him in this ward and I can do what I like with him.'

I said, 'You're a pretty evil bastard yourself, ain'cha?' I said,

'Doc, between me and you we don't fit anyone up, we leave that to the filth. I'll slip someone round to oblige him for interfering with the kid – but we don't fit anyone up.'

'Well,' he said, 'we can't help each other.'

I said, 'What do you mean?'

'You know what I mean, I'm duty bound to report that you are not co-operating.'

Fuck, he had me there so I said, 'Doc, worse can happen to him outside than anything you can risk doing, unless you're planning to cut his dick off and my boys don't get into that sort of shit. Let me sort something and, if you ain't satisfied that you got a good deal, we'll talk about the other way.

'I'll see what I can do. But you're gonna have to help me first.'

He don't like that, because he wants to keep away from trouble, like most people who hire us sort of guys to get them out the shit.

I said, 'Don't worry, all you've gotta do is get me a mobile phone so that I can get things organised. Because I won't involve my wife and I can't talk to people at visiting time because the screws are always ear'oling; now, don't that make sense?'

What a fucking mug. I didn't need a phone to make arrangements, but I did need one to keep in touch with my Val and a few pals. He got me the phone next day and I don't suppose he had one minute's trouble getting it in, because doctors are more important then the screws and what they say goes – you know that, don't you, Pete? Well, the guy kept his side of things and I don't rump no one so I kept my part of the bargain and that actor was out of the business for a very long time. Terrible what goes on sometimes. Anyway, I kept the phone in the shower room wrapped in a bit of plastic, right under the bath. So I used to go in there every night, shut myself in the bath house and talk to Val.

This went on for ages, then one day the door's open and in come this kid. He's looking at me – well, more staring, really. Now if I know you and you stare at me, that's only friendship, but, if you're a stranger and you're staring, that's a challenge. You watch animals before they fight, they stare at each other, so why is this fucking mug staring at me? I went, 'Who you fucking staring at you, you mug?'

He said, 'Len, Len, I'm only staring because I know of you. My name's Danny.'

I've gone, 'And?'

He said, 'You know my brother-in-law.' And he told me who it was.

I said, 'Yeah, I know them, they're good people, but I don't know you. What's the problem?'

He said, 'I ain't got nothing. I just come straight from the Bailey; I ain't got a pot to piss in.'

So I said, 'That's funny 'cos a pot to piss in is one of the few things we get for nothing in here.'

He's gone, 'No, what I mean is I'm brassic.'

'Yeah I got the picture I'm just having a laugh with you, I don't mind helping out – take this,' and I give him tobacco, coffee and some biscuits. I said, 'OK, you can grab the bed next to me.'

He got settled then he said, 'Len, this is my first time in prison and I've heard stories, you know.'

I said, 'No, when we go on exercise you stay with me. They give me a lot of respect,' I said, 'you walk round with me you'll be well minded.'

He went, 'Lovely, Len.'

But I said, 'I ain't doing it for you, I'm doing it for your family.'

I've gotta say, this kid sucked me right in, and that's very unusual because I can normally suss people out in two minutes after I've met them. It's all in the eyes, Pete, dunno what it is really, but them who can't look at you when you're talking to them or look away when they're answering a question, well I reckon they've got something going on inside their nut. So put it down to the stress I was under or being in that pisshole, but I got taken for a mug.

This Danny come in my cell one night and he was proper upset because he was desperate to get hold of his missus. I said, 'Can't you wait until eight o'clock tomorrow, when you can use the phone on the landing?' No, it was desperate that he got hold of her. I said, 'Well, you're fucked then, unless you go and see the PO and he might let you make a call, but I wouldn't hold your breath.'

He got himself in a state so after a bit I thought, 'Poor fucker, it's taking a risk, but I can help him.' I went to the showers, dug out the mobile phone and gave it to him and said, 'Don't ever talk to anybody about this, but you can make a call for a couple of minutes.'

He's give me a hug and promised that when his family heard what I'd done they'd owe me a big favour.

I said, 'I don't need favours off anybody, but if there's a bit of cash flying about I wouldn't say no.' I wasn't too serious about that.

Anyway, he's made his call, give me the phone back and he's over the moon. Half-hour later, he's told me he's gotta slip up the landing to have a word with the screw in charge, because he ain't feeling too good. This was about nine o'clock, so I said, 'Well, don't make a noise when you come back,' because I was having an early night. He never come back and in the morning he still didn't come back. I thought it was all a bit strange then – crash – the door's opened and the screws come in mob-handed with sticks, the heavy mob with those plastic things, the shields. The PO come in saying, 'McLean, you know what we want.'

I said, 'I ain't got a fucking clue what you're doing busting in here, but if your monkeys wave them sticks at me once more I will unload you and every one of them.'

The PO got red in the face saying, 'Don't even think about causing trouble McLean, for me or my officers because you can't win.'

I said, 'You're right, p'raps I won't win in the end, but I'll tell you what, you'll be short-staffed on this landing for a while because I'll fuckin' well hurt most of you before you get me down, I'm warning you.'

Then one of the screws come in and said, 'Got it, guv, it was in the shower room.'

These muggy c**ts have only got hold of my mobile, so I knew the shit had hit the fan.

Me having a mobile was fuck all, really. I mean, what can they do? I'm sitting on a murder, how much worse could they make it for me just because I've got myself a phone? The doctor on the other hand, fuck me, he couldn't have done any worse if he'd brought me a gun in, because he'd gone against all the rules and broken his trust. Later on, it all got in the papers about what he'd done and he either killed himself or the stress brought on a heart attack and he died; poor fucker, because he wasn't a bad fella, really. Since then I've seen that actor and you've seen him as well, Pete, and I think he deserves to be fucking murdered because he's walking around being the flash star and a kid's life is fucked up and a good man's dead because he gets it off rumping young boys. Scum, Pete, scum.

'OK,' the PO said, 'you're on your way to Belmarsh, McLean.'

I've gone, 'Why didn't you say that in the first place, why do you come in here with sticks and shields looking like you're up for a riot?'

He said, 'Well, we knew how you would react.'

I said, 'React? Let me tell you how I'm gonna react. Belmarsh is brand spanking new, six months old or so. This piss'ole has got to be 2,000 years old... Belmarsh has got to be a million miles in front of this, so I'm well pleased. I'll get my bag then I'm fuckin' well gone.'

[To Val, who has just entered] Just right, babe, we was just thinking about having a break. Doughnuts? You must be after something.

Get stuck in, Pete.

Talking about mobiles, do you remember when we was at Ronnie's funeral and that little geezer's phone went off in the church?

Yeah, that was embarrassing because everyone looked as us two because we were the tallest, like it was us. I've got that on video somewhere and our faces are a picture.

And the driver got lost, didn't he? Fucking good laugh that day – no disrespect to Ron, but you better not put I said that in the book.

When I got to Belmarsh, I wasn't there long when a guy come over the wing and introduced me to this young fella. I said, 'Who is this guy?' And he said it was a brother-in-law of the same family Danny was related to. I went, 'What, is every fucking brother-in-law of that family banged up, or what?'

He said, 'What do you mean?'

So I explained that I'd been looking after a bloke called Danny and he was related to this family, so this kid in front of me has to be shooting a line to get hisself some favours.

He said, 'No, Len, I can vouch for this fella, because I know the family very well.'

So I said, 'Well, who's this fucking bloke I been protecting? I've took him under me wing, I give him a mobile phone, I've looked after him, so who is this Danny?'

He said, 'He's police plant, a fucking no-good grass, they've been putting him round all the nicks.'

I went, 'Fuck me. I've been telling him some things. Well, if he's a grass his fucking days are numbered except he disappeared just before I got lifted for having a phone.'

This guy said, 'They brought him here to Belmarsh; he's over in the hospital, because I suppose they think he's safe there.'

OK, I'll get myself over there and do him some damage and then they'll have to stick a year on top of the 25 I'm looking at.

Next thing I know, Danny's been shunted off to Durham, well away from me, because a screw has heard I want to get over there and hurt him. I was fucked for the time being, but when I got the chance I got word to a mate, who knows everybody who's in the nick and he arranged for Danny to be well obliged. From what I heard he won't be doing any more grassing up.

I was sitting on my bed one time and all of a sudden the door's opened and the screws have brought this black guy in. They wheeled him in on a bed and he was in terrible pain. His hair was covered in blood, he was cut and bruised and he was moaning and groaning. I didn't take a lot of notice, I just thought he was a likely lad that had come in and had had a tear-up somewhere. They was a bit rough with him, the screws, and I've said, 'Oi you c**ts, I don't know what this geezer's done but if you don't treat him with a bit more respect I'll knock the pair of you out before you blow them fucking whistles.'

They walked out quick and locked up.

I've gone over to him and said, 'What's up, pal? Who are you?'

He said, 'My name's Gilbert and I've had a bit of agg with some blokes. They kicked me to pieces, they done my spine, they done my head. I don't know who in the system could have done this.'

I went, 'Who you with?'

And he mentioned a good family out of east London. Now, because he stuck up these respected people, he's got to be looked after.

So I said, 'OK, Gilbert, listen to me. While you're in here, nobody – no con, no screws – will get near you while you are in that state. Until you can stand on your own two feet, I'll mind you and look after you.'

After a bit they come and took him to the hospital and before he went I said, 'Get back on your feet, son, and show them fuckers they ain't beat you and don't forget I'll be minding your back when they put you back on the landings.'

About this time I got another job and this was in the kitchen and the bonus was I was the only one allowed in there after the dinners were all cleared up and the place cleaned up. Instead of fucking about in my cell, I could wander over and knock myself up a nice cuppa tea or a bacon sandwich. That was OK for a bit, then this new screw turned up. He was a Scotchman and a miserable c**t. I'm walking over to make myself some tea...

[Val from kitchen] **I've never seen you do that here, Len.**

No, you wouldn't, because you make better tea than I do and you love looking after me, don'cha?

You made me lose my place now.

The Scots screw and making tea.

Yeah, so I was walking over to make a cuppa and this screw, he didn't even look up from his newspaper, he didn't even look up, he went, 'Where do you think you're going, *Maclain*?'

I said, 'Excuse me?'

He said, 'I asked you where you were going at this time of night.'

I've gone over, got him by the throat and dragged him out of his chair and said to him, 'First off, my name is Mclean, like the toothpaste, you ignorant muggy c**t, and I reckon your attitude is diabolical. What is it with you mugs? Do you think you're better than me 'cos you're on that side and I'm on this one? You might think I'm an arse'ole and a mug but I guarantee you'll change very, very quick.'

I've let go of him and he's trying to puff hisself up and shouting, 'I'm putting you on report for assaulting me.'

I said, 'Assault? Fucking assault, I'll tell you what, if I do assault you, you'll know all about it.'

Anyway, next day I found out what his full name was in a roundabout way from one of the decent screws, then when Val come in for a visit I asked her to give Arthur a ring in Scotland. He's the guv'nor of Glasgow, have you heard of him, Pete?

Yeah, I have, Arthur Thomson.

That's him, he was on the same level as the Twins. He's dead now. He was a good man; I went to the funeral.

So I told my Val to say to him there's a Scotch screw giving Lenny and a lot of other good chaps a lot of hassle and will he get somebody to go round to his family, to the house, and to tell their boy in London to keep off Lenny's back and behave himself. Know what, Pete? A week later this screw was a changed man.

I had to go over to the hospital for something or other and, as I've walked in, who come steaming up to me in a wheelchair but the black fella Gilbert. He said, 'Hello Lenny, how are you?'

I went, 'Fucking hell, Gilbert, a lot better than you stuck there in a wheelchair, what's the word?'

He said, 'It turned out them bastards damaged my spine, but they're saying I did it to myself.'

I said, 'Well, they would, wouldn't they? Get yourself a good brief and he'll sort them out.'

Eventually, he come back to the cells and me and him came good pals and we had a right laugh and a giggle. Every night he would sit on his bed – his bed was perfect, he was spotless, his hair was all done nice, he was immaculate and every night he used to say his prayers and every night I used to interrupt him so he would start all over again. I wasn't taking the piss out of his religious beliefs. I was having a joke and he knew it.

Gilbert was up on a gun charge, him and a member of a well-respected family, and they both got a not guilty. He's out now and cracking away. I see him a couple of times and he's out of the wheelchair and on a pair of crutches. One day, he will walk proper again and prove that you can't keep a good man down.

Are we doing all right, Pete, is it average or good?

Gilbert didn't deserve what he got, but one guy I came across did. When I was in Brixton, they brought in this black guy who'd just been nicked for killing two women. I can't think of his name. This guy was very posh and very polite and I could hardly understand him. I said, 'Fuck me, now there are four of us on a murder charge in this block.' I said, 'How are you, son?'

He said, 'I am innocent, I never murdered those women.'

I said, 'I never fucking done mine either, nor did Tommy and Phil, none of us done ours.'

He said, 'But really, I did not do what they are accusing me of.'

I said, 'Yeah, they all say that.'

Anyway, we was talking one day, I am sitting in his cell – and this is months after we came pals – and I said, 'When are you up in court, son?'

He said, 'A fortnight.'

I went, 'Keep strong, you must keep strong and if you didn't do it the truth will come out because these barristers and judges don't miss a trick.'

We were sitting there and he said, 'Len, honestly and just between ourselves, did you do yours?'

I said, 'At first I did, because the evidence at the time

suggested that he died after I hit him, but since then my bloke has found out a few things and now I know I didn't do it. Did you do yours?' I said to him.

He thought about it for a bit, then said, 'Well, according to the evidence.'

I said, 'Hold up, I'm asking you the same question as you asked me and it stays between me and the fucking cell door. I don't want details; I ain't a grass, but I'd like to know. Did you do it, bruv? Did you kill the two women?'

He got up went out of the cell, came back, closed the door, made a roll-up, sat back on the bed and said, 'Yeah, I done the two of them.'

I said, 'You fucking muppet, you been saying you didn't do it.'

He said, 'Len, you have got to be so careful who you talk to in here.'

'Well,' I said, 'after I've been to court, I will either be coming home or doing life. It would be a miscarriage of justice if they send me down, but at least I know in my heart I didn't do it. But you just turned round and told me you done the two of them, so your chances of getting out are pretty slim.'

He said, 'Yeah, I done the two of them but if my lawyer does his job there is a very good chance I will walk out of here.'

Now like I said before, Pete, I don't judge and I never consider grassing somebody up but inside I'm thinking those two women were somebody's daughters, somebody's wife and I hope he gets what's due to him. On the other hand, if he'd confessed to killing a couple of kids I would've strangled him right there in the cell. I know I'm sort of contradicting myself but it's a very fine line.

Anyway, he goes to court and comes back every night.

'How's it looking?' I'm saying.

'Don't look bad, Len, don't look bad.'

Well, this went on for about four days and every night he's saying it's looking good. He went up on the fifth day and he didn't come back. Someone said, 'I saw your mate in the reception – fucking hell, he's turned white. As they're bringing him through he's crying and saying to the people handing out the prison gear, "It wasn't me, I didn't kill 'em, I didn't kill 'em, I didn't kill 'em."'

I said, 'Where is he now?'

He said, 'They've took him over the hospital and doped him up, so he'll be on suicide watch a long while. Seemed he got life with a rec.'

Is that a good story, Pete? Or is it average or is it blinding? It's little bit of inside information. Unless he told anybody else that he killed those two women, I'm the only one who knows the truth – and now you and in a bit a million people who read this book are gonna know – but back then I was the only one, apart from him, that knew the absolute truth. OK, they gave him a guilty based on evidence but it could've gone the other way 'cos the jury can never be 110 per cent sure that the evidence is what it seems to be.

Did you like that story, Pete?

It's all good, Len.

OK, good boy. Let's shoot out and stretch our legs – few people I want you to meet.

* * * * *

I was in the reception area talking to a pal of mine, Ritchie Anderson, and I was telling him how I was planning to come and visit him the day I got lifted. We had a laugh over that, because I only intended to visit him for two hours, not fucking 18 months. Why Ritchie was inside was because he's a fiery little fucker and don't take any shit from anybody. He was brought up in the toughest part of Glasgow, and those guys are born with a knife between their teeth. He was crossing the road one day and this car come round the corner and nearly hit him. Two guys got out and they was drunk, so Ritch plunged the fucking pair of them. He said to me it wasn't just because they nearly knocked him down but c**ts like that are gonna kill some little baby playing in the street one day. They should've given him a medal, but they gave him six years for a Section 18. So we were sitting there talking and there was this screw, one of them fucking Nazi screws, you know with his hat right over his eyes, shouting and bawling and making himself look the hard man; to be honest, he was getting on our tits. All of a sudden, Ritchie's looked over – and though Ritchie really is a placid man, a very nice man, if you get his back up, he's a lunatic. This screw's said something to Ritchie and I managed to grab him before he done this screw some damage and got another couple of years. I put my arm across him. I said, 'Remember, you're doing six, let me deal with this pratt.' I've done my usual trick with these pompous little pricks: I picked him up, and I know that makes people feel fucking stupid and very vulnerable. While I'm doing it, I was laughing, so anybody clocking the cameras thinks it's a bit of fun, but while he's up in the air I whispered, 'Listen, you c**t, keep away from me and keep away from my Scotch pal or I will have you killed inside your house when you least expect.' To be honest, I didn't mean it, but he couldn't be sure whether I did or not. But he must've read my report so it was up to him to make a judgement.

My cell was like a magnet to all the young fellas, the young tearaways. I think they thought if they hung around me it gave them a bit of cred and perhaps they thought they could pick up some tips about this and that. They was disappointed, though, because I did my best to steer them away from causing and getting aggro on the outside. You see them knocking about the streets and they think they're as hard as fuck when they're 20-handed, but one on one they are what they are: kids. How clever and how tough is it to spend the best years of your life behind the door? Telling all their mates that they're going down or are already inside might make them look like gangsters, but every one of them has cried himself to sleep more nights than they can remember.

Still, whatever, they still liked coming into Lenny's cell and listening to a few of my stories. There was a white kid and a black kid and they was both livewires and they was in my cell one time and they're both puffing away on the weed. I mean, the fucking smell of that shit must've been all over the landing. I said, 'Listen, be fucking careful, don't get caught smoking that shit in here or you'll both end up down the block and take me with you.'

We heard footsteps coming along the landing and quick as a flash these two kids have flung their roaches under my bed and fucked off out the door, leaving me standing there in the middle of all their smoke.

Bang! The door's opened again and two screws walk in sniffing like bloodhounds. They looked round the cell, then one them bent down and picked up the dog ends, looked at me and walked out again. Five minutes and the two kids slunk back in looking a bit sheepish and I said, 'I wanna punch your fucking heads in because I warned you this would happen. It's down to you if I get a month down the block with no visitors.' They don't look too happy so I said, 'Look, I ain't gonna say nothing, I'll suffer the block.'

The black kid said, 'Sorry, Len, we didn't think, but there's no way you're gonna do a month, we've been bang out of order so we'll put our hands up.'

I said, 'No, you're not gonna put your hands up to it, you ain't gonna say nothing, let's just see what happens.'

Anyway, two hours later I'm asked to go to the office. When I got up there, they said, 'You know what we found in your cell?'

I said, 'I like to keep fit because I'm a fighter, as you know.'

And they said, 'Yes.'

'Well, I don't smoke that shit, I don't like it, but I ain't gonna grass anybody up, so don't even ask me.'

They said, 'There will be no charge, because we don't know who was smoking a controlled substance, but this is a warning: if it happens again you will be held responsible.'

I stopped the boys from bringing their shit into my cell after that, because with my trial coming up I couldn't afford to suffer anymore agg than I had already.

Pete, son, I've been telling you some funny stories about my time inside, but what I haven't talked about is the times when I felt like shit. It might sound like a holiday camp when it's all behind you, but believe me it ain't. For a start, day after day after day I had it in the back of my nut that eventually I'd be standing up in court and fighting for my life. Can you imagine being on a murder charge and you haven't done it? You are living and breathing that charge every single day. When you wake up in the morning, for a few seconds it ain't there, but seconds later it hits you in the stomach – bosh! – murder, life, murder, life, then it's on your mind until you go to sleep, if you can, and even then you dream about it. It's on your mind 20 hours a day. It's terrible, because you only have three or four hours' peace a night. That's month in, month out. The system don't know what it's doing to people, especially innocent people. It wasn't the time I done in prison that done my head in, because you adapt your life round prison. What done my head up was the threat of life imprisonment. I like to think I'm a strong man, but the stress and strain was unbelievable and a lot of people say I've never been the same after that.

How did you feel as your court appearance was getting closer and closer?

How did I feel? Well, funnily enough, the closer I got, the less I seemed to worry about it. I mean, I wasn't too confident that it was gonna go my way, but I suppose getting close to fighting what had kept me awake for months and months seemed to give me a boost. I'd given up looking through my papers, because I knew them off by heart, and knowing that didn't make me any wiser anyway. When I was bunking in with Frankie at the beginning, I used to keep him awake or get him up really early to go over my papers in case he picked up something I'd missed. He used to say, 'When are we gonna look through mine?'

And I'd say, 'As soon as we've sorted mine we'll get stuck into yours.'

After we'd done my papers to death he said, 'OK, Len, I'll get my papers out,' and I went, 'Frank, I'm too fucking tired for all that shit.' He did his nut.

Well, the day finally come round and I got myself suited and booted to face up to whatever was coming. Once they get you inside the court for a couple of days it's all bollocks with the barristers playing at Ironsides – that guy on the telly who was in a wheelchair, remember? Boring as fuck even though my future depended on it. No wonder the black geezer used to come back every night saying it was going well. 'Course it was, because nothing was happening. I used to sit there in the heat, sweating my nuts off and wishing I was back in my cell.

Bobby Warren came to the Bailey every single day without fail, because he was more or less minding my wife and making sure everything was OK. I'd already had the pre-trial and that was a waste of time as well, because I knew there was no chance of me getting bail and I know the guy in front of me is not gonna hear my case, he's only gonna see if he's got enough evidence to be sent up to the Bailey. It's obvious there was plenty of that, because there I was standing in the Bailey, listening to a load of old shit. When I was stuck in the dock, I wouldn't face the judge. I ain't got to look at him and I don't want to look at him. All I wanted to do was turn my back on this man and look at my wife, and that's what I done; I disregarded the court.

While I was standing there, it must've been about 80 degrees, and I was sweating cobs. I had a box of Kleenex tissues in the dock and over in the corner there was DI Cater, who was hoping I would go down, and another guy, and what I kept doing was, as I was wiping the sweat off me I was rolling the tissues up into a ball and every time the judge looked the other way or looked down at his papers I'd flick them at the two of them. They kept looking at me and they was fuming but they couldn't do nothing. What could they do? I was on a fucking murder charge. The only one that was rucking was Bobby. He was making faces and pointing at me and I got the message that he didn't like me lobbing them balls at them coppers, so I packed it in. Why I was throwing stuff at Cater was because I couldn't belt him and he deserved one of my right-handers.

It was funny looking round – well, not funny so much as strange, because though I had a lot of supporters in court, there were loads of people who'd more or less come in off the streets and I thought, 'You lot are no different to people a hundred years ago who'd go to a public hanging for a day out, or like them who put the thumbs down for gladiators in the olden days.' Bunch of bloodsucking, thrill-seeking c**ts. I could imagine them going home at night and while they're having their tea telling the wife, 'Blinding day in court today, saw this bloke get sent down for 25 years. Any more of that cake, love?'

I could see the bloke's family, the one I was supposed to have murdered, and I felt sick. Up to that moment, he was just a faceless fucking nuisance who'd caused me to get in the deepest shit ever, but seeing his family sitting there brought home to me that he was a real person.

The truth is, Pete, if I'd known he was a sick boy who'd forgot to take his medication, I would've helped him. I would've made sure he was properly looked after. But how was I to know he had a problem? I've dealt with drunks for 20 years and every one of them is the same. Good as gold when they're sober, but once they're full of piss they become violent, aggressive and to all appearances nutty as fruitcakes. How am I, or any other doorman, supposed to sort out who's drunk and who's got some sort of mental problem? Impossible, ain't it?

I couldn't look at his family. Not because I felt guilty – though I've always had this niggle inside me – but because I didn't want them to think I was some cocky thug who knew he'd killed their son or brother and didn't give a fuck. My heart bled for his mum, but I didn't kill her boy and that's what I'd spent months and months in prison for, to end up here and prove it to her and everyone else that I was innocent.

You'd hardly think I was the biggest news of the week, but going to and from the court was a fucking nightmare with newspaper photographers flashing their cameras through the van windows. I palled up with a guy named John and as we shared the van we kept saying to each other, 'Look out, look out,' as these pratts tried to get a picture.

I tell you, son, being in the Bailey is one of the most draining experiences I've ever suffered. I'd get back to my cell and fall into bed and the funny thing is I slept better over them few days than I had since I was first lifted.

Don't get me wrong, I still had my moments of depression, but things was happening so fast I didn't really have too much time to dwell on what might happen. And, of course, all the guys inside was looking out for me, because it was like they was on trial as well. When a con went to court and got a result it cheered all of us up, and when it went wrong for him we was gutted to fuck and the place would be all quiet for a while. That's because we were in this little world of our own, miles from the outside.

Anyway, things hotted up when this doctor expert took the stand – a bird called Paula Lannas. In her opinion there was no doubt that when I give Gary a slap I broke his jaw and that led directly to his death. In fact, she said she'd known of loads of cases where a broken jaw was more than enough to kill somebody. I wanted to shout out, 'You stupid c**t, who's more of an expert on broken jaws, you or me?'

I could feel my heart sinking as she went on and on and on, playing the same old record about fucking jaws.

When we had a break, or recess as they call it, I said to my barrister, 'For fuck's sake, that woman is crucifying me out there. And when she come out of the box, do you know what she said to him? She said, "How did I do?" Whose fucking side is she on anyway?'

That made Martin and Kenny smile. 'Well, even though she's impartial, as she's the prosecution's star expert, obviously she's on the other side.'

'Sorry, Lenny, that's the way the system works.'

'Fuck the system then,' I went, 'I might as well put my hands up now.'

The barrister said, 'You wait until our witness takes the stand; I've got a feeling the smile will be knocked off a few faces.'

'Why's that?' I said.

'Well, the expert we have, Professor Gresham, is the number-one pathologist in the world and he actually taught Paula Lannas, so presumably he has vastly more experience and he has certainly spoken out on many world-famous cases – the Australian dingo case springs to mind.'

I could've kissed them both, because for the first time since it all started I felt I had much more than a chance.

'But,' the barrister said, 'there are no guarantees that the jury will accept his evidence – after all, you are a well-known man: well known for being violent and dangerous.'

'Fucking thanks very much,' I thought, 'give me hope then kick me in the bollocks.'

You finding this interesting, Pete?

Very much, Len, it's fascinating.

That's good. I didn't find it too interesting at the time, but I suppose it's different when you're liberty ain't at stake.

Anyway, Pete, the day come for our bloke to do his bit and, when the little guy at the front shouted out, 'Call Professor Gresham,' my stomach turned over and I was thinking, 'Go on my son, give to them.'

I dunno what I expected, I suppose I thought he'd stand up and say, 'In my opinion, Lenny didn't do it so you can let him go home,' but it was much more drawn out than that. He come out with all this technical medical stuff, and photos and bits of paper were handed out to the jury until I felt like shouting at him to get to the point where he pulls a bit of evidence out the bag and everybody cheers like they do on telly. I mean, what I'm saying to you in a couple of minutes, in that court it took all day. He said Gary Humphreys did have a broken jaw, and my heart sank, but then he said he'd never known anybody to die through that, and that was two fingers to Lannas. But, best of all, and the thing that put a grin on my face, was that he said, in his opinion, you couldn't seriously rule out the chance that the boy had died when the police got hold of him. He wasn't saying they deliberately killed him, but, what with him kicking off all over the place, he said you couldn't completely rule out that he might've died when they were trying to control him. The professor saying that was a right fucking result for me, so kiss my arse, Cater. Now it was my turn to smirk at Cater like he'd been doing to me through the trial and that man couldn't look at me.

I think I laid awake all that night running things through my nut. I might've fallen asleep, but if I did I carried on weighing up all the ins and outs. Bottom line was, would the jury believe my side of it or the side of the police? Few hours and I'd know.

I suppose you could say that day was going to be the biggest and most important in my life. I could be going home to my lovely wife Val and my two kids, who I loved more than life itself, or I could be going back to prison to spend years and years and years, just like Reg and Ron. Could I accept it the way they did? Well, you can't tell, can you, Pete? You can never tell nothing until you're actually faced with it.

OK, so I'm back in court and the sun was streaming through them windows in the roof and while the mumbling and the paper rustling was going on I stood looking up and thought, 'Is this how I'm gonna see the sun for the next quarter of a century, through dirty glass?' I was stood there like somebody waiting for that last number in the Lottery, that one number that's gonna change their life for ever.

It went all quiet when the judge come in, and it made me look down and around at all the people waiting to see me either go free or go to fucking hell. My Val, bless her, I thought I'd suffered on my own, but she suffered just as much as me and she was looking old and tired.

Sorry, babe, if you're ear'oling in the kitchen, but you was and it was all my fault.

I wanted to jump down and give her a cuddle and tell her whatever happened I'd make it up to her somehow. There was Bobby – diamond, diamond man, always there for me.

I looked at all my pals who were praying for me and then I looked at them jury people. Judged by my peers? Fuck off, these people weren't my peers. I wasn't knocking them, but, come on, if were talking peers there should be 12 people in that dock that was knocked senseless as a kid, who lost their dad when he was a nipper and their mum far too young. People who had to claw their way through life to get what they wanted, people who had to fight, fight, fight. And then they might be able to understand and judge me. But no, I've got bank clerks, milkmen, shop assistants and fuck knows who else, weighing up a lot of law stuff they haven't got a clue about. Most of them don't even wanna be there – I know I didn't when I got that summons thing through for jury service. They ain't interested, they wanna get it over and done with and get back to work; I'm nothing to them except a bully, a street fighter, a fucking raving lunatic. Will they stop and think that I'm a loving father, a good husband and loyal to my friends? Will they bollocks.

I'm too busy fucking off the jury that I only sort of come to, to hear the judge say... 'And what is your verdict?'

I nearly bent the rail running along top of the dock as I dug my fingers in. I had a quick look at my Val, but she looked like she was gonna cry and I couldn't look no more. Then the foreman said... 'NOT GUILTY!'

Peter, my son, I can still feel that feeling. The relief sort of swept over me. Val was laughing and crying and I felt that sort of prickle behind my own eyes, but I shook it off, looked at Judge Lowry and started to sing, 'Always look on the bright side of life' – you know, from that film. He didn't tell me to shut up, so he must've felt good about the decision. All he said was, 'Take that man down.'

The clapping and cheering that went on was fucking deafening. I was led back downstairs by these two screws and, as we're getting near the bottom, I said, 'You boys up for a laugh?' and I turned their caps round, put my arms in theirs and as we reached the bottom I started singing all over again. I could see John up the end of the passage and he was shouting, 'Well done, Len, well done,' and he started clapping and so did all the other screws and people down there. I mean, half of them didn't know me, but they was still clapping and cheering. I let the two screws go and, just like I did when I beat Shawie, I threw my arms in the air and shouted, 'THE GUV'NOR'S GOING HOME.'

How was that, son?

Fantastic. I was there in the courtroom with you.

That's good, that's what I want people to know, just what it feels like.

I think we should end the book right there, don't you?

Well, you're the writer, you tell me and I'll go along with it. One thing, though. I know I shouted I was going home and all that, but that was the excitement of the moment. Really, I still had to go back to the nick and finish off a sentence of 18 months for GBH. Fucking liberty, that was. For a start, they never could prove I actually hit that kid and, though I put my hands up, they didn't know exactly how hard I hit him. I didn't hit him hard at all, Pete, and I don't have to lie to you, but what I'm saying is for all they know I might've given him a little slap, like you give a naughty baby. But on the evidence they heard in court they obviously thought different.

So where do we go from here?

Well, I'll get this put on the computer, and then me and you will get together and go through the whole thing.

Can I add bits in or take bits out if I don't like them?

Yeah, I said that earlier, we'll work together on this and tighten it right up.

Good boy. Well, crack away, son, it's up to you now. Let's have a nice cuppa tea now we're finished.

Tea will be great, but we're not finished yet.

No, I know that, but we've broken the back of it and that's what counts. We've made a good team, you and me. Gimme your hand.